INSPIRATION OF THE HOLY SCRIPTURES.

A TREATISE ON THE

INSPIRATION

OF

THE HOLY SCRIPTURES.

BY

CHARLES ELLIOTT, D.D.,

PROFESSOR OF BIBLICAL LITERATURE AND EXEGESIS IN THE PRESBYTERIAN
THEOLOGICAL SEMINARY OF THE NORTH-WEST,
CHICAGO, ILLINOIS.

WIPF & STOCK · Eugene, Oregon

Wipf and Stock Publishers
199 W 8th Ave, Suite 3
Eugene, OR 97401

A Treatise on the Inspiration of The Holy Scriptures
By Elliott, Charles
ISBN 13: 978-1-60608-919-4
Publication date 1/1/2017
Previously published by T & T Clark, 1877

PREFACE.

THE author who publishes a work acknowledges by the very act that he believes such a work to be needed. There is certainly great need at present of correct views on the subject of the inspiration of the Holy Scriptures. Whether this treatise will contribute in any way to promote these views, others, not the author, must judge. He claims nothing original. The same topics, though, so far as he knows, not in the same order, have been discussed elsewhere more thoroughly, and by abler minds. He has merely collected into a small compass matter distributed through many books, which seldom come under the perusal of common readers. This treatise is intended for such readers, and not for the learned. If it shall tend to disseminate sound views on the important subject which forms its theme, to Him be the praise to whose grace we are indebted for the inestimable gift of His Holy Word.

The statement made concerning the popular aim of the work will render unnecessary any explanation of the fact that many questions, necessary in an exhaustive treatise, but out of place in one intended for popular use, have been omitted.

Due acknowledgments have been made to writers

whose works have been used. These will be found in the body of the treatise. Sometimes, however, quotations have not been indicated by inverted commas, for the reason that the author was obliged to abridge the passages cited and employ his own language.

THE AUTHOR.

EDINBURGH, 1877.

TABLE OF CONTENTS.

PART I.

CHAPTER I.

INTRODUCTORY REMARKS.

PAGE

The Bible a historical fact—Claims to be a revelation from God—Professes to give the history of redemption—Impossible to eliminate the miraculous element from it—Naturalists and rationalists deny the supernatural—Assumption of a personal God, the Creator of all things—Creation a supernatural act—No presumption against miracles—No presumption against revelation considered as miraculous—Revelation probable *à priori*—Supposing a revelation to be given, we would naturally expect it to be attested by miracles—Miracles capable of proof—How can the Infinite One reveal Himself?—A revelation having been given, may differ very much from our preconceived notions of it, hence many objections against it may be founded upon our ignorance—The Church receives the Bible as a divine revelation—General plan, . . 1

CHAPTER II.

IMPORTANCE OF THE QUESTION.

Every truth is important—Some truths more important than others—The inspiration of the Scriptures a truth of paramount importance to the Christian system—Roman Catholic Church admits tradition to be of co-ordinate authority with the Holy Scriptures, but does not deny their inspiration—Importance to the Church of maintaining the infallible authority of the Scriptures—True views of inspiration especially important at the present time—The doctrine of plenary inspiration in its relation to biblical interpretation, ... 12

CHAPTER III.

CANON OF SCRIPTURE.

Books received as canonical and inspired—Canon of the New Testament : (*a*) Origin of the idea of the New Testament canon ; (*b*) this collection

PAGE

has been considered from the beginning by the Church as a harmonious and complete whole; (c) historical division of the New Testament canon into three parts; (d) three ante-Nicene catalogues; (e) Origen's catalogue; (f) Eusebius' catalogue; (g) Council of Nice; (h) eleven authentic catalogues of the fourth century,—nine by the Fathers, and two by the Councils of Laodicea and Carthage—Recapitulation—Canon of the Old Testament: (a) The five books of Moses deposited in the ark; (b) copies made out before they were deposited; (c) Book of Joshua; (d) autograph of Moses; (e) this autograph probably destroyed when Nebuchadnezzar destroyed Jerusalem; (f) formation of the present canon attributed to Ezra; (g) probable conclusion; (h) how the books were distributed; (i) the Old Testament Scriptures received the explicit sanction of our Lord; (k) testimony of Josephus; (l) the books of the Old Testament have since the time of Christ been in the keeping of both Jews and Christians; (m) the Septuagint version; (n) the Samaritan Pentateuch — Apocrypha — Why did the Jewish Church accept as inspired only the books of the Old Testament canon? —The New Testament canon furnishes an exact parallel, . . 15

CHAPTER IV.

INTEGRITY OF THE HOLY SCRIPTURES.

Inspiration, in the strict sense of the term, limited to the original autographs, or to exact copies made from them in the same language— Origin of the various readings: (1) unintentional; (2) intentional— Origin of discrepancies of statement: (1) difference of date; (2) difference of authorship; (3) difference of standpoint or of object; (4) different principles and methods of arrangement; (5) different modes of computation; (6) peculiarities of Oriental idiom; (7) plurality of names of the same person or object, and different (sometimes opposite) significations of the same word—Not surprising that various readings and apparent discrepancies should exist in the Bible—Results of these various readings and discrepancies—Design of the discrepancies, . 38

CHAPTER V.

HISTORICAL CREDIBILITY OF THE SCRIPTURES.

Criteria of the credibility of a historian—Canons of historical criticism—Historical credibility of the Pentateuch—Authenticity of the Pentateuch—Genesis stands on a different footing from the other four books of the Pentateuch—Moses probably used documents—External evidence to the credibility of the Mosaic narrative—Berosus and Manetho—Chronologies of Berosus and Manetho—Berosus' account of the creation—His account of the deluge—His account of events between the deluge and the time of Abraham—Descendants of Noah—Expedition of Chedor-laomer—The exodus—From the exodus to the time of Solomon—Weakness of Egypt and Assyria—Conquest of Canaan—The sun's standing still—David's Syrian and other wars—Connection of Judæa with Phœnicia—Solomon's relations with Egypt—Indirect points of agreement— From the death of Solomon to the destruction of Jerusalem by Nebuchadnezzar—Closing period of Old Testament history—Book of Daniel—Captivity—Nebuchadnezzar—Return of the Jews to Palestine—Historical credibility of the New Testament, . . . 55

CHAPTER VI.

SCIENTIFIC ACCURACY OF THE SCRIPTURES.

The Bible does not pretend to teach science ; it uses popular language—The sacred writers, with a few exceptions, not scientific men—Conflict between science and the Bible often asserted, but never established— Conflicting views of scientific men on astronomy, geology, and Egyptology—Points of agreement between the Bible and science : geology, astronomy, ethnology, philology, chronology—The language of Scripture agrees, in a remarkable manner, with modern scientific discoveries —The accuracy of Scripture confirmed by discoveries in the historico-scientific field of knowledge, ... 83

PART II.

PROOFS OF THE INSPIRATION OF THE BIBLE.

CHAPTER I.

DOCTRINES AND PRECEPTS OF THE BIBLE, AND ITS UNIQUE CHARACTER.

A comparison of the Bible with other books evinces a striking difference— Comparison of the cosmogony of the Bible with the cosmogonies of Sanchoniatho, Hesiod, and Aristophanes—Doctrine of God—Doctrine concerning man—Doctrine of redemption—Doctrine of morality—Precepts of the Bible—Precepts referring to duties involving relations nowhere acknowledged except in the Bible—Unique character of the Bible—Objections to the morality of the Bible, . . . 107

CHAPTER II.

DIVERSITY AND UNITY OF THE BIBLE.

Diversity of the Bible—Illustrations of its unity in the midst of diversity— Its unity can be perceived only by careful study—The Bible consists of sixty-six books, written by different authors, in different languages, in different periods, and in different countries—All the books of the Bible agree in the same great truths—The Bible idea of God constitutes its unity—This idea of God consistent with itself throughout both Testaments—The teaching of the Bible respecting the divine government

x   CONTENTS.

                                                                    PAGE
and providence in perfect harmony with its idea and doctrine of God—
The Bible doctrine of the nature, government, and providence of God
in keeping with what the Scriptures teach of the nature, condition, and
necessities of man—Unity of teaching as to the way of salvation—Same
unity of teaching in regard to rewards and punishments—Unity of the
Scriptures illustrated by the progressive development of the doctrines
of redemption and final retribution, ... 126

CHAPTER III.

ORGANIC CHARACTER OF THE BIBLE.

General analogy of the organic character of the Bible to the system of
nature—Definition of organism—Organism of the several parts of the
Old Testament—Organism of the New Testament—Such an organism
as the Bible cannot be a merely human production, . . . 135

CHAPTER IV.

THE UNIVERSALITY OF THE BIBLE.

The Bible, in some of its features, is a national book—Notwithstanding
its national character, it is a book for all climes and all ages—Comparison of the Bible with works of literary genius among the heathen
—Ground of its adaptability to all men : illustrations from Dr.
Chalmers—To speculative minds it offers a solution of their difficulties, by requiring them to exercise faith—Faith the true rest of
the mind—It reveals an atonement for guilt—It presents an object
fitted to win the affections—It furnishes the strongest motives to
influence the will—It is adapted to the whole man—It is a comforter in the varied experience of life—It is adapted to man in his
social and domestic relations—Application of the argument, . . 141

CHAPTER V.

THE BENEFICIAL EFFECTS OF THE BIBLE ON THE WORLD.

Man left to his unaided powers retrogrades—Philosophy has made large
pretensions, but has failed to regenerate men—The means of man's
elevation found in the Bible—Nature of the knowledge derived from
the Bible, and its potency to effect the regeneration of the world :
(a) True knowledge of God ; (b) true knowledge of ourselves ; (c) a
knowledge of duties, personal and relative ; (d) knowledge of the
objects and duties of government—The power of this knowledge to
effect the regeneration of man—Purifying influence upon the individual—Influence of the Bible upon society in general—Influence of
the Bible upon the State—Testimony of history to the beneficial
effects of the Bible—Exceptional position of the Bible in the world, . 148

CHAPTER VI.

PROPHECY.

The writers of the Bible predicted future events—Prophecies relating to the Jews—Prophecies respecting the kingdoms of Judah and Samaria —Prophecies concerning Jerusalem—Prophecies concerning Nineveh, Babylon, Tyre, Egypt, Ammon, Moab, Edom, and Philistia—Prophecies concerning Christ, ... 165

CHAPTER VII.

TESTIMONY OF THE SCRIPTURES THEMSELVES.

The canon furnishes the testimony of the Church—The testimony of Scripture belongs to the external class of evidence—The Scriptures claim to be inspired—An appeal to the testimony of the Scripture is not a begging of the question—Inspiration of the Old Testament: (*a*) The prophets profess to speak for God, and by His authority ; (*b*) quotations from the Old Testament, and allusions to it contained in the New Testament ; (*c*) the general names or titles under which the Old Testament, as a whole, is spoken of in the New Testament, viz. ' Scripture ' or ' Scriptures ; ' ' Moses, Prophets, and the Psalms ; or, the Law and the Prophets ; ' ' Word of God, Oracles of God '—Inspiration of the New Testament : (*a*) Christ promised to His apostles the Holy Spirit ; (*b*) this promise fulfilled ; (*c*) the apostles claimed to be infallible organs of God ; (*d*) their claims confirmed by miracles— Mark and Luke, ... 173

PART III.

DEFINITIONS, THEORIES, DISTINCTIONS, NATURE, AND EXTENT OF THE INSPIRATION OF THE HOLY SCRIPTURES.

CHAPTER I.

MEANING OF THE TERM INSPIRATION.

Θεόπνευστος — ὑπὸ πνεύματος ἁγίου φερόμενοι — Definitions of inspiration— Knapp, Lee, Bannerman, ... 189

CHAPTER II.

OPINIONS AND THEORIES ON THE SUBJECT OF INSPIRATION.

Opinion of the apocryphal writers — Josephus — Philo Judæus — Sub-apostolic Fathers : Barnabas, Clement, Polycarp, Ignatius, Papias, and

Hermas—The apologists : Justin Martyr, Tatian, Athenagoras, Theophilus — The Fathers of the Church of Asia Minor : Hegesippus, Melito, Claudius Apollinaris, Irenæus — The Fathers of the Roman Church : Caius, Novatian, Hippolytus — The Fathers of the North African Church : Tertullian and Cyprian—The Fathers of Alexandria : Clemens Alexandrinus, Origen, Eusebius, Chrysostom, Jerome, Epiphanius, Theodore of Mopsuestia, Augustine, Gregory the Great—The Schoolmen—Reformers—Theory of verbal inspiration—Mystical theory—Theory of degrees of inspiration—Latitudinarian and rationalistic theories—Schleiermacher—Coleridge—Gracious inspiration, . 192

CHAPTER III.

DISTINCTION BETWEEN INSPIRATION AND REVELATION.

Duty of the sacred writers—How did the sacred writers acquire a knowledge of what they wrote, and under what guidance or influence did they write ?—View of Archdeacon Lee—Dr. Bannerman's view—Dr. Hodge's view—Dr. Patton's view—Comparison of the foregoing views —Conclusion, ... 237

CHAPTER IV.

NATURE AND EXTENT OF INSPIRATION.

The Bible has a twofold authorship—Proofs of human authorship—The individuality of the sacred writers preserved in Scripture—Inspiration did not destroy the conscious self-control of the writers—The two agencies, divine and human, in the composition of Scripture, were so combined as to produce one indivisible result—Their union inexplicable—The union of these two elements has an analogue in the person of Christ—The same term, 'Word of God,' is used in Scripture to designate the Son of God and the written revelation which He has given to us—Limits of this analogy—Other analogies illustrating the twofold agency in the production of the Scriptures — The effect of inspiration is to render its subject the infallible organ of the Holy Spirit in communicating truth—Inspiration is limited to the nature of the object to be accomplished—It extends equally to every part of Holy Scripture ; it is plenary—Doctrine of plenary inspiration consistent with the facts of Scripture—Bearing of the theanthropic view of inspiration upon the different theories of the subject, . . 252

PART I.

CHAPTER I.

INTRODUCTORY REMARKS.

A very remarkable book, entitled the Bible, exists in the world. This book is not of recent origin: it has come down to us from remote ages. It consists of sixty-six small books, differing from one another in various particulars, according to the authorship and design of each; the oldest of which were written about fifteen hundred years before the birth of Christ, and the last near the close of the first century of our era. A book whose composition extends over so long a period must of course have been the work of various authors, and written at different times.

This book claims to be a revelation from God, and in this character it has been received by the Church from generation to generation until the present time. Men of the highest intellectual endowments, of every rank and of every profession, have acknowledged its claim, and submitted to its authority. Others, eminent for their science and erudition, have exercised their talents and ingenuity to make it utter contradictions, and prove it false; but it still remains the Incomparable Book, and its evidences derive fresh lustre from every assault. The very means used to destroy it have been turned to its support. A divine power resides in it, which has shivered, with godlike ease, the armour of its most powerful enemies. 'He that sitteth in the heavens' has laughed at their temerity, and brought their foolish counsels into contempt.

The Bible professes to give the history of our world, so far as that history is connected with the scheme of redemption, during the period of four thousand years. This period begins with a miracle and ends with a miracle. The first is the creation of the world; the second the appearance of the Eternal Word in our flesh. These two miracles, of the creation and incarnation, stand out distinct from all others; the former constitutes the beginning of the world's history, the latter its central fact. All history revolves round the person of the God-man. Between these two great epochs lies the era of sacred history, distinguished by God's progressive revelation of Himself. It exhibits to us theophanies, miracles, and prophecy. These are not spread uniformly over its whole course, yet they are essential to it, and it ceases to be sacred when they disappear.

If we take the Bible for what it professes to be, we cannot eliminate the miraculous element from sacred history. The union of this element with what, for the sake of convenience, may be called the human element of Scripture history, is so intimate and essential, that any attempt to disunite them would result in rejecting both. This is not because of the number of miracles, but because their connection with the sacred record is of such a kind as to make them inseparable from it. They are not embellishments that can be spared from the narrative without injury to its continuity and completeness, or excrescences that can be cut off, or a foreign element that can be sorted out from its proper teaching, and set aside as no part of it. On the contrary, the shape and movement of events in the Bible are dependent on the supernatural action; and the results of the human history which it records are ruled and coloured by the superhuman influences that predominate in the midst of them. The natural and the supernatural in the narratives of the sacred volume are blended so as to form one organic whole, which cannot be analyzed into its component parts, but must be accepted or rejected in its integrity and as it stands.

'Even were it possible to separate between what has been intimately joined together in Scripture, without destroying the substance of the text, it could not be done without fatally destroying the moral character of the religion. Christianity bears upon its front a profession that it comes from God, and is attested by His miraculous attestations; the Author of Christianity pointedly and frequently appealed to the works that He did as evidence that He bore the commission of His Father, and He was contented to abide the decision which such an appeal involved, when He claimed from His enemies to be believed, if not for His own, yet at least for His work's sake. To answer this appeal by the denial or rejection of the miracles of the Bible, is to destroy at one blow both the outward evidence to which it points, and the moral character of the religion which it records. The claim made to the power of working miracles, and the appeal to them as the test and witness of His authority, leave no alternative but either to receive the teaching as a revelation from Heaven, or to reject the Teacher as One that has untruly said that he comes from God. Either the works on which he built his doctrine were supernatural, or that doctrine has wrongfully claimed a divine authority over the conscience.'[1]

---

[1] *Inspiration: The Infallible Truth and Divine Authority of the Holy Scriptures.* By James Bannerman, D.D. Edinburgh: T. & T. Clark. 1865. Pp. 12, 13.

Naturalists and rationalists deny the supernatural, and consequently reject the miraculous element of the Bible. The former explain the phenomena of the universe by a blind force acting necessarily. The latter consider reason our sufficient and only guide, exclusive of tradition and revelation. Supernaturalism is opposed to both these, and teaches that there are in nature more than physical causes in operation, and that in religion we have the guidance not merely of reason but of revelation. It holds the doctrine of a divine and supernatural agency in the production of the miracles and revelations which the Bible records, and in the grace which renews and sanctifies men.

Questions pertaining to the supernatural lie at the foundation of the subject under discussion; but as they belong properly to the department of apologetics, or evidences of Christianity, we pass them over, and assume what in that department we would be required to prove.

We assume the existence of a personal God, the creator of all things visible and invisible. The assumption that the universe was created by God necessitates the assumption that the laws which govern it are His appointments. They are uniform and permanent merely because He wills it, and not by reason of any inherent and necessary immutability; for there was a time when they were not, and a time may come when the present constitution of things may be changed, and the present laws be modified in adaptation to that change. Geological periods furnish abundant proof of such changes from time to time in the constitution of the earth, and in the laws that govern it.

The creation of 'the heaven and the earth,' with which the history of the Old Testament begins, was a supernatural act. It forms the distinctive article in the creed of those who are properly and strictly called theists, and is denied by none but atheists and pantheists. Those who admit it must necessarily admit the possibility of the supernatural.

There is, therefore, no presumption against miracles, for the beginning of the world was miraculous; and there is nothing in the constitution of things to prevent the recurrence of them, provided exigencies arise to require them. Indeed, there is a presumption in favour of their recurrence, in case such exigencies should arise; for the universe, being under the government of an Almighty Being, possessed of will and freedom, may frequently be modified to accomplish His plans and purposes.

If there is no presumption against miracles, it follows that there can be none against revelation considered as miraculous. There is none against it, as Bishop Butler remarks, at the beginning of the world; for as there was no course of nature then, or at all events we are not acquainted with it, the question about a revelation at that time is but a common question of fact. The power which was exerted to make the world, whether called miraculous or not, might just as easily be further exerted to make a revelation. We may receive, therefore, the testimony of history and tradition on this as on any common matter of fact of the same antiquity. This testimony is that religion originally came by revelation, and this has a tendency to remove any prejudices against a subsequent revelation.

There is no presumption against revelation considered as miraculous after the settlement of a course of nature, as has been already intimated; for the present course of nature is involved in so much darkness, that there seems no improbability in supposing that five or six thousand years may have given occasion for miraculous interpositions. Taking moral considerations into view, we see reasons for them. Our world is morally very much deranged. Ignorance and sin abound everywhere. The cause of this derangement, the Bible tells us, was disobedience to God on the part of our first parents. By their sin death and all our woe entered into the world. Now, suppose a plan of redemption and restoration, such as the Scriptures reveal, to have been provided by God, the communication of such a plan to man must have been made by revelation; and the only manner of authenticating this revelation, so far as we can see, must have been the working of miracles by those who were commissioned to announce it. This assumes that revelation, supposing it to have been given, was not universal, but imparted to a few, who were chosen by God for the purpose of publishing it to the world. This method is in harmony with the natural constitution and course of things under which we exist; for we see that God, in numberless instances, bestows that upon some which He does not upon others who seem equally to need it. Indeed, He bestows all His gifts, such as health and strength, capacities of prudence and knowledge, among His creatures with the most promiscuous variety, and yet He exercises a natural and moral government over the world.[1]

So far from there being any presumption against revelation considered as miraculous, there is, prior to any proof of it, a probability in its favour. This probability arises from the fact that we would remain in ignorance of truths that vitally concern our highest interests were they not revealed to us.

Some affirm that God has revealed Himself to all men by means of a spiritual or rational revelation. Such a revelation is, of course, without miracle. It implies, neither in its nature nor in the manner of its

[1] Butler's *Analogy*, Part II. chap. ii.

communication, any departure from the ordinary course of providence.

The existence of religious faculties in man is admitted, and also the existence of what is called universal religion. But this universal, subjective revelation is proved by experience and historical evidence to be deficient both in completeness and clearness. It has never been found to supersede a supernatural revelation, and render it superfluous and vain. On the contrary, the history of our race has clearly proved that natural religion in its best estate, without a supernatural communication from God, has left men in darkness, doubt, and uncertainty. 'Professing themselves to be wise, they became fools' (Rom. i. 22).

The very fact of this deficiency of a universal, subjective revelation, or natural religion, as shown by the state of religion in the heathen world, by the doubts of the greatest men on the most important subjects, and by the indifference and ignorance of mankind in general, affords an *a priori* argument in behalf of a supernatural revelation; for, seeing that God has revealed Himself in the external world and in the constitution of man in some measure, yet not in a degree adequate to satisfy our religious wants, it is probable, judging from His goodness, that He would reveal Himself more fully and more clearly. This Christians believe He has done in the Holy Scriptures, which they receive as containing an authoritative publication of natural religion, with increased light, together with an account of a dispensation of things not discoverable by reason—a scheme of mercy and of grace which, from its very nature, could be made known only by supernatural revelation.

On the supposition that a revelation has been given, the only method of attesting it, so far as we know, is by miracles. Belonging to the supernatural, it requires supernatural confirmation. Hence a history of revelation must be expected to contain narratives of supernatural events. This is a striking peculiarity of Bible history, which distinguishes it from all other history. It contains a large miraculous element interwoven with what we have styled the human, and it is so interwoven with it that the two elements cannot be separated. They form parts, equally entitled to credit, of the same narrative. In some instances the natural forms the framework of the supernatural.

Supernatural narratives throw discredit upon profane, but not upon sacred history, which the Bible claims to be. The reason of this is well stated by Horace in his 'Art of Poetry':

> 'Nec deus intersit, nisi dignus vindice nodus
> Inciderit.'[1]

In sacred history, which proceeds from the combination of the action of God and the action of the creature, we naturally expect the miraculous. It is, indeed, demanded in a book professing to be a revelation from God. So far, therefore, from forming an argument against the credibility of the Bible history, it furnishes an argument in its favour, provided miracles are capable of proof.

If it be granted that miracles are possible, which every one who believes in a personal God, the creator of the world, must admit, and that they may occur as facts, then no one can defend the position that they cannot be proved to be facts unless on principles that subvert the fundamental laws of human belief. It cannot be urged that 'all experience and analogy are against them, for this is either to judge from our own narrow and limited experience of the whole course of

---

[1] Nor let a god interfere unless a difficulty present itself worthy of a god's unravelling.—Vv. 191, 192.

nature, and so to generalize upon weak and insufficient grounds; or else, if in the phrase "all experience" we include the experience of others, it is to draw a conclusion directly in the teeth of our data, for many persons, well worthy of belief, have declared that they have witnessed and wrought miracles. Moreover, were it true that all known experience was against miracles, this would not even prove that they had not happened, much less that they are impossible.'[1]

As revelation professes to be from God, and to teach us concerning His nature and character, some ask—How can He reveal Himself? The Infinite, they affirm, is incognizable by the finite, and hence a true and proper revelation of God in human language is impossible. This conclusion makes the science of theology impossible. Christians, therefore, like the Athenians, have been worshipping an unknown God. The human mind cannot represent the infinite; it cannot form an idea commensurate with it, but it has an apprehension of it, and believes that there is and must be something beyond our power of conception. It is a necessary attribute of God that He is incomprehensible; if He were not so He would not be God, or the being that comprehended Him would be God also. But it also belongs to the idea of God that He may be apprehended though not comprehended by His rational creatures: He has made them to know Him, though not to know Him all; to apprehend, though not to comprehend Him. We represent to ourselves the Divine Being with certain attributes, and we think of God as possessing all these attributes to such a degree that no addition can be made to them. We conceive of Him as absolutely perfect. The idea of the perfect is that of something to which nothing can be added; or,

[1] Rawlinson's *Historical Evidences.* Boston: Gould & Lincoln. 1868. P. 43.

as Aristotle describes it, that which has nothing beyond. We conceive of Him as infinite. The idea of the infinite is that of something to which something can ever be added; or, as the same philosopher describes it, that which has always something beyond. These two views are not inconsistent, but supplementary the one to the other. Our conception of the infinite, therefore, is not merely negative, it has a positive side. Our knowledge of both the infinite and finite is incomplete. We apprehend both under a few, and not under all, of their properties and relations. But in each case there is real knowledge; the mind apprehends it as real, and applies it as real. All human knowledge must be partial in reference to the object known, but it may be true as far as it goes. The knowledge of a child is partial and limited compared with that of a philosopher, but it is not the less real and true within its proper limits. Indeed, the philosopher is sometimes obliged to fall back upon the native convictions of the child as proofs of his doctrines. Whatever difficulty there may be in our knowledge of God, because it is partial and incommensurate with His nature, and in a revelation of Him that is not infinite as He is infinite, is a difficulty that is found in all human knowledge. We must rest in the belief that a partial knowledge of anything may be true and valid so far as it goes, and therefore available for all the practical purposes of knowledge.

Christians believe that the knowledge of God contained in the Bible is certain and sufficient for all practical purposes. They believe, moreover, that all the teachings of the Bible are communications from God to mankind, and consequently infallible. For this belief they appeal to the most convincing evidence.

This evidence, which is of an objective and historical character, cannot be invalidated by preconceived notions of what a revelation ought to be, or of what it ought to contain, for all such objections are founded on our ignorance. 'We know not beforehand,' says Bishop Butler, 'with reference to natural information, what degree of it God would afford to men; what means or disposition to communicate it He would give; what degree of evidence it would have; whether it would be imparted with equal clearness to all, and whether knowledge would be given at once or gradually; so we are ignorant of the same things in regard to revelation. The true question is, whether the Bible contains a real revelation, not whether it is such a one as we might have expected. Hence no valid objections against it can be founded on obscurity or inaccuracy of style, on various readings, on alleged discrepancies and disputes about authors, unless it had promised the contrary.'[1]

The Church has received the Holy Scriptures from the time that they were written as a revelation from God, as an authoritative and infallible standard of truth and duty. These Scriptures do not merely contain such a standard; they are such a standard. They are plenarily inspired. 'All Scripture is given by inspiration of God, and is profitable for doctrine, for reproof, for correction, for instruction in righteousness' (2 Tim. iii. 16).

That the Scriptures are inspired in the fullest sense, it is our purpose, with the help of God, to prove. After a few observations on the importance of the question, we will consider, (1) the canonicity and integrity of the Scriptures, their historical credibility and scientific accuracy; (2) the proofs of inspiration drawn from the character of the Scriptures themselves, their own testimony, and the testimony of the Church; (3) the various theories of inspiration, the distinction between inspiration and revelation, and the nature and extent of inspiration.

[1] Butler's *Analogy*, Part II. chap. iii.

CHAPTER II.

IMPORTANCE OF THE QUESTION.

THE very least truth is important, for all truth constitutes a grand harmony, which the admission of the most trifling error disturbs. Every error is a discord; every truth an accordant note in the music of the universe. But as some errors are more hurtful than others, so some truths are more important than others, on account of their central character in relation to systems of truth. If such truths be subverted, the centripetal force, which maintains in their orbits all revolving truths, is destroyed.

Of those truths of paramount importance to the Christian system is the inspiration of the Holy Scriptures, for with them the ultimate decision of all questions of doctrine and of practice rests. This is the position held by Protestants. The very essence of Protestantism, and the whole creed of the Protestant Church, may be summed up thus: 'None but Christ, and nothing but Holy Scripture.' Salvation is found in Christ alone, and the authentic record of this is contained in the Bible. This declaration was made with clearness and decision at the time of the Reformation. The authors of that glorious movement—that return to apostolic teaching—were convinced that the remedy for all the corruptions of ecclesiastical tradition lay only in the judicial authority of God's Holy Word. They restored this word to its proper position as the teacher of the Church, the umpire in all matters of Christian faith and practice, from which there could be no appeal, for its words and teachings are the words and teachings of the Holy Spirit.

The inspiration of the Scriptures has never been denied by the Roman Catholic Church, but the admission of tradition to co-ordinate authority with them renders them of no effect. When they are robbed of sole authority in matters of faith, their power is gone. The fallible and varying tradition of the Church is put on a level with the infallible and enduring word of God.

To maintain the infallible authority of this word is essential, if not to the very existence, at least to the well-being of the Church. It cannot maintain its purity and abate one iota from the declaration of the apostle, that 'all Scripture is given by inspiration of God, and is profitable for doctrine, for reproof, for correction, for instruction in righteousness;' for the spiritual culture of its members depends upon a proper estimate of the sacred volume. It is by means of it that the 'man of God' is made 'perfect, thoroughly furnished unto all good works' (2 Tim. iii. 16, 17).

Especially at this time, when rationalistic criticism and 'science, falsely so called' (1 Tim. vi. 20), are employing all their energies to demolish the defences of Christianity, and raze its temple to the very foundation, is it important to have correct views of the nature and extent of the inspiration of the Bible; for the word of God is the sure defence of the Church in its warfare against the powers of evil. The word is both living and written. The living word leads the armies of heaven, 'clothed in fine linen, white and clean' (Rev. xix. 14). The written word is the sharp two-edged sword which goeth out of His mouth, that with it He should smite the nations (Rev. i. 16, xix. 15).

The doctrine of the plenary inspiration of the Scriptures derives, moreover, importance from the fact that it is inseparably connected with the proper idea of Biblical interpretation. Plenary inspiration, rightly understood, implies that the Holy Spirit, in a sense explained in the sequel, is the author of the entire Bible ; that a perfect unity of plan and purpose pervades the whole, and that consequently there must be consistency of parts. One who believes in the inspiration of the Scriptures will, therefore, not approach them and treat them as he would any other book, but as the oracles of God, and as such he will study and expound their contents. Thus he will be preserved from the rash and destructive methods of rationalism. In order to study and elucidate any book with success, it is necessary to apprehend its true character. To ignore the inspiration of the Scriptures in our investigations of them must therefore lead to the most egregious errors.

What books are inspired ? Or, in other words, what books constitute the Holy Scriptures? The discussion of this question will form the subject of the following chapter.

CHAPTER III.

CANON OF SCRIPTURE.

THE discussion of the canon is distinct from that of inspiration, and preliminary to it. Its object is to determine what books are entitled to be received as inspired. On this point Romanists and Protestants differ. The former say that all those which the Church has decided to be divine in their origin, and no others, are to be thus received; the latter affirm that, so far as the question pertains to the Old Testament, those books, and those only, which Christ and His apostles recognized as the written word of God are to be regarded as canonical. The recognition of these books is given in the New Testament in a twofold manner. First, many of them are quoted as the word of God, and the Spirit is said to have uttered what is recorded in them. Secondly, Christ and His apostles refer to the sacred writings constituting the volume which the Jews regarded as divine as being what they claimed to be—the oracles of God.

As to the New Testament, only those books which can be proved to have been written by the apostles, or to have received their sanction, are to be recognized as of divine authority. The reason of this rule is obvious. The apostles were the duly authenticated messengers of Christ, of whom He said, 'He that heareth you, heareth me' (Luke x. 16).[1]

The books received by the Protestant Church as

[1] Hodge's *Systematic Theology*, vol. i. pp. 152, 153. New York: Charles Scribner and Company. 1872.

canonical and inspired are the thirty-nine books of the Old Testament, written in Hebrew, and the twenty-seven books of the New Testament, written in Greek. The canonicity and inspiration of these books are acknowledged by both the Roman Catholic and the Protestant Churches; though the former, since the time of the Council of Trent, which commenced its sessions A.D. 1545, has admitted into the canon several apocryphal books, which were from the first rejected by the Jewish Church, and also by the Christian Church until the meeting of that council.

As the evidence of the canonicity of the Old Testament depends in part upon the testimony of the New, the consideration of the canonicity of the latter properly precedes that of the former.

It is probable that the idea of a collection of the writings of the New Testament arose at a very early period among all the Christian communities. It originated soon after those communities received from the apostles memoirs of the Saviour's life and teaching, together with the epistles. They were prepared for it by having in their hands the Old Testament,—a collection formed centuries before,—of the inspiration of which there was only one opinion among both Jews and Christians. This collection was venerated by Christ, who called it *the Law* and *the Prophets* (Matt. v. 17, xi. 13; Luke xvi. 16); *your Law* (John x. 34); *the Scripture* (John x. 35); *the Scriptures* (Matt. xxii. 29; John v. 39). It was venerated by the apostles, who called it *the Oracles of God* (Rom. iii. 2; Heb. v. 12; 1 Pet. iv. 11). It was venerated by the Christian Church, in whose assemblies it was read. Such a collection would naturally lead to the idea of a similar collection of the sacred books of the New Testament.

Accordingly we find that the writings of the apostles were successively gathered into one collection, which was received by the primitive Christians equally with the Old Testament, was read in the religious assemblies, and was called *the Scriptures, the Book, the New Testament, the Divine Instrument, the Sacred Digest, the Divine Oracles, the Evangelists and the Apostles.*

The custom was early adopted of calling this collection the Canon or the Rule, and of denominating the books which constitute it canonical books.[1]

The books composing the canon of the New Testament were written at various times, and in different places, during the latter half of the apostolic century, by eight inspired authors. The canon, of course, was completed gradually, and was closed toward the end of the first century or the beginning of the second. It was regarded from the beginning as a complete whole, having God for its author, and destined throughout to reveal Jesus Christ; just as ancient Israel had regarded the collection of books forming the Old Testament, received in the same manner, as a single harmonious unit, having the same God for its author, and destined, throughout all its parts, to reveal to the Jewish Church the counsel of God for the redemption of the world.

Of this high regard for the divine oracles Professor Gaussen quotes two examples, taken from the first century of the Church or the beginning of the second. 'Let every one read,' says Professor Gaussen, 'how in the beautiful Epistle to Diognetus, the author, who styles himself one of the disciples of the apostles, presents *the Law and the Prophets, the Evangelists and the Apostles*, as acting together to bring into the Church grace and joy. He says: "Thus the fear of *the Law* is proclaimed, and the grace of *the Prophets* is comprehended, and the faith of *the Gospels* is founded, and the instruction of *the Apostles* is preserved, and the grace

---

[1] *The Canon of the Holy Scriptures.* By Professor L. Gaussen. Published by the American Tract Society. Pp. 18–22.

of the Church leaps for joy." Ignatius also, about A.D. 107, in one of his epistles, said to the Philadelphians (chap. v.): "Your prayer will secure my completeness in God. . . . Giving me refuge in *the Gospel*, as in the flesh of Jesus, and in *the Apostles*, as in the presbytery of the Church. And cling also to *the Prophets*, because they have themselves announced the gospel, hoped in Christ, looked for His coming in the unity of Jesus Christ, and found their salvation in Him by faith.'[1]

Twenty books of the New Testament—viz. the four Gospels, the Acts of the Apostles, the first thirteen epistles of Paul, counting the Epistle to the Hebrews as his, the First of Peter, and the First of John—were immediately received by all Christians, without having, from the beginning and for eighteen centuries, their divine authority called in question by the Church. These books Eusebius calls *homologoumena*, or undisputed. Professor Gaussen designates them the *first canon*.

The five brief later epistles—viz. James, the Second of Peter, the Second and the Third of John, and Jude—were not received immediately by the whole Church, though they were received by the majority of the churches. The reason of this, according to Professor Gaussen, was that they were written a short time before the deaths of their respective authors, and distributed after their deaths in a distracted period; and that consequently their authors could not be appealed to to confirm them. After some hesitation on the part of some of the churches, they were universally received. These books Eusebius calls *antilegomena, contested*, because, although recognised by the majority of the churches and ecclesiastical writers, they were not at first universally received, or received with some reservation and hesitation. They constitute, according to Professor Gaussen, the *second canon*.

[1] Gaussen on the *Canon*, pp. 23, 24.

The Epistle to the Hebrews and the Revelation of the Apostle John were at first universally received, and for that reason they were placed by Eusebius among the *homologoumena;* but afterward they were contested for a time, the one principally in the West and the other in the East. They were again universally acknowledged as constituting a part of the canon. Because they were at first received, then contested, and again received, Professor Gaussen has designated them the *second-first* canon.

These three divisions made by Professor Gaussen are convenient for the purpose of method. They are also conformable to the facts of ecclesiastical history. But it must be kept in mind that they are not made for the purpose of attributing less certainty of their divine origin to some of the books than to others; for though their certainty is not the same in a purely historical point of view, yet our faith in the authority of all is founded on the same solid basis.[1]

We have three catalogues anterior to the Nicene Council. The first belongs to the period of the Apostle John's death, at the end of the first century; the second belongs to the commencement of the third century; the last to the beginning of the fourth century. The first is furnished by the ancient Syriac version of the New Testament, called the Peshito. The second is given twice by Origen; first directly, in a homily on Joshua, and then indirectly in the quotations which Eusebius has made from his commentaries on Matthew, John, and the Epistle to the Hebrews. The third is furnished by Eusebius himself, in A.D. 324, in the third book of his *Ecclesiastical History.*

The Peshito version of the New Testament is the most ancient, and is considered one of the best. It was not known in Europe until A.D. 1552, when Moses

---

[1] Gaussen on the *Canon,* pp. 26-31.

of Mardin was deputed by the Patriarch of the Maronites to Pope Julius III. Michaelis, together with many eminent philologists, attributes it to the first century, or, at latest, to the second, and declares it to be the best version known to him, whether in regard to its elegance, freedom, or fidelity as a translation.

This ancient version contains our canon complete, with the exception of the Revelation and the four shorter and later epistles—Jude, Second Peter, and Second and Third John. Such, then, at the end of the first century, or at the beginning of the second, was the canon of the Syriac churches.

Here we notice two important facts:

(1) The absence of any apocryphal book, though they had begun in the East, from the second century, to publish many books under false apostolical titles.

(2) The order assigned to the sacred books is that uniformly found in the best and oldest Greek manuscripts: first, the four Evangelists, in their invariable order, Matthew, Mark, Luke, John; then the Acts; then the Catholic Epistles; and the fourteen epistles of Paul, always in the same order as we now have them, from Romans to Hebrews.

The next catalogue of the sacred books is that given by Origen. This celebrated man was born A.D 185, and died A.D. 253. We see from this catalogue—

(1) That, at the beginning of the third century, this great teacher received our entire canon.

(2) That all the churches had continued to admit, as they have ever since done, the twenty books which Professor Gaussen designates the first canon.

(3) That they equally acknowledged the two books of the second-first canon, viz. Hebrews and Revelation.

(4) That some persons doubted the canonicity of Peter's second epistle, and of John's two smaller epistles.

(5) That Origen, according to Eusebius, speaks of no opposition in his day to the epistles of James and Jude. Nor, indeed, does he there speak of his own acceptance of these divine epistles; but this is an evident oversight of Eusebius, since Origen, more than fifteen times in his works, alludes to the Epistle of Jude, and calls it a divine scripture.

(6) If many were led in his day, by the style of the Epistle to the Hebrews, to doubt Paul's authorship, yet that involved no doubt about its canonicity.

Eusebius, the father of ecclesiastical history, and bishop of Syrian Cæsarea, was born about A.D. 270. He divides the scriptures of the New Testament into books *recognised* (ὁμολογούμενα) and books *contested* (ἀντιλεγόμενα).

In his chapter entitled, 'Of the *recognised divine scriptures, and of those which are not*,' he says: 'It will be proper that at this point we should recapitulate the scriptures of the New Testament which we have already made known. Now we must rank in the first place the holy group of the *four Gospels*, which are followed by the scripture of the *Acts of the Apostles*. After this scripture we must insert in the catalogue the Epistles of Paul; then that of John, which is called the First; and we must equally ratify also the Epistle of Peter. With these books must be ranked, if you will, the *Apocalypse of John*, on which we will take occasion to give our views. Such are, then, the books which belong to the recognised.'

The scriptures which Eusebius places among the 'contested' are the five small epistles, viz. the Second of Peter, those of James and Jude, and the Second and Third of John. 'These contested scriptures,' he says, 'which are yet recognised by the great number of the people, and the majority of ecclesiastical writers, and publicly read with the other catholic epistles in the majority of the churches, are exposed to some contradictions, and less cited by the ancient authors.'

The canon of the New Testament is often spoken of as if the first General Council, convoked by Constantine to put an end to the divisions troubling the Church at the time, had enacted some decree on the catalogue of the Scriptures. This is a mistake; it enacted no decree on the subject.

On a throne, in the midst of that assembly, was laid the sacred volume of the Gospels, to signify, as was done in all the early General Councils, that the Scriptures are the supreme rule in all controversies. And Constantine, in his address to the members of the Council, reminded them that they had the doctrine of the Holy Spirit written; and that the books of the evangelists and of the apostles, and that the oracles of the prophets, teach us clearly and certainly what we must believe concerning the things of God, so that all differences must be determined by reference to the divinely inspired oracles. And the Council, in accordance with its 'Formula of Faith,' attested that it founded its doctrines solely on the divine Scriptures, when, in its preamble proposed by Eusebius, it said: 'As we learned in the Holy Scriptures, this is our creed: "I believe in one only God, the Father Almighty,"' etc. But amid all these professions, the Council never manifested the slightest thought of forming a decree on the catalogue of the New Testament.

Though the Council of Nice maintained a reserve in regard to the canon,—a reserve perhaps unconscious,—yet from the time of the assembly there was an immediate and marked change in the dispositions of those who had before manifested some uncertainty about the contested books. Hesitations immediately began to disappear, until at last the whole body of the Christian Church reached that admirable unanimity which they have now manifested for fifteen hundred years among every nation. The Council, without doubt, contributed powerfully, though indirectly, to this important result; because, by bringing together for three months, in intimate intercourse, the most illustrious and learned representatives of Christianity, opportunity was furnished for exchanging their views and comparing their respective manuscripts, and thus removing all unfounded prejudices, and recognising their universal agreement.

The Fathers and the Councils of the fourth century have left us eleven catalogues of the sacred books, without counting that of Eusebius. All these, without exception, are unanimous in recognising as canonical, not only the twenty books constituting the first canon, but also the Epistle to the Hebrews and the five books which Eusebius calls contested, and which have been denominated the second canon. Of these eleven catalogues of the fourth century, nine are found in the writings of the Fathers, and two in the decrees of Councils.

Nine catalogues of the fourth century are given by the Fathers; and of these, three, — those of Cyril, Gregory the theologian, and Philastrius,—agreeing fully on every other point with the canon of our churches, either do not name the Apocalypse, or state, with Amphilochius, that some still doubted its canonicity. Hug, in his introduction, says: 'Notwithstanding the unanimous opinion of the churches after the Council of Nice, the discussions in opposition to the Millenarians had been in some places too vivid, and in all too recent, for this book to have regained fully its place.'

All the six other catalogues of the Fathers of the fourth century are entirely conformed to that of our churches. They are—(1) that of Athanasius; (2) that of a contemporary Father whose name is unknown to us; (3) that of Epiphanius; (4) that of Jerome; (5) that of Rufinus; (6) that of Augustine.

Two Councils of this period expressed their views of the canon, viz. that of Laodicea and that of Carthage. The former was held in Asia Minor, A.D. 364, thirty-nine years after the Council of Nice; the latter in Africa, A.D. 397, thirty-three years later. The fifty-ninth and sixtieth canons of the Council of Laodicea, which are in fact the last two, and are numbered 163 and 164 in the Universal Code, which contained 207 before the time of Dionysius the Less, read as follows: 'Private psalms are not to be read in the church, nor any uncanonical books of the Old and New Testaments. These are the books of the Old Testament to be recognised: 1. The Genesis of the world; 2. The Exodus from Egypt; 3. Leviticus; 4. Numbers; 5. Deuteronomy; 6. Joshua; 7. Judges; 8. Ruth; 9. Esther; 10. Four books of Kings; 11. Two books of Chronicles; 12. First and Second of Ezra (Ezra and Nehemiah); 13. Book of one hundred and fifty Psalms; 14. Proverbs of Solomon; 15. Ecclesiastes; 16. Song of Songs; 17. Job; 18. Twelve Prophets; 19. Isaiah; 20. Jeremiah and Baruch, Lamentations and Epistles;[1]

---

[1] Professor Gaussen says: 'It must not be imagined that the Book of Baruch is here intended, but simply an exegetical manner of indicating more explicitly that which, according to the Jewish reckoning, the twentieth book contained, which we call Jeremiah and his Lamentations. It was nearly in the same terms that Origen already, a hundred years before, designated this same book' (Euseb. *Hist. Eccl. Lib.* vi. ch. 25). He says: 'Jeremiah with his Epistles and Lamentations forms but one book' (chap. xxx.). Athanasius and Cyril, in their designation of the Book of Jeremiah, add, with the Laodicean Council, the indication of the twenty-ninth chapter and of that which relates to Baruch. Besides, we see the Council has carefully numbered all of Jeremiah as the twentieth book.

Bleek is of the opinion that 'the epistle of Jeremiah is a pretended letter of Jeremiah to the Babylonian exiles against idolatry, which in Luther and the Vulgate stands at the end of the Book of Baruch (as chap. vi.), but in ancient manuscripts of the LXX. after Lamentations. Origen must have met with it in the latter place, which was doubtless its original position in the LXX. The latter is decidedly spurious, and without doubt

21. Ezekiel; 22. Daniel. The books of the New Testament are the four Gospels, according to Matthew, Mark, Luke, and John; the Acts of the Apostles; the seven Catholic Epistles, namely, one of James, two of Peter, three of John, one of Jude; fourteen epistles of Paul, namely, one to the Romans, two to the Corinthians, one to the Galatians, one to the Ephesians, one to the Philippians, one to the Colossians, two to the Thessalonians, one to the Hebrews, two to Timothy, one to Titus, one to Philemon.'

The Apocalypse was omitted in this catalogue. Many will attribute this silence to its not having been yet restored to the canon; but this explanation is entirely incompatible with contemporary facts. It is a much more satisfactory reason to assign, that the Fathers of this Council, while admitting the canonicity of this sacred book, judged it too symbolical and mystical for public reading in the churches.

We must not lose sight of the end which the Fathers of this Council had in view. Occupied with the single question, what books were to be read in the churches, they contented themselves with two declarations. By the first they forbade the reading of any non-canonical book; by the second they ordered the reading of the twenty-two books of the Old Testament, and twenty-six books of the New. But they nowhere said that they did not consider the Apocalypse, although they did not name it, as canonical, any more than the Church of England says it, when, on the one hand, in her Prayer Book (in the sixth of the Thirty-Nine Articles

was originally written in Greek. It is possible that there was a Hebrew translation of it, and that at the time of Origen it existed in this form in some manuscripts of a Hebrew Codex. But it is more probable that Origen was acquainted with it only in the LXX., and that he was induced to mention it, as he did, in the Hebrew canon, only because he had been accustomed to read it after the canonical scriptures of Jeremiah.'—Bleek's *Introduction to the Old Testament*. London: Bell and Daldy. 1869.

of Faith) she ranks the Apocalypse among the canonical books, and, on the other hand, in the calendar and the preface to the same liturgy she does not allow the Apocalypse to be read in public.

The Council of Carthage says: 'Now these are the canonical scriptures of the Old Testament. . . . And as to the New Testament—four Gospels, one book of the Acts of the Apostles; thirteen epistles of Paul, with one of the same to the Hebrews; two of Peter; three of the Apostle John; one of Jude; one of James; and one of the Apocalypse of John.' The Council adds: 'Let this be to make known to our brother and priest Boniface, or other bishops of those countries, the confirmation of this canon, because we have learned from the Fathers that they are the books to be read in the Church. At the same time, permission is granted to read the sufferings of the martyrs on the anniversaries of their death.'

From the foregoing testimonies we see that the voice of the universal Church was always unanimous, from the times of the apostles, in regard to the first canon; that from the time of the Council of Nice, it was unanimous in regard to the second; and that, in the course of the fourth century, it ended by pronouncing definitely on the second-first. The temporary and later hesitations of the Western Church, in regard to the Epistle to the Hebrews, had already almost entirely ceased, so that the canon was thenceforward universally recognised in all the Christian Churches.[1]

We now pass to a consideration of the canonicity of the books of the Old Testament.

The five books of Moses were, when finished, carefully deposited by the side of the ark of the covenant (Deut. xxxi. 24-26).

No doubt, copies of the sacred volume were made

---

[1] Gaussen on the *Canon*, pp. 31-92.

out before it was deposited in the Most Holy Place; for since it was there inaccessible to all but the priests, the people generally must have remained ignorant of the law, had there been no copies of it. We know that copies were written, for it was one of the laws regulating the duty of a king, when such an officer should be appointed, that he should write out a copy of the law with his own hand (Deut. xvii. 18-20).

It seems that the Book of Joshua was annexed to the volume of the Pentateuch; for we read that 'Joshua wrote these words in the book of the law of God.' And the matters contained in this book were of public concern to the nation, as well as those recorded in the law. For as in the latter were written statutes and ordinances to direct them in all matters, sacred and civil, so in the former was recorded the division of the land among the tribes. The possession of each tribe was here accurately defined, so that this book served as a national deed of conveyance. When other books were added to the canon, no doubt the inspired men, who were moved by the Holy Spirit to write them, would be careful to deposit copies in the sanctuary, and to have other copies put in circulation. But on this subject we have no precise information. We know not with what degree of care the sacred books were guarded, nor to what extent copies were multiplied.

A single fact shows that the sacred autograph of Moses had well-nigh perished in the idolatrous reigns of Manasseh and Amon, but was found during the reign of the pious Josiah among the rubbish of the temple (2 Kings xxii. 8-13; 2 Chron. xxxiv. 14-21). It cannot, however, be reasonably supposed that there were no other copies of the law scattered through the nation. It does, indeed, seem that the young king had never seen the book, and was ignorant of its contents until it was now read to him; but while the original had been misplaced and buried among the ruins, many pious men might have possessed private copies.

Although at the destruction of Jerusalem and of the temple by Nebuchadnezzar this precious volume was, in all probability, destroyed with the ark and all the holy apparatus of the sanctuary, yet we are not to credit the Jewish tradition that on this occasion all the copies of the Scriptures were lost, and that Ezra restored the whole by miracle. This is a mere Jewish fable, and is utterly inconsistent with facts recorded in the sacred volume. We know that Daniel had a copy of the Scriptures, for he quotes them, and makes express mention of the prophecies of Jeremiah. And Ezra is called 'a ready scribe in the law of Moses' (Ezra vii. 6); and it is said, in Ezra vi. 18, that when the temple was finished the functions of the priests and Levites were regulated 'as it is written in the book of Moses.' And this was many years before Ezra came to Jerusalem. And in Neh. viii. 1–3 it is said that Ezra, at the request of the people, brought the law before the congregation, and read therein from the morning until mid-day. It is evident, therefore, that all the copies of the Scriptures were not lost during the captivity. This story no doubt originated from two facts—the first, that the autographs in the temple had been destroyed with the sacred edifice; and the second, that Ezra took great pains to have correct copies of the Scriptures prepared and circulated.

It seems to be agreed by all that the forming of the present canon of the Old Testament should be attributed to Ezra. To assist him in his work, the Jewish writers inform us that there existed in his time a great synagogue, consisting of one hundred and twenty men, including Daniel and his three friends, Shadrach, Meshach, and Abednego, the prophets Haggai and

Zechariah, and also Simon the Just. But it is very absurd to suppose that all these lived at one time, and formed one synagogue, for from the time of Daniel to that of Simon the Just two hundred and fifty years must have intervened.

It is, however, not improbable that Ezra was assisted in this great work by many learned and pious men, who were contemporary with him; and as prophets had always been the superintendents as well as the writers of the sacred volume, it is likely that the inspired men who lived at the same time as Ezra would give attention to this work. But in regard to this great synagogue, the only thing probable is, that the men who belonged to it did not live in one age, but successively until the time of Simon the Just, who was made high-priest about twenty-five years after the death of Alexander the Great. This opinion has its probability increased by the consideration that the canon of the Old Testament appears not to have been fully completed until about the time of Simon the Just. It is generally conceded that Malachi lived after the time of Ezra, and therefore his prophecy could not have been added to the canon by this eminent scribe; unless we adopt the opinion that Malachi was Ezra himself—Ezra being his proper name, and Malachi an appellative given to him from the circumstance of his having been sent to superintend the religious affairs of the Jews. This opinion, though it has been held by some, is very improbable.

But this is not all. In the Book of Nehemiah mention is made of the high-priest Jaddua, and of Darius Codomanus, king of Persia (Neh. xii. 12), both of whom lived at least a hundred years after the time of Ezra. In the third chapter of the First Book of Chronicles, the genealogy of the sons of Zerubbabel is carried down at least to the time of Alexander the

Great. This book, therefore, could not have been put into the canon by Ezra; nor much earlier than the time of Simon the Just. The Book of Esther also was probably added during this interval.

The probable conclusion, therefore, is, that Ezra began this work, and collected and arranged all the sacred books which belonged to the canon before his time; and that a succession of pious and learned men continued to pay attention to the canon until the whole was completed, about the time of Simon the Just. After his time, nothing was added to the canon of the Old Testament.

Most, however, are of the opinion that nothing was added after the Book of Malachi was written, except a few names and notes; and that all the books belonging to the canon of the Old Testament were collected and inserted in the sacred volume by Ezra himself. And this opinion seems to be the safest, and is not incredible in itself. It accords also with the uniform tradition of the Jews, that Ezra completed the canon of the Old Testament, and that after Malachi there arose no prophet who added anything to the sacred volume.

Whether the books were now collected into a single volume, or were bound up in several codices, is a question of no importance. If we can ascertain what books were received as canonical, it matters not in what form they were preserved. It seems probable, however, that the sacred books were at this time distributed into three volumes, the Law, the Prophets, and the Hagiographa. This division we know to be as ancient as the time of the Saviour, for He says: 'These are the words which I spake unto you, that all things might be fulfilled, which are written in the Law of Moses, and in the Prophets, and in the Psalms, concerning me' (Luke xxiv. 44). Josephus also makes mention of this division, and it is by the Jews with one consent referred to Ezra as its author.

In establishing the canon of the Old Testament, we might labour under considerable uncertainty and embarrassment in regard to several books, were it not that the whole of what were called the Scriptures, and which were included in the threefold division mentioned above, received the explicit sanction of our Lord. He was not backward to reprove the Jews for disobeying, misinterpreting, and adding their traditions to the Scriptures; but He never drops a hint that they had been unfaithful or careless in the preservation of them. So far from this, He refers to the Scriptures as an infallible rule, which must be fulfilled, and cannot be broken (Mark xiv. 49; John x. 35). 'Search the Scriptures,' said He, 'for in them ye think ye have eternal life: and they are they which testify of me' (John v. 39). The errors of the Sadducees are attributed to an ignorance of the Scriptures (Matt. xxii. 29); and they are never mentioned but with the highest respect, and as the unerring Word of God. The Apostle Paul also, referring principally, if not wholly, to the Scriptures of the Old Testament, says: 'And that from a child thou hast known the Holy Scriptures, which are able to make thee wise unto salvation through faith which is in Christ Jesus. All Scripture is given by inspiration of God' (2 Tim. iii. 15, 16). They are called by the apostle 'the oracles of God' (Rom. iii. 2); by Stephen, 'the lively oracles' (Acts vii. 38); by Christ, 'the word of God;' and when quotations are made from David, the Holy Ghost is said to speak by the mouth of David (Acts iv. 25; Heb. iii. 7, iv. 7). The testimony of Peter is not less explicit, for he says: 'The prophecy came not in old time by the will of man: but holy men of God spake as they were moved by the Holy Ghost' (2 Pet. i. 21).

And the Apostle James speaks of the Scriptures with equal confidence and respect: 'And receive with meekness,' says he, 'the engrafted Word, which is able to save your souls.' 'And the Scripture was fulfilled which saith,' etc. 'Do ye think that the Scripture saith in vain?' (Jas. i. 21, ii. 23, iv. 5).

We have, therefore, an important point established with certainty, that the volume of Scripture which existed in the time of Christ and His apostles was uncorrupted, and was esteemed by them an infallible rule. Now, if we can ascertain what books were then included in the sacred volume, we shall be able to settle the canon of the Old Testament with certainty.

But here lies the difficulty. Neither Christ nor any one of the apostles has given us a catalogue of the books which composed the Scriptures of the Old Testament. They have distinctly quoted a number of these books, and so far the evidence is complete. We know that 'the Law,' 'the Prophets,' and 'the Psalms' were included in the canon. But this does not prove whether the very same books which we now find in the Old Testament were then found in it, and no other. It is necessary, therefore, to resort to other sources of information.

The Jewish historian, Josephus, furnishes us with the very information which we want, not indeed as explicitly as we could wish, but sufficiently so to lead us to a very satisfactory conclusion. He does not name the books of the Old Testament, but he numbers them, and so describes them that there is scarcely room for any mistake. The passage to which we refer is in the first book against Apion. 'We have,' says he, 'only twenty-two books which are to be believed as of divine authority, of which five are the books of Moses. From the death of Moses to the reign of Artaxerxes, the son of Xerxes, king of Persia, the prophets, who were the successors of Moses, have written in thirteen books. The remaining four books contain hymns to God, and documents of life for the use of man.' Now the five books of Moses are universally agreed to be Genesis, Exodus, Leviticus, Numbers, and Deuteronomy. The thirteen books written by the prophets include Joshua, Judges with Ruth, Samuel, Kings, Isaiah, Jeremiah with Lamentations, Ezekiel, Daniel, the twelve Minor Prophets, Job, Ezra, Esther, and Chronicles. The four remaining books are the Psalms, Proverbs, Ecclesiastes, and the Song of Solomon, making the whole number twenty-two, to correspond with the Hebrew alphabet, which consists of twenty-two letters. To accomplish this, the Jews annexed the book of Ruth to Judges, Lamentations to Jeremiah, made one of the two books of Samuel, one of the two books of Kings, one of the two books of Chronicles, and one of the twelve Minor Prophets.

There is another source of evidence, which is conclusive on this point. It is the fact that these books have been, ever since the time of Christ and His apostles, in the keeping of both Jews and Christians, who have been constantly arrayed in opposition to each other, so that it was impossible that any change should have been made in the canon by either party without being immediately detected by the other. And the conclusive evidence that no alteration in the canon has occurred, is the perfect agreement of these hostile parties at this time in regard to the books of the Old Testament. The Hebrew Bible of the Jew is the Bible of the Christian. There is here no difference. A learned Jew and a Christian have been associated in publishing an excellent edition of the Hebrew Bible. Now, if any alteration in the canon has occurred, it must have been by the concert or collusion of both parties; but the absurdity of this idea must be manifest to all.

What is here said of the agreement of Christians and Jews can be said only in relation to Protestant Churches. For as to the Romish and the Greek Churches, they have admitted other books into the canon, which Jews and Protestants hold to be apocryphal.

It is an important fact that, a short time after the canon of the Old Testament was closed, a translation was made at Alexandria in Egypt, at the request, it is said, of Ptolemy Philadelphus, king of Egypt, that he might have a copy of these sacred books in the famous library which he was engaged in collecting. A more probable opinion is, that it was made for the use of the Hellenistic Jews, who had adopted the Greek as their ordinary language. This version is called the Septuagint, from its having been made, according to tradition, by seventy, or rather seventy-two men,—six from each of the tribes of Israel. So many fabulous things have been reported of this translation, that it is very difficult to ascertain the exact truth. But it is manifest from internal evidence that it was not the work of one hand, nor probably of one set of translators; for while some books are rendered with great accuracy, and in a very literal manner, others are translated with little care, and the meaning of the original is very imperfectly given.

The probability is, that the Pentateuch was first translated, and that the other books were added from time to time by different hands; but when the work was once begun, it is not likely that it would be long before the whole was completed. Now this Greek version contains all the books which are found in our canonical Bibles. It is a good witness, therefore, to prove that all these books were in the canon when this version was made.

There is, moreover, a distinct and remarkable testimony to the antiquity of the five books of Moses in the Samaritan Pentateuch, which has existed in a form entirely separate from the Jewish copies, and in a character totally different from that in which the Hebrew Bible has been for many ages written. It has also been preserved and handed down to us by a people who have ever been hostile to the Jews. This Pentateuch has been transmitted through a separate channel ever since the ten tribes of Israel were carried captive. It furnishes authentic testimony to the great antiquity of the books of Moses, and shows how little they have been corrupted during the lapse of nearly three thousand years.

There are fourteen apocryphal books, sometimes inserted in our Bibles between the Old and New Testaments. The meaning of the term apocrypha is 'hidden, secret,' in which sense it is used in Hellenistic as well as in classical Greek. But towards the close of the second century it seems to have been associated with the signification 'spurious,' and ultimately to have been received in that meaning. Some of these books were adopted into the canon by the Council of Trent; but there is no authority for their canonicity. The arguments against their canonicity are—

(1) They are not found in the canon of the Old Testament.

(2) Though probably written by Jews, they were never received by that people as canonical.

(3) The New Testament makes no mention of them.

(4) They are not cited by the Christian Fathers as of divine authority, nor admitted into their catalogues.

(5) The writers were not prophets, and did not claim to be inspired.[1]

Why did the Jewish Church accept as inspired no

---

[1] Alexander on the *Canon*, *passim*.

other books than those contained in the Old Testament canon? They had other books. We read of the 'Book of the Wars of the Lord' (Num. xxi. 14); the 'Book Jasher' (Josh. x. 13; 2 Sam. i. 18); and 'the Acts of Uzziah, first and last,' written by Isaiah the prophet, the son of Amoz (2 Chron. xxvi. 22). It is therefore evident that, from a multitude of writings extant among the ancient Jews, a selection of certain books was made to the exclusion of others. The books thus selected were received as divine and infallible; those which were excluded were regarded as human and fallible. In defence of these books which were received as inspired, both Jews and Christians have submitted to persecution and death. The selection of these books cannot have been owing to their antiquity; for we have seen that there was extant in the days of Moses a record entitled 'the Book of the Wars of the Lord' (Num. xxi. 14). Nor was the fact that a book was written by a prophet sufficient to confer divine authority upon it; for we did not find in the canon 'the Acts of Uzziah, first and last,' written by Isaiah.

Nor did the circumstance that a book was composed in the Hebrew language secure it a place in the canon; for the Book of Ecclesiasticus, which was written in Hebrew, and whose author assumed the prophetic tone, was never received by the Jewish Church as inspired. Add to this the astonishing fidelity and affection with which the Jews preserved the writings which they did receive into their canon, though these writings contained the record of their shame. How can these facts be explained except upon the hypothesis that the Jewish Church had the most convincing evidence of the divine origin and authority of those books which they received into their canon as the oracles of God?

We have an exact parallel in the case of the New Testament canon. It is very evident that the primitive Christians received some documents as inspired and infallible, while they rejected others. Luke, in the preface to his Gospel, says: 'Forasmuch as many have taken in hand to set forth,' etc. (Luke i. 1); and Irenæus describes the apocryphal gospels as being 'countless in number.' It is also evident that the primitive Christian Church did not consider apostles as alone qualified to compose inspired documents, for Mark and Luke were not apostles. It cannot be alleged that the writings of these evangelists were received because, being companions and friends of the apostles, they had opportunities of gaining more accurate information respecting the life and teaching of Christ than others enjoyed; for if this were so, why did the Church never recognise as canonical the epistles of Clement and Barnabas, who were companions of the Apostle Paul? The only hypothesis which will account for the facts of the case is the same as that which has been already stated in regard to the canon of the Old Testament. The Church must have had conclusive evidence that the books composing the New Testament were the writings of men who wrote 'as they were moved by the Holy Ghost.'

We have given a brief outline of the canon of Holy Scripture, and of the evidence upon which the canonicity of each book rests. The Christian has a good foundation for his belief that the whole Bible as we have received it is the inspired word of God, and that it furnishes an infallible rule of faith and practice.

CHAPTER IV.

INTEGRITY OF THE HOLY SCRIPTURES.

VARIOUS readings and alleged discrepancies exist in the Bible. These have been used as arguments against its inspiration. They do not, however, affect the question, unless they are of such a character as to destroy the integrity of the Scriptures; and even in that case they would affect only quotations made by one writer from another, copies, and versions; for the original autographs could not contain various readings, and discrepancies, if any existed, might be easily reconciled, provided we had a perfect knowledge of all the circumstances of each case.

Inspiration, in the strict sense of that term, is of course limited to the autographs of the sacred writers, or to exact copies made from them in the same language. No translation can, strictly speaking, be said to be inspired, unless it infallibly represents the original. In a modified sense, however, translations may be said to be inspired, and we may claim for them divine authority. An official document does not lose its official character when it is translated into another language. Provided it conveys the sense of the original, it is equally binding with it, notwithstanding it may contain some inaccuracies of translation. Laws written in English, and translated into German for the benefit of our Teutonic citizens (in the United States), are just as obligatory upon them as the originals are upon the English-speaking community, though every shade of meaning may not be conveyed in the translation.

Various readings owe their origin (1) to accident, and (2) design. To those of the first class belong (*a*) the mistakes of transcribers made by confounding letters similar in shape, of which there are several in the Hebrew language, *e.g.* Beth and Caph, Gimel and Nun, Daleth and Resh, He and Hheth. So striking is the resemblance of each pair of these letters to one another, that it was an easy matter to interchange them. From the same cause they omitted letters, words, and sentences, especially when two clauses or periods terminated in the same way. The technical term for such omissions is *homoioteleuton*; *e.g.*, when a person writing from a manuscript meets, after a short interval, with the same word, or with a word ending with the same letters, he may easily fall into the mistake of omitting the intervening words.

(*b*) In case the transcriber employed another person to read for him while he wrote, he might hear wrongly or imperfectly, and thus fall into mistakes. He might write one letter for another, if the letters were similar in sound. In the same way he might write one word for another. Some identifications of *lo* (לא), not, and *lo* (לו), to him, are found in the Bible, *e.g.* Ps. c. 3: 'It is He that hath made us, and not we ourselves,' should be read, 'It is He that hath made us, and we are to Him,' *i.e.* we are His.

(*c*) Transcribers very likely made mistakes from memory. They perhaps relied upon it too much, wrote freely, and were mistaken about the exact words that they set down. Hence they were liable to transpose words and sentences, to omit them altogether, to confound synonymous terms, and to make changes according to known parallels.

(*d*) Transcribers may have made mistakes in judgment. It was an easy matter for them to misapprehend the text before them, and therefore to divide words badly, to misunderstand abbreviations, and to blunder with regard to the letters called *keepers of lines*, as well as to marginal notes. Sometimes one word was improperly separated into two, or two combined into one. Abbreviations were usually made by writing the first letter of a word and appending a small stroke or two, to indicate the omission of some letter. Hence the omission was sometimes erroneously supplied, or the abbreviated word was considered complete in itself.

The Jews did not divide a word at the end of a line when the space was too small to write it in full. They added letters to fill up this space, for the purpose of preserving the uniform appearance of the copy. These supernumerary letters were generally the initials of the following word, which was written entire in the next line. Ignorant transcribers may have taken these superfluous letters, called *keepers of the lines*, into the text. On the other hand, they may have suspected the existence of these *line-keepers* in places where they did not occur, and omitted part of the text. Marginal and liturgical annotations may sometimes have been taken into the text.

Intentional errors may be divided into two classes, viz. changes made in the text for the purpose of eliciting a different sense, and changes innocently introduced through uncritical officiousness. In the former case the intention was bad, for alterations were made by those who knew them to be corruptions; but in the latter the design was good, for the alterations were intended to improve the text, and make it more intelligible.

Intentional errors, if any, are very few. Some may have arisen from uncritical officiousness, but probably none from an intention of changing the sense. Both

Jews and Christians have always held their sacred books in too much veneration to justify a charge against them of such dishonesty. The former were accused by the Samaritans of falsifying Deut. xxvii. 4; but the corruption was due to their accusers. The Hebrew text is right, and the Samaritan reading wrong. The early Christians also brought the like accusation against them, but they were not competent witnesses. When the Jews quoted from the Hebrew Bible passages differing from the Septuagint, the Christians found it easiest to say that the Jews had corrupted the Scriptures in such places. Being ignorant of the Hebrew language, this was all the reply that they could make. It is, therefore, useless to adduce passages from the Christian Fathers to show that the Jews corrupted their Bible. Our Lord accused them of making 'the commandment of God of none effect by' their 'tradition;' but neither He nor His apostles accused them of corrupting their Scriptures.[1]

What has been said relates to the errors of transcribers. But there are alleged discrepancies of statement which cannot be accounted for in that way. They exist in the same copies, and must have existed in the original autographs themselves. They are due to various causes.

Many of the so-called discrepancies are attributable to a difference in the dates of the discordant passages. A description or statement, true and pertinent at one time, and in one state of affairs, may not be true and pertinent at another time, and in a different state of affairs. Change of circumstances necessitates a change of phraseology. For example, we read in Gen. i. 31, 'God saw everything that He had made, and behold it was very good;' and in Gen. vi. 6, 'It repented the

[1] Davidson's *Biblical Criticism*, chap. vi. Edinburgh: Adam and Charles Black. 1854.

Lord that He had made man on the earth, and it grieved Him at His heart.'

A certain infidel, bent upon making the Bible contradict itself, contrasts these two passages, and taking them out of their connection, and making no mention of the interval of time which divided them, seeks to make it appear that the Bible represents God as at the same time satisfied and dissatisfied with His works. Had he told his readers that the fall of man and a period of some fifteen hundred years intervened between the two epochs respectively referred to in these texts, his 'discrepancy' would have become too transparent for his purpose.

After man had fallen, God could no longer be satisfied with him, unless a corresponding change had taken place in Himself. We thus see that differences of date and circumstances may perfectly explain apparent discrepancies, and remove every vestige of contradiction.[1]

The Bible records the words of God and of good men, and also some of the sayings of Satan and of wicked men. A collision between these two classes of utterances will not seem strange to him who is cognizant of the antagonism of good and evil. For example, we read, 'Thou shalt surely die,' and, 'Ye shall not surely die' (Gen. ii. 17, and Gen. iii. 4). When we call to mind that the former are the words of God, and the latter the words of Satan, we are at no loss to account for the incongruity.

The question of the respective authorship of conflicting texts is an important one. 'Whose are these sayings?' 'Are they recorded as inspired language?' 'Are they inserted as mere matter of history?' 'Does the sacred writer endorse, or merely narrate, these statements?' The answer to these questions will often

---

[1] *Alleged Discrepancies of the Bible.* By John W. Haley, M.A. Andover: Warren F. Draper. 1874. P. 4.

be the only solution which the supposed discrepancy needs.[1]

Seeming disagreements are occasioned by differences of standpoint or of object. Truth is many-sided, flinging back from each of its countless facets a ray of different hue. Single texts of Scripture may be so interpreted, if not compared together and explained by each other, as to contradict one another, and to be each of them at variance with the truth. The Scriptures, if so studied, will no less mislead their readers than if they were actually false; for half the truth will very often amount to absolute falsehood.

In looking from different positions, or at different objects, we often follow lines of thought, or employ language, which seems inconsistent with something elsewhere propounded by us; yet there may be no real inconsistency in the case. Thus we say in the same breath, 'Man is mortal,' and 'Man is immortal.' Both statements are true; they do not collide in the least. In respect to his material, visible, tangible organism, he is mortal; but with reference to the deathless, intelligent spirit within, he is immortal.

In the *Christian Paradoxes*, published in Basil Montagu's edition of Lord Bacon's works, we find striking contrarieties. Thus, concerning the pious man,—

'He is one that fears always, yet is he bold as a lion.'

'He loseth his life, and gains by it; and whilst he loseth it, he saveth it.'

'He is a peacemaker, yet is a continual fighter, and is an irreconcilable enemy.'

In these cases no uncommon acuteness is requisite to see that there is no contradiction, since the conflicting sayings lie in different plains of thought, or contemplate different ends.

[1] *Alleged Discrepancies of the Bible.* By John W. Haley, M.A. P. 6.

The principle that every truth presents different aspects, and bears different relations, is one of great importance. Sometimes these aspects or relations may seem inconsistent or incompatible with each other; yet if we trace back the divergent rays to their source, we will find that they meet in a common centre.

The principle just enunciated serves to reconcile the apparent disagreement between Paul and James respecting faith and works, and to evince the profound underlying harmony between them. Looking from different points of view, they present different, yet not inconsistent, aspects of the same great truth.

In studying the Scriptures, therefore, we should carefully look for and keep in mind the particular point of view and the object of each of the authors. Unless we do this, we risk a total misapprehension of them.[1]

Discrepancies of a historical character are occasioned by the adoption, on the part of the several authors, of different principles and methods of arrangement. One writer follows the strict chronological order; another disposes his materials according to the principle of the association of ideas. One writes history minutely and consecutively; another omits, condenses, or expands, to suit his purpose.

The methods of the several authors being thus different, their narratives, when compared, will present appearances of dislocation, deficiency, redundancy, anachronism, or even antagonism. But if we were fully acquainted with their different principles and methods of arrangement, all these seeming discrepancies would disappear.

The Gospels furnish illustrations of this point.[2]

Other apparent discrepancies arise from the use of

---

[1] *Alleged Discrepancies of the Bible.* By John W. Haley, M.A. Pp. 7-9.
[2] *Ibid.* pp. 9, 10.

different modes of computation, particularly of reckoning time. Phenomena of this description are not confined to the Scriptures or to the domain of theology, they are found in scientific and other literature. Anatomists disagree in regard to the number of bones that compose the human skeleton. Some compute 204 bones; others, 246; some, 240; others, 208. There is, however, no real discrepancy in the case, since these authors reckon differently.

A historical illustration is also in point. The family record in an old Bible which belonged to Washington's mother asserts that he was born 'ye 11th day of February $173\frac{1}{2}$.' On the other hand, a recent biography of Washington gives the date as the '22d of February 1732, new style.' To those who understand the difference between 'old style' and 'new style' this discrepancy of eleven days will furnish no difficulty. When one historian reckons from one epoch, and another from a different one, there will of necessity be an apparent if not a real disagreement.

Many ancient and several modern nations have two kinds of year in use, the civil and the sacred. The Jews employed both reckonings. The sacred reckoning was that instituted at the exodus, according to which the first month was Abib; by the civil reckoning the first month was the seventh. The interval between the two commencements was thus exactly half a year.

The Egyptians, Chaldeans, Persians, Syrians, Phœnicians, and Carthaginians each began the year at the autumnal equinox, about September 22. The Jews also began their civil year at that time; but in their ecclesiastical reckoning the year dated from the vernal equinox, about March 22.

Among the Latin Christian nations there were seven different dates for the commencement of the year. In the era of Constantinople, which was in use in the

Byzantine empire, and in Russia till the time of Peter the Great, the civil year began with September 1, and the ecclesiastical sometimes with March 21 and sometimes with April 1. Even among us the academic and the fiscal do not begin and end with the civil year.

It follows, therefore, that when two ancient writers fail to agree as to the month and day of a given event, we must inquire whether or not they employ the same chronological reckoning. If not, their disagreement furnishes no proof that either is wrong. Each, according to his own method of computation, may be perfectly correct. When in the Fahrenheit thermometer the mercury stands at 212 degrees, in the Reamur at 80, and in the Centigrade at 100, the inference is not valid that any one of the instruments is inaccurate. The different methods of graduating the scale account for the different indications.

It was a peculiarity of the Jewish reckoning that fractional years were counted for whole ones. The very first day of the year may stand in computation for that year, or any part of the foregoing year may be reckoned a whole year. Thus, a child born in the last week of December would be reckoned a year old on the first day of January, because it was born in the old year.

The Jews often employed round numbers, or, omitting fractions, made use of the nearest whole number. Thus the ages of the patriarchs in the fifth chapter of Genesis are given in this manner, unless we adopt the improbable supposition that each of them died upon some anniversary of his birth.

The foregoing considerations evince the folly of hasty decisions in regard to biblical chronology. When the sacred writers disagree as to numbers and dates, unless there is evidence that they intended to reckon from the same point of time, and by the same method, we must not conclude that a discrepancy exists. The verdict must be: 'Discrepancy not proven.'[1]

Peculiarities of Oriental idiom are another source of discrepancies. The people of the East are fervid and impassioned in their modes of thought and expression. They think and speak in poetry. Bold metaphors and startling hyperboles abound in their writings and conversation. Passion and feeling predominate. In the Psalms pre-eminently we see the theology of the feelings rather than of the intellect. Logic is out of place there. Dogmas cannot be established on such a basis, nor was it ever meant to be so.

Such being the genius and idiom of the Orientals, it cannot be deemed strange that their metaphors and hyperboles overlap and collide with one another; that we find David, for example, at one time calling God a rock, and elsewhere speaking of his wings and feathers. Such bold and free imagery, when properly interpreted, develops a felicitous meaning; but when expounded according to literalistic, matter-of-fact methods, it yields discrepancies in abundance. To the interpreter of Scripture, no two qualifications are more indispensable than common sense and honesty.[2]

It is an Eastern custom to apply a plurality of names to the same person or object. In matters of everyday life this custom is widely prevalent. Thus in the Arabic there are 1000 different words or names for 'sword;' 500 for 'lion;' 200 for 'serpent;' 400 for 'misfortune;' 80 for 'honey.'

The Hebrew language has also many different words to denote the same thing. Gesenius gives many examples of this.

The usage in respect to proper names is quite similar. Thus, we find Jacob and Israel, Edom and

[1] *Alleged Discrepancies of the Bible.* By J. W. Haley, M.A. Pp. 11-13.
[2] *Ibid.* pp. 14-16.

Esau, Gideon and Jerubbaal, Hoshea or Oshea, and Jehoshua or Joshua. One of the apostles bore the following appellations:—Simon, Simeon, Peter, Cephas, Simon Peter, Simon Bar-jona, and Simon son of Jonas. So we find Joseph, Barsabas, and Justus designating the same individual.

Not infrequently the names of persons and places were exchanged on account of some important event. This custom prevails to some extent in modern times, *e.g.* the changing of the names of the popes at the time of their accession to the Papacy.

In the Bible the name of the head of a tribe or nation is frequently put for his posterity. Thus in many cases 'Israel' means the Israelitish nation; 'Ephraim' and 'Moab' signify the descendants of these men respectively. Keeping in mind the great latitude allowed by the Orientals in the use of names, we see the ready solution of many difficulties in the biblical record.

Some verbal contradictions arise from the use of the same word with different, sometimes opposite, significations. The Hebrew word 'barak' is used in the opposite senses of *to bless* and *to curse*. So 'yarash' means both *to possess* and *to dispossess*; 'nakar,' *to know* and *not to know*; 'shabar,' *to buy grain* and *to sell grain*. So the Latin word 'sacer' means both *holy* and *accursed*.

In our version of the Scriptures, and in early English literature, the word 'let' is employed with the contradictory meanings *to permit* and *to hinder*. Sometimes a word is employed in our version in an unusual or obsolete sense. Thus we find 'prevent' signifying *to anticipate* or *precede*; 'thought' in the sense of *anxiety*. Such examples, however, do not exist in the original. They are due to the infelicity of our own language.[1]

---

[1] *Alleged Discrepancies of the Bible.* By J. W. Haley, M.A. Pp. 17–19.

In view of the foregoing considerations, it is not surprising that various readings and seeming discrepancies should exist in the Bible. It is a book of high antiquity. The greater part of it was written in a language differing in genius, structure, and idiom from our own; among a people differing from us in manners, customs, and modes of thought; and in a country whose political institutions, history, geography, physical features, fauna, and flora, all contributed their share to mould its style and forms of thought. Some of its books have undergone transcription during more than three thousand years, and others during eighteen hundred years. Is it strange, then, that variations should exist?

The Bible in this respect has not fared worse than other books of much later date. The Latin and Greek classics exhibit great variety of readings, and many discrepancies. The works of Shakespeare, which have been in existence about two centuries and a half, have suffered within that brief period the common fate of all writings. The readings are very numerous, and furnish a wide field for literary criticism for those ambitious to settle the original Shakespearian text.

The various readings of the sacred text neither unsettle it nor essentially impair its integrity. They do not vitiate it in any appreciable degree. The conclusion reached by eminent scholars and critics, after protracted and thorough investigation, is, that the text of the Bible has been transmitted to us virtually unaltered.

'In the Hebrew manuscripts,' says Professor Stuart, 'that have been examined, some eight hundred thousand various readings actually occur as to the Hebrew consonants. How many as to vowel-points and accents no man knows. And the like to this is true of the New Testament. But, at the same time, it is equally true that all these taken together do not change or materially affect any important point of doctrine, precept, or even history. A great proportion, indeed the mass, of variations in Hebrew manuscripts, when minutely scanned, amount to nothing more than the difference in spelling a multitude of words. What matters it as to the meaning whether one writes *honour* or *honor*, whether he writes *centre* or *center?*'

Isaac Taylor remarks: 'The evidence of the genuineness and authenticity of the Jewish and Christian Scriptures has, for no other reason than a thought of the consequences that are involved in an admission of their truth, been treated with an unwarrantable disregard of logical equity, and even of the dictates of common sense. The poems of Anacreon, the tragedies of Sophocles, the plays of Terence, the epistles of Pliny, are adjudged to be safe from the imputation of spuriousness or of material corruption, and yet evidence ten times greater as to its quantity, variety, and force supports the genuineness of the poems of Isaiah and the epistles of Paul.'

Such scholars as Buxtorf, Bleek, Hävernick, Keil, and others affirm that the Jews took such extraordinary care in copying their sacred books, that it was their practice to count not only the number of verses, but also that of the words, and even of the letters of the various books, in order to ascertain the middle verse, the middle word, and the middle letter of each book. Such an enumeration of verses, words, and letters is found in the *Masora*, a rabbinic critical work upon the Old Testament.

In view of the scrupulous care practised by the Jews in the preservation of their Scriptures, Bishop Herbert Marsh observes: 'When we consider the rules which were observed by the Jews in transcribing the sacred writings,—rules which were carried to an accuracy that bordered on superstition,—there is reason to believe that no work of antiquity has descended to the present age so free from alteration as the Hebrew Bible.'

Notwithstanding its various readings and minute discrepancies, the text of the New Testament is better established than that of any other ancient book. No one of the so-called classics, not Homer nor Herodotus, compares favourably in this respect with the New Testament. Of the manuscript copies of the Greek Testament, from seven hundred to one thousand of all kinds have been examined already by critics; and of these at least fifty are more than one thousand years old, and some are known to be at least fifteen hundred years old, while the oldest manuscripts of the Greek classics scarcely reach the antiquity of nine hundred years, and of these the number is very small compared with those of the Greek Testament.

Among the Greek classical writers, Herodotus and Plato are of the first importance. The earliest manuscripts of Herodotus extant are, one in the Imperial Library at Paris, executed in the twelfth century; one in the Florentine Library, assigned to the tenth century; and one in the Library of Emmanuel College, Cambridge, England, which may possibly have been written in the ninth century. One of the earliest manuscripts of Plato is in the Bodleian Library at Oxford, and was executed not earlier than the ninth century.

Among the manuscripts of the New Testament we have the Alexandrian, written about A.D. 350; the Vatican, written about A.D. 325; the Sinaitic, of an equally early date; the Ephraim manuscript, probably somewhat later than the Alexandrian, but of great critical value; and the Beza manuscript, dating about A.D. 490. Scholars, though not entirely, yet substantially concur in these dates.

Here, then, we find five manuscripts of the Greek New Testament, the latest of which is about fourteen hundred years old, and all of which may have been prepared by persons who had studied the original manuscripts written by the apostles themselves.

So far, therefore, as an authenticated and settled text is concerned, the classics are very far behind the New Testament. There is not, says Tregelles, such a mass of transmissional evidence in favour of any classical work. The existing manuscripts of Herodotus and Thucydides are modern enough when compared with some of those of the New Testament.

Such is the conclusion of one well qualified to express an opinion on the matter, and it is the conclusion arrived at by all the most celebrated textual critics.

Scrivener says, in his *Criticism of the New Testament*: 'Now the experience we gain from a critical examination of the few classical manuscripts that survive should make us thankful for the quality and abundance of those of the New Testament. These last present us with a vast and almost inexhaustible supply of materials for tracing the history and upholding (at least within certain limits) the purity of the sacred text; every copy, if used diligently and with judgment, will contribute somewhat to these ends. So far is the copiousness of our stores from causing doubt or perplexity to the genuine student of Holy Scripture, that it leads him to recognise the more fully its general integrity in the midst of partial variation.'[1]

Many of the discrepancies of statement are the product of the imagination of the critic, or of his dogmatic prejudices. Some critics, such as Strauss and Colenso, seem resolved either to find a discrepancy or to make one. Moses and the evangelists must be

---

[1] *Alleged Discrepancies of the Bible.* By J. W. Haley, M.A. Pp. 41–54.

made to contradict themselves, whether they will or not, because the critical and dogmatic aims of these men require it. Such men, of course, would reject any solution that would vindicate the historical accuracy and truth of the Bible. 'They have a convenient method of disposing of answers to the objections adduced by them. They begin at once to talk loftily of the higher criticism, and to deride the answers and solutions as gratuitous assumptions.' All that can be done with such men is to show the absurdity of their canons of criticism, their unfairness in handling the Scriptures, their inconsistency, pertness, and ignorance.

Discrepancies which are purely subjective, originating not in the sacred books, but in the prejudices and disordered imagination of the critic or reader, must remain unsolved until these subjective obstacles to a candid and impartial consideration of them are removed. When that is done many discrepancies and difficulties will disappear. Should any remain after the most diligent and persistent efforts to remove them, true candour and honest impartiality would lead us to conclude, not that they are inexplicable, but that some facts necessary to their explanation are wanting.

Alleged discrepancies of the Bible are very numerous, but real discrepancies are very few; and those which are such are not greater than many that are found in historical writings of admitted veracity and credibility. Solutions of them have been given satisfactory to many minds of great critical acumen, and capable of estimating the results of historical criticism. The conclusion which has been reached by many such minds may be expressed in the words of one[1] who has devoted a work of nearly five hundred pages to an

---

[1] John W. Haley, M.A., author of the *Alleged Discrepancies of the Bible*. Andover: Warren F. Draper. 1874.

examination of the subject—a work 'adapted to the wants of men at the present time, and taking due account of modern investigation and discovery.' In the preface to that work, the author remarks: 'I may be allowed to say, that the more thoroughly I have investigated the subject the more clearly have I seen the flimsy and disingenuous character of the objections alleged by infidels. And whether or not my labours shall result in inducing a similar belief in the minds of my readers, I cannot but avow, as the issue of my investigations, the profound conviction that *every difficulty and discrepancy in the Scriptures* are, and will yet be seen to be, capable of a fair and reasonable solution.'[1]

It is not pertinent to the aim of this treatise to do more than to indicate in the briefest manner the design of these discrepancies. They evidently serve a high moral end by stimulating the intellect, by illustrating the analogy of the Bible and nature, by disproving collusion on the part of the sacred writers, by leading us to value the spirit above the letter of the Bible, and by serving as a test of moral character. They furnish an opportunity of testing the saying of our blessed Saviour: 'If any man will do His will, he shall know of the doctrine, whether it be of God, or whether I speak of myself' (John vii. 17).

[1] *Alleged Discrepancies of the Bible*, Preface, p. ix.

CHAPTER V.

HISTORICAL CREDIBILITY OF THE SCRIPTURES.

THE Holy Scriptures of both the Old and the New Testament are distinguished from all other religious books by their objective, or historical, character. They contain an important body of facts, which may by investigation be duly attested, and shown to be in accordance with other known facts. As historical science advances, questions are raised afresh concerning the real character of those events which form the basis of our holy religion, and the real character of those documents to which it appeals. By appealing to those documents, it invites historical inquiry, and feels confident that it can stand the test of the most thorough and repeated investigation. It only asks that sound principles be assumed as proper criteria of historic truth, and that they be fairly and legitimately applied.

A brief statement of the criteria of the credibility of a historian, and of the canons of historical criticism, will conduce to a clearer understanding of the subject under present consideration.

The criteria of the credibility of a historian are two: (1) purpose to relate facts; (2) means of knowing the facts. The purpose to relate facts is easily discernible in the book itself. Take, for example, Livy, Tacitus, Virgil, and Ovid. We cannot conceive of any one being so devoid of understanding as to imagine that the former two intended to relate fiction, and the latter two, facts. So in regard to the books of the Bible. The authors of the historical books intended to relate facts, or they were guilty of fraud, —a supposition impossible under the circumstances of the case. These authors had also the means of knowing the facts which they relate. They were many of them contemporary with the facts, and of course had personal knowledge of them. They were also in possession of official records or pre-existing documents, and of popular tradition.

The laws of modern historical criticism, which are assumed in the writings of our best historians, and involved in their criticisms, are formulated by Mr. Rawlinson in the four following propositions:—

(1) 'When the record which we possess of an event is the writing of a contemporary, supposing that he is a credible witness, and had means of observing the fact to which he testifies, the fact is to be accepted as possessing the first or highest degree of historical credibility. Such evidence is on a par with that of witnesses in a court of justice; with the drawback, on the one hand, that the man who gives it is not sworn to speak the truth, and with the advantage, on the other, that he is less likely than the legal witness to have a personal interest in the matter concerning which he testifies.

(2) 'When the event recorded is one which the writer may be reasonably supposed to have obtained directly from those who witnessed it, we should accept it as probably true, unless it be in itself very improbable. Such evidence possesses the second degree of historical credibility.

(3) 'When the event recorded is removed considerably from the age of the recorder of it, and there is no reason to believe that he obtained it from a contemporary writing, but the probable source of his

information was oral tradition; still, if the event be one of great importance, and of public notoriety, if it affected the national life or prosperity, especially if it be of a nature to have been at once commemorated by the establishment of any rite or practice—then it has a claim to belief as probably true, at least in its grand outline. This, however, is the third, and a comparatively low, degree of historical credibility.

(4) 'When the traditions of one race, which, if unsupported, would have had but small claim to attention, and none to belief, are corroborated by the traditions of another, especially if a distant or hostile race, the event which has this double testimony obtains thereby a high amount of credibility, and if not very unlikely in itself, thoroughly deserves acceptance. The degree of historical credibility in this case is not exactly commensurable with that in the others, since a new and distinct ground of likelihood comes into play. It may be as strong as the highest, and it may be almost as weak as the lowest, though this is not often the case in fact. In a general way, we may say that the weight of this kind of evidence exceeds that which has been called the third degree of historical credibility, and nearly approaches to the second.'

To these four canons 'modern rationalism would add a fifth, an *à priori* opinion of its own, the admission of which would put a stop at once ' to any investigation of the truth of the Scripture records. 'No just perception of the true nature of history is possible,' says the modern rationalist, 'without a perception of the inviolability of the chain of finite causes, and of the *impossibility* of miracles.'[1]

The fact that a narrative deals in the supernatural destroys in the mind of the rationalist its historical

[1] Rawlinson's *Historical Evidences*, Lect. I. pp. 39, 40, 42.

character; and, according to his principles of interpretation, relegates it into the realm of the mythical.

If miracles cannot take place, our present inquiry is in vain; for revelation is itself miraculous, and therefore by the hypothesis impossible. But we have already seen that, on the assumption of the existence of a personal God, the Creator of the world, miracles are neither impossible nor improbable.[1] It is a bold and unwarrantable assertion to say that God cannot, if it seems good to Him, suspend the working of those laws by which He commonly acts upon matter, and act on special occasions differently. His immutability does not stand in the way of miracles; for if we apply the notion of law to God at all, it is plain that miraculous interpositions may, on fitting occasions, be as much a regular, fixed, and established rule of His government, as the ordinary working of what are called natural laws.

It is unnecessary to discuss this point, as we have assumed that the world was created; and on this postulate, the occurrence of one stupendous miracle at least is proved. The occurrence of others must be determined by the ordinary rules of evidence. No man can, without the highest presumption, affirm that miracles cannot take place, unless he knows all the relations that the laws of nature sustain to Him who established them; and no man can say that miracles have never occurred, unless he possesses all the experience of the whole world, from the beginning until now. We reject, therefore, the canon of the modern rationalists, that 'no just perception of the true nature of history is possible without the perception of the inviolability of the chain of finite causes, and of the *impossibility* of miracles.' It is an *ex post facto* canon, enacted as a last resort by rationalists, in their

[1] Introductory Remarks, chap. i.

desperate efforts to destroy the historical credibility of the Scripture records.

A full examination of the historical evidences of the Bible, in accordance with the four canons which have been stated, and whose truth is admitted, would require many volumes. A brief outline is all that can be attempted consistently with the plan of the present treatise. Any one who wishes to read a masterly treatment of the subject will find it in the scholarly work of George Rawlinson, M.A., on *The Historical Evidences of the Truth of the Scripture Records*, which combines a complete survey and a logical method, with copious specific proofs and illustrations. From that work the materials of this outline are principally drawn.

If we proceed down the stream of history, the proper starting-point is the Pentateuch. With that we will begin.

(1) The ancient, positive, and uniform tradition of the Jews has assigned the authorship of the Pentateuch, with the exception of the last chapter of Deuteronomy, to Moses. It being an admitted rule of all sound criticism, that books are to be recognised as proceeding from the writers whose names they bear, unless very strong reasons can be adduced to the contrary, we must receive this tradition as *prima facie* evidence of its Mosaic authorship, so far at least as to throw the burden of proof upon those who call it in question. The reasons of critics who do so, rest upon misconceptions of the meaning of passages, upon arbitrary and unproved hypotheses, and upon such *à priori* conceptions as might be urged against any writer in advance of his age.

(2) Doubts have been expressed as to the existence of writing in the time of Moses. The evidence of the Mosaic records themselves, if the true date of their

composition be allowed, is conclusive upon this point, for they speak of writing as a common practice. Apart from this evidence, there are hieroglyphical inscriptions upon stone, known in Egypt at least as early as the fourth dynasty, or B.C. 2450;[1] inscribed bricks, which were common in Babylon about two centuries later; and writing upon papyrus, both in the hieroglyphic and hieratic characters, which was familiar to the Egyptians under the eighteenth and nineteenth dynasties, the time to which the Mosaic records belong. If Moses was educated by a daughter of one of the Ramesside kings, and learned, as we are told (Acts vii. 22), in all the wisdom of the Egyptians, it seems certain that he would be acquainted with the Egyptian method of writing with ink upon papyrus. It is also probable that Abraham, who emigrated not earlier than the nineteenth century B.C. from 'Ur of the Chaldees' (Gen. xi. 31), would bring with him, and transmit to his descendants, the alphabetic system of his country.

(3) Many heathen writers—Hecatæus of Abdera, Manetho, Lysimachus of Alexandria, Eupolemus, Tacitus, Juvenal, and Longinus—ascribe to Moses the institution of that code of laws by which the Jews were distinguished from other nations; and the majority distinctly note that he committed his laws to writing. This is equivalent to ascribing to him the authorship of the Pentateuch. If we had the complete works of those many other writers to whom Josephus, Clement, and Eusebius refer as mentioning Moses, the amount of heathen evidence on this point would be greatly increased.

(4) The Pentateuch itself furnishes internal testimony to its Mosaic authorship. It tells us that God

---

[1] According to the Hebrew chronology, this date would be prior to the flood; but according to that of the Septuagint, it would be some centuries after that event.

commanded Moses to 'write' the discomfiture of Amalek 'in a book' (Heb. in *the* book, Ex. xvii. 14); that Moses wrote all the words of the Lord (Ex. xxiv. 4), and 'took the book of the covenant and read it in the audience of the people' (Ex. xxiv. 7); and 'wrote the goings out of the people of Israel according to their journeys by the commandment of the Lord' (Num. xxxiii. 2); and 'made an end of writing the words of this law in a book, until they were finished' (Deut. xxxi. 24); and 'commanded the Levites, which bare the ark of the covenant of the Lord, saying, Take this book of the law, and put it in the side of the ark of the covenant of the Lord your God, that it may be there for a witness against thee' (Deut. xxxi. 25, 26). A book, therefore,—a book of the covenant, a book out of which he could read the whole law (Deut. xxviii. 58, xxix. 20, 27),—was certainly written by Moses; and this book was deposited in the ark of the covenant, and given into the special custody of the Levites, who bore it, with the strict injunction, 'Ye shall not add to the word which I command you, neither shall ye diminish aught from it' (Deut. iv. 2); and they were charged 'at the end of every seven years, in the year of release, at the feast of Tabernacles, to read it before all Israel in their hearing' (Deut. xxxi. 10, 11); and further, a command was given that, when the Israelites should have kings, each king should 'write him a copy of the law in a book, out of that which was before the priests the Levites, that he might read therein all the days of his life' (Deut. xvii. 18, 19). We must, therefore, either admit the Pentateuch to be genuine, or we must suppose that the book which the Jews ascribed to Moses as its author, which was placed in the ark of God, over which the Levites were commanded to watch with jealous care, which was to be read to the people every seven years, and which was guarded by awful sanctions from additions and diminutions, perished, and that another book was substituted in its place by an unknown author, for unknown objects, professing to be the work of Moses, and believed to be his thenceforth, without so much as a doubt being expressed on the subject, either by the nation, its teachers, or even its enemies, for many hundred years. Those who deny the Pentateuch to be genuine must suppose all this. The supposition is certainly very improbable, and cannot be entertained. As to the date of the introduction of the forged volume, they vary by more than a thousand years, and differ also from one another in every detail in which they venture to clothe the transaction.

The admission of the Mosaic authorship of the Pentateuch involves the admission of the authenticity of the narrative in all its main particulars. For the most sceptical acknowledge it to be an argument of decisive weight in favour of the credibility of the Bible, if it can be shown that it was written by eye-witnesses. Moses was such a witness. He was the leader of the Israelites during their forty years' journeying between Egypt and Canaan. He was consequently conversant with all the events connected with that journey, and was qualified to give a faithful history of them. Deception under the circumstances was impossible. If, then, he wrote the account which we possess of the exodus and of the wanderings in the wilderness, and delivered it to those who knew the events as well as he, the conditions which secure the highest degree of historical credibility, so far at least as regards the events of the last four books, are obtained. We have for them the direct witness of a contemporary writer—not an actor only, but the leader in the transactions which he relates. The record shows him to be honest, for he mentions his own sins and the transgressions of the people. He is honest necessarily, for he writes of events which were public and known to all.

(5) The book of Genesis stands on a different footing from that of the other books of the Pentateuch. Our confidence in it must rest mainly on our conviction of the inspiration of the writer. But apart from that, as an ordinary historian he would naturally possess that knowledge of the time of the first going down into Egypt, and of the history of Joseph,—which the most sceptical of the historical critics allow,—that men have of their own family and nation, from the days of their grandfathers to their own time. His mother was the daughter of Levi; and consequently he would be good authority for the details of Joseph's history, and for the latter part of the life of Jacob. With respect to the earlier history, it passed, according to the Hebrew chronology, through very few hands to Moses. According to this chronology, Moses might, by mere oral tradition, have obtained the history of Abraham, and even of the deluge, at third or fourth hand; and that of the temptation and the fall at fifth or sixth hand. The longevity of the patriarchs had the effect of reducing centuries to little more than lustrums, so far as the safe transmission of historical events was concerned, for this does not depend upon years or upon generations, but upon the number of links in the chain through which the transmission takes place. Moses, therefore, would have little difficulty in acquiring his historical information of the early events of our world by oral tradition.

It is highly probable, however, that he made use of documents. Without lending any countenance to the fanciful speculations which have been advanced in connection with the documentary and fragmentary hypotheses, we may affirm, without dogmatizing in the matter, that both antecedent probability and the internal evidence seem to favour the opinion that Moses consulted monuments or records of former ages, which had descended from the patriarchs, for the composition of his history. This is the opinion of Vitringa and Calmet, and certainly far from being improbable. Written documents existed before the time of Moses; for our knowledge of the antiquity of writing, both in Egypt and Babylon, renders it probable that the art was known and practised soon after the flood, if it was not even, as some have supposed, a legacy from the antediluvian world.

(6) Hitherto we have considered the weight which attaches to the Pentateuch itself, viewed as a historical work, written by a certain individual, under certain circumstances, and at a certain period. We now proceed to examine the external evidence to the character of the Mosaic narrative furnished by the other ancient records in our possession, so far at least as these have a fair claim to be regarded as of any real historic value.

The only reliable records besides the Pentateuch for the history of the period which it embraces, are some fragments of Berosus and Manetho, an epitome of the early Egyptian history of the latter, a certain number of Egyptian and Babylonian inscriptions, and two or three valuable papyri. A preference is assigned to these materials, for the reason that they are the records of Egypt and Babylon, two countries which, according to the most trustworthy accounts, both sacred and profane, were the first seats of civilisation. In them writing seems to have been practised earlier than elsewhere. They paid from the first great attention to history, and possessed, when the Greeks became acquainted with them, historical records of an antiquity confessedly greater than that which could be claimed for the documents of any other nation.

Manetho the Sebennyte, and Berosus the Chaldean,

had free access to the national records, and so could draw their histories directly from the fountain-head; and though they were long suspected by the learned, yet monuments which have been recovered furnish the strongest evidence of their honesty, diligence, and carefulness.

(7) On comparing the Mosaic account of the first period of the world's history with the outline obtained from Egyptian and Babylonian sources, we are struck at first sight with what seems an enormous difference in chronology. The sum of the years in Manetho's scheme, as it has come down to us in Eusebius, is little short of thirty thousand, while that in the scheme of Berosus, as reported by the same author, exceeds four hundred and sixty thousand. Omitting what in each case is plainly a mythic computation, we have in the Babylonian scheme a chronology which mounts up no higher than 2458 years before Christ, or 800 years after the deluge according to the numbers of the Septuagint; and in the Egyptian scheme a discrepancy of a few hundred years between it and the Scripture chronology. This is a discrepancy of very little moment, and one which might easily arise from slight errors of the copyists, or from an insufficient allowance being made in Manetho's scheme in respect of either or both of the causes from which Egyptian chronology is always liable to be exaggerated. Some of the most celebrated Egyptologists are in favour of a chronology almost as moderate as the historic Babylonian. The accession of Menes, according to them, falls about 2660 years before Christ, or more than 600 years after the Septuagint date of the deluge.

(8) The removal of the chronological difficulty opens the way to a consideration of the positive points of agreement between the Scripture narrative and that of the profane authorities.

The cosmogony of Berosus is in close agreement with that of Moses. According to the Chaldean historian, the earth was 'without form and void,' and 'darkness was upon the face of the deep.' He represents the Creator as dividing the watery mass, and making the two firmaments, that of the heaven and that of the earth. The light is spoken of before the sun and moon. A divine element is infused into man at his creation, and he is formed 'from the dust of the ground.' Between the first man (including the first man) and the deluge are ten generations, the exact number given in the fifth chapter of Genesis. The duration of human life is very much exaggerated by Berosus; but we see in this exaggeration a glimpse of the truth, that the lives of the patriarchs were extended far beyond the term which has been the limit in later ages.

(9) Berosus' account of the deluge is still more strikingly in accordance with the narrative of Scripture; and though the events following that catastrophe are reported with some disagreement by writers whose Babylonian history seems drawn directly from him, or from sources which he used, yet there is reason to believe that he mentions the building of the tower of Babel and the confusion of tongues. These writers make distinct allusion to both these events.

(10) The confusion of tongues is represented by the sacred historian as the occasion of the dispersion of the human family over the earth (Gen. xi. 7-9). The preceding chapter, which chronologically succeeds, gives, with wonderful grasp, and still more wonderful accuracy, a sketch of the nations of the earth, their ethnic affinities, and to some extent their geographical position and boundaries. This sketch has extorted the admiration of modern ethnologists, who continually find in it anticipations of their greatest discoveries.

One of the most recent and unexpected results of modern linguistic inquiry is the proof which it has furnished of an ethnic connection between the Ethiopians or Cushites, who adjoined on Egypt, and the primitive inhabitants of Babylonia; a connection which was positively denied by an eminent ethnologist only a few years ago, but which has now been sufficiently established from the cuneiform monuments. In the tenth chapter of Genesis, we find this truth briefly but clearly stated. 'And Cush begat Nimrod, the beginning of whose kingdom was Babel' (Gen. x. 8–10). So we have had it recently made evident from the same monuments that 'out of that land went forth Asshur and builded Nineveh' (ver. 11); or that the Semitic Assyrians proceeded from Babylonia and founded Nineveh long after the Cushite foundation of Babylon. Again, the Hamitic descent of the early inhabitants of Canaan, which had often been called in question, has recently come to be looked upon as almost certain, apart from the evidence of Scripture; and the double mention of Sheba, both among the sons of Ham and also those of Shem, has been illustrated by the discovery that there are two races of Arabs—one (the Joktanim) Semitic, the other (the Himyaric) Cushite or Ethiopic. On the whole, the scheme of ethnic affiliation given in the tenth chapter of Genesis is pronounced safer to follow than any other, and commends itself to the ethnic inquirer as the most authentic record that we possess for the affiliation of nations, and as a document of the very highest antiquity.

(11) At the time of Abraham, the narrative of the Book of Genesis passes from a general to a specific character. It gives the history of that patriarch and his descendants from the time that he left Ur of the Chaldees until the death of Joseph in Egypt. The confirmation which profane history lends to this special

narrative is only occasional, and for the most part incidental. There are several very interesting notices of Abraham and his successors from heathen pens; but they are of far inferior moment to the authorities hitherto cited, since they do not indicate a separate and distinct line of information, but are in all probability derived from the Hebrew records. They consist of passages which Eusebius produces in his *Gospel Preparation*, from Eupolemus, Artapanus, Molo, Philo, and Cleodamus or Malchas, with regard to Abraham; and from Demetrius, Theodotus, Artapanus, and Philo, with respect to Isaac and Jacob.

There are three points only in this portion of the narrative which, being of the nature of public and important events, might be expected to obtain notice in the Babylonian or Egyptian records. Did we possess the complete monumental annals of the two countries, or the complete works of Berosus and Manetho, we might adduce evidence from them of all these events; but with the fragmentary remains that have come down to us, we are able to produce a decisive confirmation of only two. These two are the expedition of Chedor-laomer and the exodus of the Jews. The event of which they are silent is the great famine in the days of Joseph.

The monumental records of Babylonia bear marks of an interruption in the line of native kings about the date which from Scripture we would assign to Chedor-laomer, and point to Elymais (or Elam) as the country from which the interruption came. We have mention of a king, whose name is on good grounds identified with Chedor-laomer, as paramount in Babylon at this time—a king apparently of Elamitic origin; and this monarch bears in the inscriptions the unusual and significant title of *Apda Marta*, or 'Ravager of the West.' The fragments of Berosus give no names at this period; but his dynasties exhibit a transition at about the date required, which is in accordance with the break indicated by the monuments. We thus obtain a double witness to the remarkable fact of an interruption of pure Babylonian supremacy at this time; and from the monuments we are able to pronounce that the supremacy was transferred to Elam, and that under a king, the Semitic form of whose name would be Chedor-laomer, a great expedition was organized, which proceeded to the distant and then almost unknown west.

The exodus of the Jews was an event which Manetho could scarcely omit. It was one, however, of such a character, so repugnant to the feelings of an Egyptian, that we could not expect a fair representation of it in his history. Accordingly, the fragments of Manetho present us with a distinct, but very distorted, notice of the occurrence. They mention the oppression, Moses the national leader, the Hebrews under the disguise of *Abaris*, and the true direction of the retreat; but we have all the special circumstances of the occasion concealed under a general confession of disaster.

(12) There are certain historico-scientific arguments which will be noticed in the following chapter. These arguments are derived from the agreement of the sacred narrative with the conclusions reached by those sciences which have a partially historical character. Again, there is an argument, of immense compass, deducible from the indirect and incidental points of agreement between the Mosaic records and the best profane authorities.

We may add, that there are geographic and ethnological notices in the books of Moses which are of such a veracious character as to stamp the whole narrative with an unmistakeable air of authority. And this is an argument to which modern research is perpetually adding fresh weight. For instance, if we look to the geography, we shall find, till within these few years, that 'Erech, and Accad, and Calneh, in the land of Shinar—Calah and Resen, in the country peopled by Asshur—Ellasar, and Ur of the Chaldees,' were mere names, and that beyond the mention of them in Genesis, scarcely a trace was discoverable of their existence. Recently, however, the mounds of Mesopotamia have been searched, and stones buried for near three thousand years have found a tongue, and tell us exactly where each of those cities stood, and sufficiently indicate their importance. Again, the power of Og, and his threescore cities, all 'fenced with high walls, gates, and bars, besides unwalled towns a great many' (Deut. iii. 4, 5), in such a country as that to the east of the Sea of Galilee, whose old name of Trachonitis indicates its barrenness, seemed to many improbable; but modern research has found in this very country a vast number of walled cities still standing, which show the habits of the ancient people, and prove that the population must at one time have been considerable. So the careful examination that has been made of the valley of the Jordan, which has resulted in a proof that it is a unique phenomenon, utterly unlike anything elsewhere on the whole face of the earth, tends greatly to confirm the Mosaic account that it became what it now is by a great convulsion; and by believers in the Bible it will be considered as confirming the miraculous character of that convulsion. Such facts as these, the absence of any counter evidence, and the constant accession to our knowledge of the ancient times, whether historic, or geographic, or ethnic, help to remove difficulties, and to produce a perpetual supply of fresh illustrations of the Mosaic narrative. They all tend to show that we possess in the Pentateuch, not only the most authentic account of ancient times that has come down to us, but a history absolutely, and in every respect, true.

(13) On the credibility of the Pentateuch we might rest the credibility of all subsequent Bible history; for it forms the foundation of the whole fabric of that history. The whole Bible, as a history, and as an organic evolution, stands or falls with it. It is certainly the most remarkable historical production in existence; and it seems incredible how any candid mind that reads it carefully, observes its air of honesty and truthfulness, considers its circumstantiality, its vast superiority to all ancient documents, and its substantial accord with them, can deny it the character of true history.

(14) In the subsequent part of this outline of the credibility of the Scripture records it is necessary to observe still greater brevity than we have hitherto done. A mere syllabus is all that will be attempted.

The Book of Joshua is the production of an eye-witness. The writer includes himself among those who passed over Jordan (Josh. v. 1). He speaks of Rahab the harlot still 'dwelling in Israel' when he wrote (Josh. vi. 25); and of Hebron as still in the possession of Caleb the son of Jephunneh (Josh. xiv. 14). If the author of the book was not Joshua himself, which some doubt, he must have belonged to the 'elders that outlived Joshua, which had known all the works of the Lord that He had done for Israel' (Josh. xxiv. 31); and he is, therefore, a credible witness of the events of the settlement of the Israelites in Palestine.

The Book of Judges, according to the tradition of the Jews, was written by Samuel. There is nothing in the work that very distinctly marks the date of its composition. From its contents we can only say that it must have been composed about Samuel's time—that is, after the death of Samson, and before the capture of Jerusalem by David. As the events related in it cover a space of some hundreds of years, the writer, whoever he was, cannot be regarded as a contemporary witness for more than a small portion of the time. But as national records, of which we have a specimen in the song of Deborah and Barak, were doubtless kept by the successors of Moses and Joshua, it is reasonable to suppose that he made use of them.

The two books of Samuel are thought by some to form, together with the two books of Kings, a single work, and are referred to the time of the Babylonish captivity; but this view is contrary both to the internal and to the external evidence. The tradition of the Jews is, that the work was commenced by Samuel, continued by Gad, David's seer, and concluded by Nathan the prophet; and this is a very probable supposition. We know from a statement in the 'First Book of Chronicles,' that 'the acts of David the king, *first and last*, were written in the book of Samuel the seer, and the book of Nathan the prophet, and in the book of Gad the seer' (1 Chron. xxix. 29); and these writings, it is plain, were still extant in the chronicler's time.

The writer of the First Book of Kings derives his account of Solomon from a document, which he calls 'the Book of the Acts of Solomon' (1 Kings xi. 41); while the author of the Second Book of Chronicles cites three works as furnishing him with materials for this part of his history—'the book of Nathan the prophet, the prophecy of Ahijah the Shilonite, and the visions of Iddo the seer against Jeroboam, the son of Nebat' (2 Chron. ix. 29). These last were certainly the works of contemporaries; and the same may be presumed of the other, since the later compiler is not likely to have possessed better materials than the earlier.

The histories of David and Solomon are drawn from two separate and distinct authorities. The writer of Chronicles does not take even his account of David wholly from Samuel, but adds various particulars, which show that he had further sources of information. And the account of Solomon appears not to have been drawn from Kings at all, but to have been taken independently from the original documents.

We have, moreover, in the Book of Psalms a running commentary illustrative of David's personal history, the close agreement of which with the historical books is striking; and also a work affording abundant evidence that the history of the nation, as it is delivered to us in the Pentateuch, in Joshua, and in Judges, was at least believed by the Jews in the time of David to be their true and real history.

(15) We have now to consider what amount of confirmation profane history lends to the truth of the sacred narrative during this period.

The first point of agreement is of a negative character, and relates to the weakness of Egypt and Assyria at this time. This weakness appears both from the Scripture narrative and from the monuments. The expeditions of the latter were still confined within the Euphrates, or if they crossed it on rare occasions, at any rate went no farther than Cappadocia and Upper Syria, or the country about Aleppo and Antioch. And Egypt, from the time of Ramesses the Third, which was not long after the exodus, to that of Shishak, the contemporary of Solomon, seems to have sent no expedition beyond its own frontier. Thus the annals of the two countries are necessarily silent concerning the Jews during the period in question; and no agreement between them and the Jewish records is possible, except that tacit one which is found in fact to exist. The Jewish records are silent concerning Egypt from the exodus to the reign of Solomon, which is exactly the time during which the Egyptian records are silent concerning the Jews. And Assyria does not appear in Scripture as an influential power in Lower Syria and Palestine till a time considerably later than the separation of the kingdoms; while similarly the Assyrian monuments are without any mention of expeditions into these parts during the earlier period of the empire.

The following point of agreement is direct and positive, and is a striking illustration, from a profane source, of the veracity of Scripture. Moses of Chorêna, the Armenian historian, Procopius, the secretary of Belisarius, and Suidas, the lexicographer, relate that there existed in their day at Tingis (or Tangiers) in Africa an inscription, to the effect that the inhabitants were descendants of those fugitives who were driven from the land of Canaan by Joshua the plunderer. Procopius says that the inscription was in Phœnician characters and in the Phœnician language. This fact renders it probable that it was made prior to the Christian era; and the epithet, 'plunderer,' applied to Joshua renders it certain that it was not a Jewish or Christian monument.

Profane history, in the opinion of some, confirms the miracle of the sun standing still (Josh. x. 12, 13); and of his returning ten degrees backward on the sun-dial of Ahaz (Isa. xxxviii. 8). Herodotus says (B. II. 142) that the Egyptians declare that since Egypt was a kingdom the sun has on four several occasions moved from his wonted course, twice rising where he now sets, and twice setting where he now rises. This statement may not be confirmatory of the two miracles mentioned, but it evidently alludes to some unusual celestial phenomena.

The period of Jewish history which commences with the reign of David brought the people of Israel once more into contact with those principal nations of the earth whose history has to some extent come down to us. David carried on war with the Syrians, Philistines, Moabites, Ammonites, Idumæans, and Amalekites. His victory over the Syrians of Damascus, when they came to the assistance of Hadadezer, king of Zobah (2 Sam. viii. 3–13; comp. 1 Chron. xviii. 6), is mentioned by Eupolemus, and also by Nicolas of Damascus, the friend of Augustus Cæsar. Eupolemus mentions, too, the most of David's successes over the Philistines, Moabites, Ammonites, Idumæans, and Amalekites.

The connection of Judæa with Phœnicia is another point which receives illustration from profane history.

A firm friendship was established between the two powers, which continued beyond the reign of David into that of Solomon (2 Sam. v. 11, 12; 1 Kings v. 1; 1 Chron. xxii. 4). Hiram, the Tyrian king who was contemporary with David and Solomon, is mentioned in the Assyrian inscriptions, by Herodotus, and by the Phœnician historians, Dius and Menander. They do not mention David; but they speak distinctly of the close connection between Hiram and Solomon, and of the puzzling questions which they put to one another.

In the time of David and Solomon, the Scripture records imply the superiority of Tyre over Sidon. At a period prior to this, they imply the contrary. With this profane authorities agree. Homer implies, and Strabo and Justin distinctly assert, the ancient superiority of Sidon over Tyre. On the other hand, Dius and Menander, who draw their Phœnician histories from the native records, clearly show that, at a time anterior to David, Tyre had become the leading city, which she continued to be until the time of Alexander.

The Egyptian marriage of Solomon, and his friendly connection with Pharaoh, receive no confirmation from profane sources, beyond that which they receive from Eupolemus; but the change in the relations between the two courts towards the close of Solomon's reign, which is indicated by the protection extended to his enemy Jeroboam by a new king Shiskah, receives some illustration and confirmation both from the monuments and from the native historian Manetho.

What the Scriptures say of Solomon's kingdom corresponds to a condition of things with which we are perfectly familiar from profane sources. We read that he 'reigned over all the kingdoms from the river (Euphrates) unto the land of the Philistines, and unto the border of Egypt' (1 Kings iv. 21); again, that 'he had dominion over all the region on this side the river, from Tiphsah (or Thapsacus on the Euphrates) to Azzah (or Gaza), over all the kings on this side the river' (1 Kings iv. 24); and that 'they brought presents' (1 Kings iv. 21),—'a rate year by year' (1 Kings x. 25),—'and served Solomon all the days of his life.' This account is in entire harmony with the political notions and practices of his day. In his time the modern system of centralized government, and the satrapial system of Darius Hystaspis, which has prevailed generally throughout the East since its first introduction, were unknown. The empires of that time were composed of a number of separate kingdoms, each under its own native king; and the sole link uniting them together was the subjection of these petty monarchs to a single suzerain. Such, from the account given of it in Scripture, was the character of Solomon's empire.

Similarly, with respect to the buildings of Solomon, it may be remarked that they appear, from the description of them in Kings and Chronicles, to have belonged exactly to that style of architecture which we find to have prevailed over Western Asia in the earliest times, and of which we have still remains in the ancient cities of Nineveh, Susa, and Persepolis.

(16) The period between the death of Solomon and the destruction of Jerusalem by Nebuchadnezzar embraces about four centuries.

The documents which furnish the history of this period are Kings and Chronicles, which are compilations from the State Archives of the two kingdoms of Israel and Judah, made probably by prophets at the time of their composition.

The Books of Kings and Chronicles are distinct and independent authorities, and confirm each other. They also receive a large amount of illustration, and so of confirmation, from the writings of the contemporary prophets, who exhibit the feelings natural under the circumstances described by the historians, and incidentally allude to the facts recorded by them.

The points of agreement between these documents and profane history will be exhibited in the briefest manner possible.

The separate existence of the two kingdoms of Israel and Judah is abundantly confirmed by the Assyrian inscriptions. The conquest of Judæa by Sheshonk [Shishak] (2 Chron. xii. 2–5) is recorded in the great temple at Carnac. Menander mentions Ethbaal (1 Kings xvi. 31), the father of Jezebel; and also that during his reign there was a remarkable drought, that continued in Phœnicia for the full space of a year. This drought is fairly connected with the still longer one in the land of Israel which Elijah announced to Ahab (1 Kings xvii. 1). The power of Benhadad, and the nature of the force under his command (1 Kings xx. 1 seq.), receive a confirmation in the cuneiform annals of an Assyrian king. The same record verifies the historical accuracy of the Book of Kings, by mentioning Hazael as king of Damascus immediately after Benhadad; and also by the synchronism which it establishes between this prince and Jehu, who is the first Israelite king mentioned by name on any inscription hitherto discovered. Berosus mentions Pul, or Phul, who is probably identified with a monumental king who took tribute from Samaria (2 Kings xv. 19; 1 Chron. v. 26). Two invasions of Israel by Tiglath-Pileser are related in Scripture (2 Kings xv. 29, xvi. 7-9). Of the first of these two campaigns we have no mention in profane history; but some account of the second is given in an Assyrian fragment, in which Tiglath-Pileser speaks of his defeating Rezin, and capturing Damascus, and also of his taking tribute from the king of Judah. Isaiah states (xx. 1) 'that Tartan came unto Ashdod (when Sargon the king of Assyria sent him), and fought against Ashdod, and took it.' This is confirmed by the Assyrian annals, which relate that he made war in Southern Syria, and took Ashdod. If we may presume that Sargon is intended by the king of Assyria who took Samaria (2 Kings xvii. 6), and carried the Israelites away captive (xviii. 11), then there is derivable from the monuments a very curious illustration of the statement of Scripture, that the monarch who did this placed his captives, or at least a portion of them, 'in the cities of the Medes' (2 Kings xviii. 11). The Scripture account of Sennacherib's two expeditions against Hezekiah agrees exactly with the inscription of that Assyrian king. The historians Polyhistor and Abydenus relate the murder of that prince; and Moses of Chorêne notices the escape of the murderers into Armenia. The succession of Esarhaddon is confirmed by the monuments. So Seveh, king of Egypt, is identified with Shebek or Sabaco;

Tirhakah, with Tehrak or Taracus; Necho, with Neku or Nechao; Hophra, with Haifra or Apries. Herodotus confirms the battle of Megiddo, and the calamitous end of Apries. Inscriptions, Berosus, and Ptolemy confirm the reign of Merodach-Baladan at Babylon. Berosus relates the recovery of Syria and Palestine by Nebuchadnezzar, and his deportation of the Jews, and destruction of Jerusalem.

(17) The closing period of Old Testament history is that of the captivity and return. The historian of the captivity is Daniel, who combines history with prophecy, and unites in a single book the visions with which he was favoured with an account of various remarkable events which he witnessed.

The character of Nebuchadnezzar, the length of his reign, and the fact of his having uttered prophecies, are points in which there is a remarkable agreement between the sacred record and the profane authorities. Berosus and Abydenus speak of his splendour and magnificence, his military successes, his devotion to his gods, and the pride which he took in adorning Babylon.

Berosus, Polyhistor, and Ptolemy state, without any variety, that the length of Nebuchadnezzar's reign was forty-three years. The Babylonian monuments go near to prove the same, for the forty-second year of Nebuchadnezzar has been found on a clay tablet. Here Scripture is in exact accordance; for as the first year of Evil-Merodach, the son and successor of Nebuchadnezzar, is the thirty-seventh of the captivity of Jehoiachin, who was taken to Babylon in Nebuchadnezzar's eighth year, it is evident that just forty-three years are required for the reign of the great Chaldean monarch.

In the inscription known as the 'Standard Inscription' of Nebuchadnezzar, that monarch seems to refer to his mysterious malady. He relates that during a considerable time—four years apparently—all his great works were at a stand : he did not build high places; he did not lay up treasures ; he did not sing the praises of his lord Merodach; he did not offer sacrifice; he did not keep up the works of irrigation.

Berosus confirms the succession of Evil-Merodach. The supposed difference between Scripture and profane history in the narrative concerning Belshazzar has been explained by the discovery that Nabonadius, the last native king named in Ptolemy's canon, associated with him on the throne, during the later years of his reign, his son *Bil-shar-uzur* (Belshazzar), and allowed him the royal title. The capture of Babylon by the Medo-Persians during a feast, and the transfer of the empire, have been confirmed by many writers. It can be clearly shown by a comparison of Berosus with Ptolemy's canon, that, according to the reckoning of the Babylonians, the time between Nebuchadnezzar's first conquest of Judæa, in the reign of Jehoiakim, and the year following the fall of Babylon, when Daniel made his prayer (Dan. ix.), was sixty-eight years, or two years only short of the seventy which had been fixed by Jeremiah as the duration of the captivity. Thus the chronology is confirmed.

The re-establishment of the Jews in Palestine is related in the books of Ezra and Nehemiah, the authenticity of which is generally allowed ; and of their genuineness there is no reason to doubt.

Attacks have been made upon the authenticity of the Book of Esther. The story of the book in its leading features may seem wonderful and antecedently improbable ; but the contemplated massacre of the Jews, and the actual slaughter of their enemies, which are the points objected to, are proved by the commemorative festival of Purim. And it may lessen the seeming antecedent improbability of the story, to bear in mind that open massacres of obnoxious persons were not unknown to the Persians of Xerxes' time. There had once been a general massacre of all the Magi who could be found; and the annual observance of this day, which was known as the 'Magophonia,' would serve to keep up the recollection of the circumstance.

The portion of Jewish history contained in Ezra and Nehemiah finds ample confirmation from profane sources. The religious spirit of the Persian kings, as evinced in their proclamations (Ezra i. 2, 3; comp. 2 Chron. xxxvi. 23; Ezra vi. 8–10, vii. 12, 23), is in keeping with their inscriptions. The succession of the kings is correctly given. The interruption of the building of the temple by the Pseudo-Smerdis accords with his other religious changes; and the reversal of his religious policy by Darius agrees with the Behistun inscription. The break in the history, as recorded by Ezra, is filled up by the Book of Esther. The name Ahasuerus is the proper equivalent of Xerxes; and if Xerxes is intended in the Book of Esther, the portrait of him and the history are in harmony with the facts recorded by the Greeks. The character of Artaxerxes Longimanus, and the length of his reign, agree with the statements of Nehemiah.

With the restoration of the Jews from captivity, the history of the Old Testament terminates. All the evidence which we possess from profane sources, of a really important and trustworthy character, tends to confirm its truth. The veracity of the writers who have delivered it to us is illustrated and established by the monumental records of past ages—Assyrian, Babylonian, Egyptian, Persian, and Phœnician; by the writings of historians who have based their histories on contemporary annals, as Manetho, Berosus, Dius, Menander, and Nicolas of Damascus; by descriptions given by eye-witnesses of the Oriental manners and customs;

F

and by proofs obtained by modern research of the condition of art in the time and country in which the Old Testament was written.

(18) The Old Testament is principally historical; the New Testament is chiefly biographical and epistolary. There is, therefore, as might be expected, a scantiness of points of contact between the main facts of the New Testament and profane records. Their harmony is seen chiefly through the incidental allusions of the New Testament writers. A strong argument has been constructed by Archdeacon Paley out of the undesigned coincidences that abound in their writings.

The historical books of the New Testament are the productions of contemporaries and eye-witnesses. Two of those who wrote lives of Christ were apostles, and were consequently His close and intimate friends. Luke, the author of the Gospel that bears his name, and also of the Acts of the Apostles, and Mark, the author of the second Gospel, were companions of the apostles. The truth of the narrative contained in their writings is evidenced by their sober, simple, and unexaggerated tone, and by their agreement, often undesigned, with each other. The incidental allusions to it found in the speeches of the apostles, and in their epistolary correspondence with their converts, are confirmations of its truth. A comparison of its incidental facts with the civil history of the times, reveals an agreement so minute as to constitute an overwhelming argument in proof of its authenticity. It was received and believed at the time when the truth of every part of it could have been readily tested. Consider the rapid spread of the religion that it teaches, and the great numbers of early converts, some of whom were men of erudition and culture. All these things establish beyond doubt the truth of the New Testament history.

CHAPTER VI.

SCIENTIFIC ACCURACY OF THE SCRIPTURES.

THE Bible does not profess to teach science. Its aim is higher. It reveals the plan of salvation for our fallen race, gives a history of the development of that plan until 'the fulness of the time was come,' when 'God sent forth His Son' (Gal. iv. 4) into our world, furnishes a brief sketch of the establishment and progress of Christianity until near the end of Paul's ministry, and closes with a revelation of the Church's fortunes until the consummation of the present dispensation.

In the progress of its history, it touches upon many scientific and historical questions connected with geology, astronomy, philology, chronology, geography, archæology, and some other branches of knowledge. In speaking of these, it uses popular language—not the language of science, which is unsuitable to its purpose. It uses such language as scientific men themselves use in common conversation, or when addressing popular uneducated audiences. A lecturer on astronomy would employ the terms 'sunrise' and 'sunset,' though, scientifically speaking, there is no such thing.

With the exception of Moses and Solomon, we have no evidence that the sacred writers were scientific men. Paul was learned and a profound dialectician; but there is no proof that he was a scientific man, in the popular acceptation of that term. He was a theologian, pre-eminently skilled in biblical knowledge. Apart from their inspiration, the sacred writers were on a level with the times in which they lived. Unless they were otherwise taught by special revelation, their scientific views were those of their countrymen contemporary with them. In their statements they sometimes referred to the opinions of the times as containing substantial truth, without regard to strictly scientific or historical accuracy. Such a statement we may consider that of Paul: 'And after that he gave them judges about the space of four hundred and fifty years, until Samuel the prophet' (Acts xiii. 20). Yet a careful examination, in the original languages, of all the passages of Scripture (with the exceptions indicated) will establish the scientific accuracy of their phraseology, and show that their authors were under supernatural guidance.

It is the custom, in certain quarters, to speak of the conflict between science and the Bible; and to intimate, with a confident air, that this conflict, occasioned in many instances by the subjective condition of the heart and mind, is irreconcilable. The Bible, according to these self-constituted oracles of science, is a book of the past, written before the age of scientific discovery, and consequently unworthy of the consideration of the advanced thinkers of the present age. The discoveries of science, they affirm, have proved it to be unreliable, and therefore of no authority in all matters of a scientific character.

These opponents of the Bible 'are willingly ignorant' (2 Pet. iii. 5) of some things, and 'speak evil of what they know not' (Jude 10). They 'are willingly ignorant' of the Bible itself—of its history and its teachings—of the accumulative evidence of its historical and scientific accuracy—of the victories that it has achieved over the many assaults that have been made upon it, from the earliest times down to the present, by the pretended masters of science, oftentimes 'falsely so called'—and speak of it with an indifference, or with a contempt, which can only be justified by the clearest proof that it is nothing but a 'cunningly devised fable.' These men, like 'Jannes and Jambres, who withstood Moses, do also resist the truth;' they are 'men of corrupt minds, reprobate concerning the faith' (2 Tim. iii. 8).

This, however, is not the character of all those who believe that there is a want of agreement between science and the Bible. Some are willing to admit that the Bible is a good book in the sphere of morals and religion, though even there it may not be infallible, and think that to this sphere its authority should be limited. They yield an easy assent to its teachings, because they have been educated in the belief of them, and because their own moral judgments accord with them. Whatever doubts may arise in their minds, they cannot bring themselves to reject the Bible entirely; for the very thought of such a thing would give a shock to their moral nature which they are unwilling to incur. Therefore, they continue in the belief that the Bible is a very good book in its place; but that place, they say, is entirely out of the field of science.

But there are men of science—men deserving of the name, men of earnest moral nature and honest purpose — who find real difficulties in the Bible in its scientific relations, at least difficulties real to themselves, and are desirous of resolving them; but instead of resorting to the Bible itself, and examining its credibility and claims to be a divine revelation, they have recourse to special expositions of their difficulties by scientific biblical scholars—expositions in which they find great variety of opinion, and perhaps no satisfactory solution of the questions that perplex them. Their conclusion is that a solution is impossible. This is unphilosophical; at least it is founded upon a false premise. We are not at liberty to infer that a difficulty is insolvable because it has not been solved. It is not the course which these very same men pursue in their scientific researches, in which they meet with many difficulties, and a great many attempted solutions of them, all equally unsatisfactory. Yet this does not shake their faith in the order and constancy of the constitution and course of nature. They know that there is harmony throughout the universe, though some things seem to be in conflict with one another. So we are persuaded in regard to the Bible, if it is a revelation from God. Whatever conflict may seem to exist between it and science, we know there is harmony, if the facts of both are known and understood. They constitute parts of one concordant system.

Some scientists, and unbelievers generally, make great use of the various and conflicting views of theologians on many biblical questions and Scripture doctrines, for the purpose of justifying their belief that the teachings of the Bible are uncertain and unreliable. In some instances, indeed, they are made the ground of rejecting the Bible altogether. If its professed expounders differ so much among themselves in their expositions of it, others, it is concluded, need not trouble themselves to give it any serious consideration.

As an offset against this, we will give a brief exhibition of conflicting views of scientific men on questions of science, guarding against the inference, however, that science is on that account unworthy of attention. The foundation of science stands sure, notwithstanding many of its self-styled builders either entirely miss it, or erect upon it a structure of destructible materials. The instances are not rare in which some of these ambitious builders have piled their 'wood, hay, and stubble' so high as to attract the lightning from heaven and bring swift destruction upon their combustible fabric.

We will begin with astronomy. The scientific world, with the exception of Pythagoras, Aristotle, and a few others, who appear to have had some doubts on the subject, was convinced of the truth of the Ptolemaic system until the time of Copernicus, when it was persuaded to believe the reverse. There was then a complete revolution in the science of astronomy.

The existence of the law of gravitation is admitted, but the application of it by scientific men is not always infallible. This is seen in the discovery of the planet Neptune by the astronomers Adams and Le Verrier, whose calculations of the position of the planet which caused the perturbations of Uranus, dependent as they were upon the application of the law of gravitation, did not by any means agree. The nebular hypothesis was accepted by the scientific world, under the influence of great names that supported it, until Lord Rosse's telescope rendered it doubtful. Professor Sedgwick, in reply to Dean Cockburn's challenge, after the York meeting of the British Association in 1844, stated that he declined to support it; and Professor Nichol believed that, in due time, all the nebulæ would be resolved into clusters of stars.

The Milky Way was considered by astronomers to be an enormous ring of stars; but Mr. Proctor advocates the view that it is not a ring, but a meandering wisp of nebulæ and stars of all magnitudes. This astronomer adduces reasons for maintaining that Sir W. Herschel's method of judging of the probable distance of stars by their apparent magnitudes is altogether erroneous; and he adopts what may be called the meteoric theory respecting the development of the solar system, in contradistinction to the nebular theory.

The theory respecting the motion of the solar system in space propounded by Sir William, and upheld by astronomers as true science, has been recently assailed as untenable, and is now pronounced by the Astronomer-Royal to be in doubt and abeyance.

With reference to the sun's mass, recent theories put forth by Professor Thomson and others are utterly irreconcilable, the one making it 1000 times, the other 350,000 times greater than the bulk of the earth. And as regards the way by which the sun's mass is constantly sustained, in order to meet what it loses by radiation, instead of the theory of Newton, that this is accomplished by comets and meteoric matter falling into the sun, thus supplying the required fuel for its continuance, a certain astronomer, who once supported that idea, has turned round and proposed another theory diametrically opposed to it. Instead of the sun being fed with meteors to keep it from burning out, he makes it, in rotating rapidly on its axis, throw off meteoric bodies, from which the earth and planets were probably formed.

With reference to a recent discovery by Professor Adams respecting the acceleration of the moon's mean motion, which necessarily affects the calculation of all ancient eclipses, it is a singular fact that at the discussion on this subject which took place at the British Association meeting at Oxford in 1860, it was found that there were three great mathematicians on the one side, and three equally distinguished on the other.

The subject of light, too, has occasioned disputes in the scientific world. Newton taught the theory of emission from the sun, and Huygens the undulatory theory.

Conflicting views are still more numerous and more marked among geologists.

At the close of the last century the Neptunists and Vulcanists carried on a fierce warfare about the origin of the earth. The former, finding everywhere hardened sand and mud filled with organic remains, contended that the land was a deposit from water; the latter, fixing their attention on the basalts, traps, and granites, held that the configuration of the earth's surface was due to the agency of fire. Each one insisted that the opinion of his party was the only right one, until a third school arose, which proved that, in the multifarious strata of our globe, both agencies must be recognised.

Once granite was universally considered to form the earth's crust, and to be of igneous origin, and of older date than all the fossiliferous strata; now another opinion has been advanced. 'It has been demonstrated,' says Savile, quoting from Sir Charles Lyell's *Principles of Geology*, 'that it is difficult to point to a mass of volcanic or plutonic rock which is more ancient than the oldest known organic remains.'

Connected with the differences among geologists respecting the earth's central heat, the question arose as to the number of years that had elapsed before its surface obtained its present mean temperature, and received answers differing very widely. Professor Thomson is of the opinion that the gradual cooling of the earth's crust from a state of fusion must have occupied about 98,000,000 years. M. Boué contends that, as 9,000,000 years are required for the earth to lose 14° Reaumur, the period of cooling must be estimated at 350,000,000 years. Professor Haughton thinks the cooling must have continued 2,298,000,000 years. And Mr. Darwin calculates that 306,662,400 years must be allowed for the denudation of the weald alone.

There are also wide differences of opinion among the savans of the present day on the question of the length of time required for the formation of different portions of the earth's surface. Take, for example, the growth of peat. M. Boucher de Perthes teaches that it can only be computed at the rate of about one-fifth of an inch in a hundred years; whereas Sir Charles Lyell, in his *Principles of Geology*, shows that a peat-moss in Ross-shire, North Britain, has grown at the rate of eight feet in fifty-eight years. The same author maintains also that the Roman roads in Scotland are now in some instances covered over with peat-moss to that thickness; so that, according to the estimate of M. Boucher de Perthes, these Roman roads must have been formed nearly 50,000 years ago.

We might proceed to speak of the diversity of opinion among scientific men on other geological questions,—concerning geological breaks, climatic differences, geological fossils, successive creations, the contemporaneity of man and extinct mammalia, the atomic hypothesis, alluvial deposits, and the antiquity of man,—but the instances given are enough to show that scientists cannot boast of the unity and certainty of some of their scientific theories relating to the time required for nature's operations.

Variations of opinion on anthropology, Egyptology, and archæology might be adduced in proof that infallibility is not an attribute of our savans. Let two examples from Egyptology suffice.

The first is the age of the great pyramid of Ghizeh. Le Sueur determines its date to be certainly as old as B.C. 4975; Brugsch, B.C. 3657; Lepsius, B.C. 3426; Poole, B.C. 2352; Piazzi Smyth, B.C. 2170; Sir G. C. Lewis, B.C. 903.

The second is the zodiac discovered on the ceiling of the hall at Dendera, in Upper Egypt, which was regarded, and at once accepted by men of science, as proof that astronomy had attained a very high standard in that country from the so-called Solstitial Period B.C.; until Champollion's detection of the names of several Roman emperors, intermingled with the zodiacal signs, proved that the painting belonged to a period subsequent to the Christian era.[1]

These variations of scientific opinion, which have been adduced as an offset against the conclusion, drawn by some scientists from the conflicting views of theologians in their expositions of Scripture, that the Bible is an uncertain and unreliable authority, do not affect the facts or truth of science. They only prove that hypotheses and inferences from insufficient data are not to be received as facts of science; just as in the case of biblical interpretation, the views of interpreters are not to be accepted as the infallible teachings of Scripture. A little more caution and a little more modesty, on both sides, would prevent much misunderstanding and consequent difficulty.

We will now indicate some of the points of agreement between the Bible and modern science. This, though the materials are abundant, we can do only to a very limited extent. These materials, moreover, are always increasing with the progress of discovery. Cardinal Wiseman remarked, in his lectures on the connection between the natural sciences and revelation, that the natural sciences during their incipiency seemed to be in antagonism to revelation; but in proportion as they advanced, in that proportion the points of agreement between them and the Bible became the more numerous.[2] This statement of Cardinal Wiseman has been, in the opinion of some scientific men qualified to pronounce a judgment on the matter, fully verified.

In the illustration of this part of our subject, we will begin with geology, the discoveries of which,

[1] *The Truth of the Bible.* By the Rev. Bourchier Wrey Savile, M.A. London: Longmans, Green, & Co. 1871.

[2] This quotation from Cardinal Wiseman is made from memory. The work referred to is out of print. The writer, however, though unable to procure a copy of the work, is positive as to the reality of the statement.

according to some, completely overthrow the Mosaic account of the creation of the world.

(1) Geology points us to a beginning, if not to the matter of the world, yet to the present system of nature. This agrees with the statement of the Bible. In the very first verse we have the announcement, 'In the beginning God created the heaven and the earth.' This is the starting-point of biblical theology: it is the last position that natural science can reach.

(2) Geology furnishes a new phase of the argument from design for the divine existence and personality. This argument is of little worth, unless we assume a beginning of the existing system of nature, organic and inorganic. Geology proves such a beginning. And in the modifications of matter, which constitute the chief beauty of the world, we find full proof of a creating Deity; and in the wise and exact adaptation of one thing to another, and especially in the modifications of structure to adapt animals and plants to a changing world, we see evidence of a personal God. For a blind, unintelligent force, like law, could not have made such alterations in the successive races, and made them wisely.

(3) Geology throws light upon the statements of the Bible respecting the age of the world, its cosmogony, or mode of formation, and its final destruction by fire.

This head admits of various specifications.

(a) The Bible does not fix the time when the world was created. It says: 'In the beginning God created the heaven and the earth.' But when was 'the beginning'? On this point geology is equally silent.

(b) The Bible does fix the time when man first appeared on the globe; and it represents him as the last animal created. Geology has discovered a long pre-human period, and the late appearance of man on the earth.

(c) The Bible represents the creation as the special result of God's efficiency, to the exclusion of every other cause. Geology teaches the same lesson. It shows that the successive races, in the different formations, came in by groups at once, which can only be explained by the interposition of creative power.

(d) The Bible represents God as employing instrumentalities in the work of creation. 'God said, Let the earth bring forth grass' (Gen. i. 11). Geological records show that immense periods were consumed in the preparation, by natural operations, of the earth, the water, and the air, for their inhabitants.

(e) The Bible teaches that the creation was a gradual work, completed by successive exhibitions of divine power, with intervals of repose. Here, too, geology corresponds closely with Scripture.

(f) The Bible describes the emergence of the land from the waters before the creation of animals and plants (Gen. i. 9). Previous to this 'the earth was without form and void; and darkness was upon the face of the deep' (ver. 2). Geology has discovered that the primitive globe was covered with a uniform ocean, and that there was a long azoic period, during which neither plant nor animal could live.

(g) The Bible does not describe a chaos, in the popular acceptation of that term. The earth was desolate, or waste, and unfurnished. Geology shows that the matter of the globe has never been free from the same laws that now govern it.

(h) Moses states that there was a time when the earth was not dependent upon the sun for light or heat, when, therefore, there could be no climatic differences. Geology has verified this statement by finding tropical plants and animals scattered over all parts of the earth.

(*i*) The order of creation in Genesis, in its general outlines, corresponds to that of geology.[1]

(*k*) Geology gives plausibility to the Scripture statement of the limited period during which the human species is to occupy this world, and of the future destruction and renovation of the earth. This it does by showing that there is a limited amount of fossil fuel, ores, and other substances buried in the earth, which are necessary for man's use, and indispensable to the comfort, and even existence, of a large population and high civilisation upon the globe. There are no processes going on by which these substances can be renewed to any great extent, and consequently they must be finally exhausted. Moreover, it is a very common opinion among scientific men, that the earth is a vast fiery furnace beneath its crust. Pliny of old expressed his astonishment that a single day should pass without a general conflagration. Did not Peter, then, utter the prediction of science itself, when he wrote: 'The elements shall melt with fervent heat, the earth also and the works that are therein shall be burned up'? (2 Pet. iii. 10.)

(*a.*) Moses affirms that there was light before the sun, and that the sun, as well as the moon, is only a light-holder[2] (Gen. i. 3, 14). Astronomy proves that the sun is a non-luminous body, depending for its light on a luminous atmosphere; and the discoveries with regard to heat, combustion, electricity, and galvanism show that light may be independent of it.[3]

(*b.*) The Bible intimates that the earth had a very

---

[1] Dana's *Manual of Geology*, pp. 742-746. Philadelphia: Theodore Bliss & Co. 1866.

[2] Moses does not call the sun ' Or,' light, but ' Maor,' a place or instrument of light, a luminary.

[3] *Aids to Faith*, Essay V. pp. 241-246. *The Truth of the Bible*, Savile, pp. 72-74. *Blending Lights*, pp. 39-45. New York: Robert Carter and Brothers. 1874.

early revolution on its axis. 'God divided the light from the darkness' (Gen. i. 4). Science shows that the spheroidal form of the earth is due to such a revolution when the globe was in a fluid state.[1]

We may now ask the question: Where did Moses get all the knowledge which he has recorded in the first chapter of Genesis? How was it that he worded his rapid sketch with such scientific accuracy? If he, in his day, possessed the knowledge which genius and science have attained only recently, that knowledge is superhuman. If he did not possess that knowledge, he must have been guided by wisdom superior to that of man.[2]

Ethnology has also been brought into conflict with the Bible.

The Scriptures clearly teach that all mankind have descended from a single pair. Of the creation of this pair they give a full and explicit account. And the Apostle Paul declared, on Mars hill, to the Athenians, that God 'hath made of one blood all nations of men for to dwell on all the face of the earth' (Acts xvii. 26).

The intelligibility of the Christian system rests upon this scriptural doctrine respecting the origin of our race. Salvation is offered to us on the ground that we are sinners—fallen in Adam. Now, if it can be proved that any portion of mankind have not fallen in Adam, how do we know that salvation is intended for them? Their character and actions may prove that they are sinners; but how can we know that they became sinful in the way that the descendants of Adam did, viz. as a race in their first progenitor?

Some naturalists deny that all mankind have descended from a single pair. They speak of the Adamic race as distinct from other races, such as Negroes,

---

[1] *Aids to Faith*, Essay V. pp. 242, 243.
[2] Hitchcock's *Religion and Geology*, passim.

Hottentots, Esquimaux, and Australians, whom they consider as a kind of μιξόθηρα, half-men, half-brutes. Were such a doctrine true, it would of course be a mistaken philanthropy to manumit Negro slaves, and carry the gospel to the Hottentots and Esquimaux.

The question of the unity of the human species is now pretty well established as a scientific fact,—so well, indeed, that nothing but wilful prejudice can gainsay the arguments by which it is supported.

These arguments are well stated and fully and ably illustrated by James Cowles Prichard, M.D., in his work entitled *The Natural History of Man*. In that work Dr. Prichard considers species as simply tribes of animals, which are certainly known, or may be inferred on satisfactory grounds, to have descended from the same stocks, or from parentages precisely similar, and no way distinguished from each other. The object which he then proposes to himself is to point out the most important diversities by which mankind are distinguished and separated into different races, and to determine whether these races constitute separate species, or are merely varieties of the same species.

When any given tribes of animals are so distinguished from each other as to render it doubtful whether they belong to one species or not, several ways have been proposed for the solution of this inquiry. The most obvious and direct one is to show that the same differences commonly, and within ordinary experience, have arisen in the same stock to which both the tribes are referred. If that can be done, the question is at once answered. But when the tribes about which the inquiry is made are either permanent varieties or separate species, there is greater difficulty in arriving at a determination.

In such instances there is one way of coming to a

conclusion, which many naturalists prefer to adopt; and it is altogethor satisfactory, if we can rely on the universality of the observation on which it is founded. The reference is to the facts connected with what is termed hybridity. Dr. Prichard has shown, by an induction of particulars, that there is no such thing as hybridity among the different races of the human family. They all intermix, and the mixed races are just as prolific as the parent races. He has shown, moreover, that greater varieties than any that exist among the various races of the human family, exist within the limits of the same species among the lower animals.

All tribes of men have the same bodily structure. Anatomists and physiologists of the highest standing assign to it a place distinct from that of all other animals. The following conclusions have been established, whatever may be the variety of race:—

(1) All have the same number of teeth, and of bones in their body.

(2) They all shed their teeth in the same way.

(3) They all have the same upright posture.

(4) The head is set, in every variety, in the same way.

(5) They possess two hands and two feet.

(6) They possess smooth bodies, and heads covered with hair.

(7) Every muscle and every nerve, in every variety, are the same.

(8) They eat different kinds of food, and live in all climates.

(9) They are more helpless, and grow more slowly, than other animals.

They have also the same intellectual and moral endowments:

(1) They all have the faculties of reason and language.

(2) They all have the same moral and spiritual endowments. We find everywhere the existence of moral distinctions and of religion.

It has been affirmed by some that, in view of the many and widely different languages of the world, the statement of the Bible, that 'the whole earth was originally of one language and of one speech' (Gen. xi. 1), cannot be true. This statement of the Holy Scripture has, however, been triumphantly vindicated by recent philological investigations. These all tend to establish the veracity of the Bible statement. 'We are already so far advanced,' says Dr. Donaldson in his *New Cratylus*, ' as to be able to divide all the known languages of the world into three classes; and although we do not yet possess sufficient knowledge of the whole body of languages to be able to say what affinity exists between the three great divisions, approximations have been made to the conclusion that there are certain points in which they osculate; and, judging from the progress of linguistic studies hitherto, we may fairly hope that, as in the case of languages now known to be cognate we were impressed with the differences long before we perceived the similarities, which are now the most prominent features, so it will be hereafter with all the languages of the world.' The ' approximations ' of which Dr. Donaldson speaks incline to the conclusion that all the languages of the world have sprung from a common source, thus confirming the assertion of Moses.

The historical credibility of the Mosaic history has been called in question on the ground of chronology.

According to Baron Bunsen, the historic records of Egypt reach up to the year B.C. 9085; and Egyptian nationality commenced as early as B.C. 10,000. These conclusions are said to be drawn from Egyptian monuments, but they do not rest on any satisfactory basis.

The Egyptian monuments contain no continuous chronology, and no materials from which a continuous chronological scheme can be framed. The possibility of constructing such a scheme depends entirely upon the outline which has been preserved to us of the Sebennytic priest Manetho, who composed a history of Egypt under the early Ptolemies. This outline is in a very imperfect condition; and the two versions of it which we find in Syncellus and in the Armenian Eusebius differ considerably. Still both agree in representing Egypt as governed by thirty dynasties of kings, from Menes to Alexander, and the sum of the years which they assign to these dynasties is a little above (or a little below) 5000. The monuments have proved two things with respect to these lists: they have shown, in the first place, that, speaking generally, they are historical—that the persons mentioned were real men, who actually lived and reigned in Egypt; while, secondly, they have shown that though all reigned in Egypt, all did not reign over the whole of Egypt, but while some were kings in one part of the country, others ruled in another. It is allowed on all hands—by M. Bunsen no less than others—that no chronological scheme of any real value can be formed from Manetho's lists until it be first determined either which dynasties and monarchs were contemporary, or what deduction from the sum total of the dynastic years is to be made on account of contemporaneousness. M. Bunsen regards this point as one which Manetho himself determined, and assumes that he was sure to determine it aright. He finds a statement in Syncellus that Manetho made his dynasties cover a space of 113 generations, or 3555 years; and he accepts this statement as completely removing the difficulty, and absolutely establishing the historic fact that the accession of Menes to the crown of Egypt took place more than thirty-six centuries before our era. He then professes to follow Manetho for the preceding period; but here he distorts and misrepresents him. Manetho gave his Egyptian dynasties altogether about 30,000 years. This long space he divided, however, into a natural and supernatural period. To the supernatural period, during which Egypt was governed by gods, demi-gods, and spirits, he assigned 24,925 years. To the natural period, which began with Menes, he gave, at any rate, not much more than 5000. M. Bunsen, not content with this antiquity, but determining to find (or make) a greater, changes the order of Manetho's early dynasties, and by removing to a higher position, without authority, and of his own mere fancy, one which is plainly supernatural, obtains for the natural period four dynasties, covering a space of 5212 years (or, as he makes it, 5462 years), which are capable of being represented as human. This, then, is the mode in which the date B.C. 9085 is reached. It is not obtained from the monuments, which have no chronology, or at any rate none earlier than B.C. 1525. It is not derived from Manetho, for it is in direct contradiction of his views, more than doubling the period during which, according to him, Egypt had had human kings. It is a mere theory of M. Bunsen's, to square with which Manetho's lists have been violently disturbed, and above 5000 years subtracted from his divine to be added to his human period.

Even with respect to Menes, and the supposed date of B.C. 3892 (according to Lepsius), or B.C. 3623 (according to M. Bunsen), for his accession, on what does it in reality depend? Not on any monumental evidence; but simply on the supposition that in a certain passage (greatly disputed) of Syncellus he has correctly represented Manetho's views, and on the further supposition that Manetho's were absolutely right.

The conclusion to which eminent chronologers have arrived is, that no profane history of an authentic character mounts up to an earlier date than the twenty-seventh or twenty-eighth century before Christ. Egyptian history begins about B.C. 2700; Chinese, perhaps B.C. 2637; Babylonian, B.C. 2458; Assyrian, B.C. 1273; Greek, with the Trojan war, B.C. 1250, or perhaps with Hercules, a century earlier; Lydian, B.C. 1229; Phœnician, about the same period; Carthaginian, B.C. 880; Macedonian, about B.C. 720; Median, about B.C. 708; Roman, in the middle of the same century; Persian, B.C. 558; Indian, about B.C. 350; Mexican and Peruvian, not until after our era. The oldest human constructions remaining upon the earth are the Pyramids, and these date from about B.C. 2400; the brick temples of Babylonia seem, none of them, earlier than B.C. 2300; B.C. 2000 would be a high date for the first cyclopean walls in Greece or Italy; the earliest rock inscriptions belong to nearly the same period. Now, if man has existed upon the earth ten or twenty thousand years, as M. Bunsen supposes, why has he left no vestiges of himself till within the last five thousand? This fact renders it probable that he has existed no longer on the earth than the period assigned by the Bible.[1]

On the subject of chronology, it must be borne in mind that the chronologies of the Hebrew Bible, the Samaritan Pentateuch, and the Septuagint do not agree. In case of necessity, we can adopt the longest. That of the Septuagint affords time for all the facts of Egyptology and Sinology.

The longevity of the patriarchs appears to some modern scientists 'at variance with the laws of human

[1] *Aids to Faith*, Essay VI. pp. 273–327.

and animal organism,' and, therefore, 'as contrary to common sense as the notion of there being any real chronology in astronomical cycles of hundreds of thousands of years.' Man, we are told, can never have lived more than one hundred and fifty, or, at most, two hundred years; and a document which assigns him lives of three hundred, six hundred, eight hundred, and even nine hundred years, must be unhistorical, and is either, in respect of its numbers, worthless, or to be explained in some not very obvious way. This argument is supposed to be drawn from physiology. But this science has not spoken on the point before us. It can only say that human bodies are mortal; and, so far as modern testimony goes, men do not seem now able to resist the tendency to decay beyond the term of one hundred and fifty, or at the utmost two hundred years, while the average term of human life is very far below these numbers. But the possible duration of human life, when the species was but recently created, and had its vigour unimpaired by the taint of hereditary disease, is beyond the cognizance of physiological science, which, by the mouth of its most celebrated professors, declines to pronounce a positive judgment. Haller, when led to speak on the subject, declared the problem one which could not be solved, on account of the absence of sufficient data; while Buffon accepted the scriptural account, and thought he could see physical reasons why life should in the early ages have been so greatly extended.

It cannot, therefore, be said with truth that the longevity of the patriarchs is 'at variance with all,' or indeed with any, 'of the laws of human and animal organism.' We do not know on what longevity depends. We could not possibly tell beforehand whether man, or any other animal, would live one, ten, twenty, fifty, a hundred, or a thousand years. The whole question is one of fact, and so of evidence. We have Hindoo, Babylonian, Egyptian, Phœnician, Grecian, and Roman traditions that men in the early ages of the world lived from four hundred up to one thousand years. It seems, therefore, to be quite certain that a very widespread tradition existed in the ancient world, to the effect that the term of human life at man's first appearance upon earth greatly exceeded the present.[1]

The language of Scripture is often scientifically accurate, showing that the sacred writers were either acquainted with modern scientific discoveries, or guided by a Superior Intelligence.

We have an instance of this in Gen. i. 14, already quoted, in which the general term for sun and moon signifies, in the Hebrew language, light-holder.

Leviticus xvii. 11 states that 'the life of the flesh is in the blood'—an important scientific truth, found in the Bible more than three thousand years before the attention of any philosopher was drawn to the subject. That the blood actually possesses a living principle, and that the life of the whole body is derived from it, is a doctrine of divine revelation which the observations and experiments of modern philosophers have served strongly to confirm. The circulation of the blood through the whole human system was also taught by Solomon in the figurative language of Ecclesiastes xii. 6; the truth of which was not scientifically proved until the seventeenth century, when Dr. Harvey revived the doctrine of the vitality and circulation of the blood. This doctrine was subsequently confirmed by Dr. John Hunter, who proved by a variety of experiments that the blood unites living parts in some circumstances as certainly as the yet recent juices of the branch of one tree unite with that of another. He showed that the blood taken from the arm in the most intense cold will

[1] *Aids to Faith*, Essay VI.

raise the thermometer to the same height as blood taken in the most sultry heat, which is a very strong argument for the vitality of the blood, as living bodies alone have the power of maintaining the temperature which is known to us as animal heat. Dr. Hunter further proved that the blood preserves life in different parts of the body; for when a nerve is tied or cut the part loses all power of motion, but does not mortify; whereas let an artery be cut, the part dies, and mortification ensues, which shows that it must be the vital principle of the blood which keeps the part alive; and thus we have ample proof from science of the accuracy of the Mosaic statement that 'the life of the flesh is in the blood.'

We find another example of the scientific accuracy of Scripture language in Deut. xxxii. 24, in which we read of being '*burnt* with hunger.' The celebrated Liebig, more than three thousand years after Moses had written these words, discovered what had never been previously suspected, that when any one is starved to death a slow combustion of the body takes place at the same time.

Job says that 'God stretcheth out the north over the empty place, and hangeth the earth upon nothing' (xxvi. 7).

It is supposed that, as the Hebrew word rendered 'stretch out' signifies also 'to turn,' there is an allusion in the first clause to the motion of the earth round the sun, the effect being that the North Pole is virtually barren, desolate, and empty. However this may be, the second clause, 'hangeth the earth upon nothing,' seems to point to the law of gravitation, discovered by Sir Isaac Newton about two centuries ago.

The Pythagoreans, according to the report of Philolaus of Croton, taught the progressive movement of a non-rotating earth; and Aristarchus of Samos and Seleucus of Babylon are said to have taught that the earth not only rotated on its axis, but also moved round the sun; Plato and Aristotle spoke of the rotation of the earth round the cosmical pole; but these ideas were so much in advance of their age that they were rejected by the learned, who still thought that the earth neither rotated on its axis nor advanced in space, but that it was fixed in one central point.

In Job xxviii. 25 God is said 'to make the weight for the winds; and He weigheth the waters by measure.'

The weight of the air, or winds, was unknown until Torricelli invented the barometer. By the expression 'He weigheth the waters by measure,' we are reminded of the proportion of water to dry land. The aqueous surface of the globe is as three to one of the terrene; and experiments on evaporation respecting the quantity of vapours which arise from a given space in a given time, prove that it requires such a proportion of aqueous surface to afford moisture sufficient for the other proportion of dry land. Thus we see the scientific accuracy of Job's language, when he records that God has given the waters in due measure, as He has also made the proper proportion of weight for the winds.[1]

Materials are not wanting to illustrate to a much greater extent the points already specified, and to illustrate many others that might be mentioned. The examples which have been adduced will convey to the mind of the reader an idea of the general scientific accuracy of Scripture statement, and incline him to the belief that were every passage of Scripture having a scientific bearing carefully examined, it might be

The Truth of the Bible. By the Rev. Bourchier Wrey Savile, M.A. Pp. 200–228.

shown to be in exact harmony with true science, provided we make the same allowance in the use of popular language to the sacred writers that we accord to scientific writers.

The history of the past has shown that the Bible has nothing to fear, but much to hope, from the progress of real science. They both proceed from the same source, the Fountain of Eternal Light. They are both beams of that Light, and reflect the glory of His intellectual and moral character. Let them unite their beams, and then we will be able to walk in the light without stumbling.

PART II.

PROOFS OF THE INSPIRATION OF THE BIBLE.

CHAPTER I.

DOCTRINES AND PRECEPTS OF THE BIBLE, AND ITS UNIQUE CHARACTER.

THE first part has been merely introductory to the subject. It has been intended to secure a favourable, or at least an impartial, consideration of the claims of the Bible to be a divine revelation on the part of those who have prejudices against it, founded on the representations of its enemies that its text is corrupt, that it is unhistoric and unscientific. A full discussion of all the subjects indicated in the preceding chapters could not be expected in this treatise; but perhaps enough has been said to provoke investigation, which, conducted with an honest purpose, cannot fail to produce good results.

The way having been thus prepared, we are now ready to consider the direct proofs of the inspiration of the Scriptures. These proofs may be arranged under the two heads of *subjective* and *objective,* or *internal* and *external,*—the former being drawn from the character of the Bible itself, the latter from its influence upon the world, from the fulfilment of prophecy, and from testimony. These two classes of proofs may not always be kept distinct; for in the case of prophecy especially it will be necessary to consider predictions and their fulfilment together. But as a general order, the internal proofs will be exhibited first, and then the external.

In accordance with this general order, it seems proper to begin with a consideration of those characteristics of the Bible which would be most likely to impress the mind of the reader with the conviction that it is a wonderful book, altogether unique among the literary productions of the world. Suppose a person to undertake its perusal, what would most likely arrest his attention? Would it not be that the Bible, whatever else it may be, is pre-eminently a book of God? It speaks much of Him, and subordinates all things to Him. He is the Alpha and Omega, the beginning and the end. It would occur to him, too, on a comparison of the doctrines and precepts of the Bible with those of other books, that there is a remarkable difference, — such a difference as clearly indicates that they do not proceed from the same source. Those of the Bible bear the impress not merely of a higher, but of a supernatural style of thought. There is something about them which forces the conviction that they were dictated by an intelligence more than human. We have no such conviction when we read the teachings of Menu, Confucius, Zoroaster, Socrates, Plato, Cicero, and Seneca. These present to us nothing above the sphere of human reason; but the Bible carries us beyond the range of created thought, and introduces us to the counsels of Him whose understanding is infinite.

Take the very first chapter of the Bible: how majestically it stands alone among all the cosmogonies that have ever been written! how incongruous, absurd, and irrational do these seem compared with the clear, simple, common-sense account of Moses!

Reference has already been made to this subject in another connection,[1] but the introduction of it here, under a new aspect, is not irrelevant to the design of the present chapter. A comparison of the heathen cosmogonies with the cosmogony of the Bible will manifest the vast superiority of the latter, and prompt the question, Whence came Moses by his information?

Sanchoniatho supposes that the beginning of all things was a dark and condensed windy air, and a chaos, turbid and black as Erebus; and that these were unbounded, and for a long series of ages destitute of form. But when this wind became enamoured of its own first principles (the chaos), and an intimate union took place, that connection was called Pothos; and it was the beginning of the creation of all things. And it (the chaos) knew not its own production; but from its embrace with the wind was generated Mot, which some call Ilus (mud), but others the putrefaction of a watery mixture. And from this sprang all the seed of creation and the generation of the universe.

And there were certain animals without sensation, from which intelligent animals were produced; and these were called Zophasemin, that is, the overseers of the heavens; and they were formed in the shape of an egg; and from Mot shone forth the sun and moon, and the less and the greater stars.[2]

Hesiod, one of the earliest Greek poets, speaks as follows on this subject:—

> 'First chaos was; next ample-bosom'd earth,
> The seat immoveable for evermore
> Of those immortals who the snow-topp'd heights
> Inhabit of Olympus, or the glooms
> Tartarean in the broad-track'd ground's abyss.
> Love then arose, most beautiful among
> The deathless deities: resistless, he
> Of every god and every mortal man

---

[1] *Supra*, 'Historical Credibility of the Scriptures,' chap. v. p. 59. *Patriarchal Age.* G. Smith, F.S.A. Pp. 108, 109.

> Unnerves the limbs, dissolves the wiser breast
> By reason steel'd, and quells the very soul.
> From chaos, Erebus and ebon night;
> From night the day sprang forth and shining air,
> Whom to the love of Erebus she gave.
> Earth first produc'd the heaven, whose starry cope,
> Like herself immense.
>   'She brought
> The lofty mountains forth, the pleasant haunts
> Of nymphs, who dwell 'midst thickets of the hills.
> And next the sea, the swoll'n and chafing sea,
> Apart from love's enchantment. Then with heaven
> Consorting, ocean from her bosom burst,
> With its deep, deep-eddying waters.'

Aristophanes, following the Hesiodic cosmogony, uses the following language in his 'Aves':—

'Chaos, and night, and black Erebus, and wide Tartarus, first existed. At that time there was neither earth, air, nor heaven. But in the bosom of Erebus, black-wing'd night produced an aerial egg, from which, in due season, beautiful love, deck'd with golden wings, was born. Out of chaos, in the midst of wide-spreading Tartarus, he begot our race, and called us forth into light.'[1]

These three examples of heathen cosmogony may be taken to represent all. They are fair specimens, and not chosen on the ground of any special incongruity, or for the purpose of presenting an unduly striking contrast with the Bible narrative.

Moses enunciates this sublime and comprehensive proposition: 'In the beginning God created the heaven and the earth' (Gen. i. 1). 'This simple statement denies atheism; for it assumes the being of a God. It denies polytheism, and, among its various forms, the doctrine of two eternal principles—the one good, and the other evil; for it confesses the one Eternal Creator. It denies materialism; for it asserts the creation of matter. It denies polytheism; for it assumes the

[1] *Patriarchal Age.* G. Smith, F.S.A. Pp. 115, 116.

existence of God before all things, and apart from them. It denies fatalism; for it involves the freedom of the Eternal Being.

'It indicates the relative superiority, in point of magnitude, of the heavens to the earth, by giving the former the first place in the order of worlds. It is in accordance with the first elements of astronomical science.

'It is, therefore, pregnant with physical and metaphysical, with ethical and theological, instruction for the first man, for the predecessors and contemporaries of Moses, and for all the succeeding generations of mankind.'[1]

We might say of it what the great German philosopher, Schelling, said of Rom. xi. 36 to a friend, who asked him what he considered the first principle of all philosophy: 'This,' replied Schelling, pointing to the verse mentioned, 'is the first principle of all philosophy.' Gen. i. 1 is the first principle of all philosophy less fully expressed.

But the essential unity, underived existence, and eternity of God are not left to be implied; they are directly stated and reiterated. His unity is asserted: 'Hear, O Israel; the Lord our God is one Lord' (Deut. vi. 4); 'The Lord, He is God in heaven above, and upon the earth beneath; there is none else' (Deut. iv. 39). Self-existence: 'And God said unto Moses, I am that I am' (Ex. iii. 14). Eternity: 'The everlasting God' (Gen. xxi. 33); 'The eternal God is thy refuge' (Deut. xxxiii. 27). His nature is revealed: 'God is a Spirit' (John iv. 24). Every perfection is ascribed to Him. He is unchangeable: 'God is not a man that He should lie; neither the son of man that He should repent' (Num. xxiii. 19; comp. Jas. i. 17). He is righteous: 'Righteous art Thou, O Lord, and

[1] Murphy's *Commentary on Genesis*. Edinburgh, 1865. P. 30.

upright are Thy judgments' (Ps. cxix. 137). He is holy: 'Holy, holy, holy, Lord God Almighty, which was, and is, and is to come' (Rev. iv. 8). He is 'merciful and gracious, long-suffering, and abundant in goodness and truth' (Ex. xxxiv. 6).

To this idea of God, and to the claims of His universal, natural, and moral government, the Bible subordinates everything (Isa. xl. 12-26; Dan. iv. 34, 35). It passes by the achievements of men, the victorious march of armies, the rise and fall of empires, with a casual notice; but abounds in glowing descriptions of the divine Majesty, and of 'His wondrous works.' It speaks of 'the glory of His kingdom and of His power' (Ps. cxlv. 11). Viewed under this aspect, as the work of man, the Bible has an unnatural sublimity, and seems to invert the relative importance of events.

But though God is so infinitely exalted, yet He exercises a kind and condescending care over all His creatures (Ps. cxlv. 15). His providence directs the establishment of an empire and the fall of a sparrow (Dan. iv. 17; Matt. x. 29).

In no other book do we find these exalted views of God; neither have they been entertained by any people except Jews and Christians. That the ancient Jews, and all nations in possession of the Bible, should so far excel the most cultivated nations of antiquity, and all modern nations without the Bible, in their doctrine concerning God, is unaccountable on any rational principle, except that the Scriptures which teach that doctrine are the word of God.

As it is in respect to the divine nature and character, so it is in respect to the origin, nature, character, and condition of man. The only consistent and rational account of them is contained in the Holy Scriptures. The body of man was formed of dust. God animated that body with a living soul. He came perfect from the hands of his Maker; but he fell, and lost his integrity. By means of his fall he entailed upon the world all the moral evils that afflict it. Human nature is in ruins. To rescue it, and to restore it to more than its original glory and blessedness, the Second Person of the glorious Trinity assumed human nature, offered Himself a sacrifice to satisfy divine justice, arose from the dead, ascended into heaven, and opened it to all believers.

The scheme of redemption through Jesus Christ is of itself sufficient to stamp the Holy Scriptures with the seal of divinity. Heathen writings contain traditions of man's primitive innocence and felicity, and descriptions of his present wickedness and misery; but they make no mention of redemption, or remedy from sin and punishment. Human reason could never have devised the scheme of salvation revealed in the Bible. As man became a sinner by the use of his free agency, so the wisdom of the world has taught that he has power, by the same agency, to restore himself to rectitude and holiness. Hence the preaching of the cross has been to those professing to be wise, foolishness; but to them that believe, it is the power of God and the wisdom of God (1 Cor. i. 23, 24).

The morality of the Bible differs from that of all other systems. It seems so palpably in the face of human nature as to make it difficult to believe that it can be the teaching of men. It makes prominent the passive virtues,—patience, meekness, humility, and forgiveness of injuries. These are not moral excellences which the world admires. They are not the excellences of its great ones, whose deeds it has chronicled, and whose praises it has sung. The Alexanders, Cæsars, and Napoleons are its models of greatness. The Bible determines moral turpitude by thought and feeling, and not by the act alone. In this it exhibits a striking originality compared with other systems. It pronounces unresisted evil inclinations to be equally guilty with evil actions. Lascivious looks are adultery. Hatred is murder. The world does not sympathize with this sternness.

In a similar manner the Bible determines moral conduct by the motive, so that guilt is incurred, even by the performance of a good act, when a right motive is wanting (Matt. vi. 1). Nebuchadnezzar is represented in Scripture as God's instrument appointed to punish the nations; but because he was actuated by personal ambition, and not by a desire to accomplish the divine purposes, he was humbled, and made to know that the 'heavens do rule' (Dan. iv. 26). In social morality a great difference is made between a criminal purpose and the act, though an outward barrier, instead of conscience, has prevented the execution of it. This is very proper in human legislation; but the divine law does not recognise it.

Men in general would not have propounded an ethical system like that of the gospel, nor the Jews in particular, who have always exhibited as much of human nature, in nearly all its features, as any other people. They chafed under the yoke of the Mosaic law, which was less spiritual than that of the New Testament. They made the law of God of no effect by their traditions. They exaggerated what was ceremonial at the expense of what was spiritual, or rather they substituted the one for the other.

Equally above the sphere of human wisdom are the precepts of the Bible. When an untutored Indian heard a Christian missionary read the passage, 'But I say unto you, Love your enemies, bless them that curse you, do good to them that hate you, and pray for them which despitefully use you and persecute you,' he immediately exclaimed, 'That is from the Great Spirit.'

He felt that no human mind ever dictated such a sentiment. It is opposed to the feelings and practice of unrenewed men. It is a hard saying to many good men. None but those who already breathe the atmosphere of heaven can unhesitatingly adopt it and act upon it.

The precepts of the Bible have reference to the duties arising out of every relation of life, and in every case they contemplate more than the performance of merely outward acts. They regard, as we have seen, the motives that prompt these acts. 'Whether we eat or drink, or whatsoever we do, we are commanded to do all to the glory of God' (1 Cor. x. 31). No heathen moralist ever uttered a precept recognising a principle so high, so all-embracing, and so ennobling.

Some of these precepts refer to duties involving relations nowhere acknowledged except in the Bible. Our duties to God are enforced by the consideration that He is not only our Creator, but also our Redeemer. 'What! know ye not that your body is the temple of the Holy Ghost which is in you, which ye have of God, and ye are not your own? For ye are bought with a price: therefore glorify God in your body and in your spirit, which are God's' (1 Cor. vi. 19, 20). We are commanded to be baptized 'in the name of the Father, and of the Son, and of the Holy Ghost' (Matt. xxviii. 19).

Our duties to our fellow-men are enhanced by a fact taught directly only in the Scriptures. All men are brethren. God 'hath made of one blood all nations of men to dwell on all the face of the earth' (Acts xvii. 26). This fact gives us an interest in every member of the human family, which we could not feel if mankind were divided into different species, descended from different origins. Being the children of one common father, we feel bound to each other by peculiar ties, and experience a sympathy for one another which otherwise could have no existence.

The preceding brief outline of some of the leading doctrines and precepts of the Bible shows that they possess a unique character, which separates them widely from the doctrines and precepts of all the sages of the world. They exhibit a character so unique as to remove them into an entirely different sphere of intelligence and morality. The only inference admissible is, that the former contain elements which are more than human. They must have originated with Him who speaks as man does not speak.

The unique character of the Holy Scriptures has been developed in an able and scholarly manner by Henry Rogers, in his work on *The Superhuman Origin of the Bible.*[1] He shows that human nature in general, as known to us by consciousness and experience, would not warrant us to expect many traits of Scripture, if it be a book of purely human authorship. What follows on this point is a mere abridgment of some of his thoughts.

Consider the inveterate proneness of mankind to idolatry, which is attested by the nearly universal condition of the world from the dawn of authentic history down to the present day. The progenitors of the Jews practised it. The Jews themselves relapsed into it from time to time, in spite of instruction and chastisement. Even Christianity has been transformed by the Roman Catholic Church into something like paganism. Is it not, then, strange that the Bible, which is more varied in its contents than any other book, composed by different writers, who lived in far different ages, utters from beginning to end a solitary and persistent protest against this practice, and every-

[1] *The Superhuman Origin of the Bible inferred from itself.* By Henry Rogers. London, 1874.

where maintains the doctrine of a sublime, elevated, uncompromising monotheism? Considering that human nature has always shown so intense a sympathy with this general tendency to idolatry, how is it that the Jewish nation, which manifested that tendency as much as any other people, preserved in their sacred writings the doctrine of one God, the Maker of heaven and earth?

Assuming the Scriptures to be of mere human origin, we meet with certain paradoxes which, on that assumption, have no parallel in all other history or literature. They constitute a long libel on the Jewish nation, and yet the Jews clung to them with a desperate tenacity and boundless veneration. Consider especially the New Testament. How could the Jews have originated such a book and the religion which it contains? Its authors predicted its rejection by the Jews, and its acceptance, though not without violent opposition, by the Gentiles, among whom it proceeds to narrate its rapid progress. This New Testament, too, while recognising the rights of conscience, and consecrating the principle of toleration, propounds a religion which aspires to universal dominion, which is to be achieved by moral force alone.

Take the character of Christ, the founder and exemplar of the system of morality taught in the gospel, and the difficulty just touched is only one of a knot of difficulties of the same kind. What was a single paradox in contemplating the morality alone, becomes, when we contemplate the history and character of Him who propounded it, a bundle of paradoxes. The problem is a very complex one—moral, intellectual, and literary all at once. Neither among Greeks nor Romans can we discover the elements which could have evolved so peculiar a creation, whether supposed to be real or fictitious; among the Jews, to whom the problem historically limits us, as little as among any other people. These had none of the conditions under which such a character, if real, could have spontaneously risen among them as a simple growth of the national genius, culture, or institutions, or been ideally conceived as a deliberate fiction, or developed as a gradual aggregation of myth or legend. The first is clearly proved by the shock which such a Messiah gave to all their prejudices, and the vivid indignation which He evoked; by their persecution and crucifixion of Him; by their incessant hostility to those who espoused His cause; and by their bitter and constant hatred of Him from that day to this. Eighteen hundred years have not exhausted, or even sensibly abated, their prejudice; and its inveteracy and constancy bear evidence how little such a character was likely to be generated as an actual phenomenon, or conceived as an ideal creation, in a nation thus conditioned.

On the hypothesis that Christ is a mere fiction or myth, the argument is strengthened. For how should the Jews be either able or willing to paint such a portrait or embody such a myth, the mere exhibition of which has roused the undying animosity of their nation for eighteen hundred years?

If the character of Christ portrayed in the Gospels is regarded as a phenomenon which human nature might have produced, or human nature could have invented, the most startling incongruities embarrass us on every side. Suppose that Jesus Christ was a real personage, but simply a man, born under those ordinary conditions of humanity, which might have given to the world many Christs before Him, or which may give us many after Him. On this supposition, how do we account for the miracles which are ascribed to Him? Of course, on this hypothesis they were never wrought. How shall we consider His absurd and fantastical claims if He was only a mere man? They must be treated with the same indifference and contempt with which we would treat those of a wild dreamer or madman.

Suppose that Christ never existed, and that the Gospels are mere myths. It is admitted that His professed portrait exists. Now, if it is not a portrait, it is, in the first place, a curious paradox that a painting has to a large extent changed the great facts of the world's history; or, which comes to the same thing, only more difficult to be believed, if it be the embodiment of myth, then the casual illusions of a multitude of imaginations have issued in a painting of such exquisite skill as to produce the same effects. We are told of an ancient painter, who, finding that he could not depict to his mind the foam about a fiery steed's mouth, dashed his brush against the canvas in a paroxysm of despair, and, lo, what skill could not do, chance did for him. It is much the same with the mythical hypothesis, as applied to account for such a transcendent creation as that of Christ.

On the supposition that it is an ideal creation, we are no longer met by the conflict of heterogeneous qualities, such as would make the reality, if a mere man, simply a monster; for, on this supposition, the incongruous attributes must be supposed to form part of the ideal, and we are left only to wonder at the marvellous art which has blended them, however incongruous, in such exquisite union and harmony, that the most heterogeneous qualities do not instantly give the impression of incongruity. But we are still met with a paradox in human nature—namely, that the very qualities which should have warned the world that it was a mere ideal on which it was gazing, have not prevented its mistaking it for a reality. The painter has so overdone his part that the world has vehemently contended, and generally believed, that the painting is no painting at all; nay, rather than believe it such, it has been willing to receive all those supernatural traits with which it is fraught as also copied from reality.

It is a still greater paradox in human nature that the artists who executed this painting were, so far as we can judge, as utterly incapable of imagining or executing such a portrait as the merest dauber of emulating the divinest performances of a Raphael or a Michael Angelo. In the ordinary Jew of those days, in the class of men to which this problem limits us, there was not one single attribute, moral or intellectual, to account for this masterpiece. It is a favourite maxim in modern times, and sometimes strained into an apology for the most egregious follies or the most atrocious crimes, that a man cannot rise far above the spirit and prejudices of his age. It is at least equally true in relation to extraordinary excellence. Now, in contemplating the Jews of that age, it is impossible to imagine men more destitute of the moral and intellectual qualifications essential to the creation of such an ideal as Christ. Their national predilections, which had been fondly cherished for ages, tended in a totally different direction. They gloried in their exclusive privileges; they were steeped in religious bigotry; and they consoled themselves, amidst their calamities, with the dream of a conquering Messiah, who should restore and augment the glories of ancient Israel. How came the authors of the Gospels to divest themselves of these prejudices, and conceive a Messiah whose life is depicted as one series of humiliation and ignominy, whose glories were all to be in the future and invisible world, who shrank from every attempt to force Him to a practical assertion of His sovereignty, and who at last died the death of a malefactor? His career of obloquy and suffering is relieved by glimpses of a species of moral greatness, which their education and associations disqualified them from fully appreciating, and which they themselves, so far from being able to invent it, confess their 'slowness of heart' to perceive and apprehend. How came they to originate a Messiah who, in direct opposition to their national narrowness and intense bigotry, inculcated universal brotherhood and a worldwide charity—who proclaimed the approaching abolition of all those privileges on which a Jew prided himself, in favour of a religion which should no longer know the badge of Jew or Gentile? How was it possible for human nature, conditioned as were the Jews of that age, to rise to a conception like this?

It is inconceivable that one man should successfully execute a portrait like that of Christ; and yet four have executed it with similar success. They have transmitted to us a portrait, in which the combination of the human elements, and their mode of presentation, are of the most singular originality; in which obscurity, poverty, and suffering are covered with a halo of glory, which belongs to no hero of history or romance; in which a boundless sympathy with human frailty is conciliated with a holiness that knows no frailty; in which virtue, perfect as it is, is untinctured with that austerity which is almost always its shadow, and which so often detracts from its loveliness; in which patience and meekness, which can bear all wrongs and forgive them, are united with a courage on behalf of truth which the frowns of an opposing world cannot daunt, a gentleness which will not 'break the bruised reed or quench the smoking flax,' with an indignation which launched at hypocrisy more bitter and burning invectives than ever before fell from human lips. All these, and many traits more, equally unlikely to be combined in human nature, are conjoined with supernatural qualities, which, far from betraying discordance with the human elements, are so skilfully wrought into the picture, that, as already said, instead of at once convincing the world that Christ was a mere ideal, they have beguiled it into accepting Him as a historic reality. Whence came these four obscure painters to possess this power? Who instructed them to dip their pencils in the colours of the rainbow, and handle them with such skill as to cheat the world into the notion that incredibilities are true, and chimeras realities?

They have done this, too, in the most difficult of all forms, that of dramatic exhibition. They have made Christ speak, and act, and live before us, and move our sympathies more deeply than it is possible for all other dramatic personations put together to do.

These, and many other arguments of a similar nature which might be adduced, admit of only one conclusion, viz.: *'That the Bible is not such a book as man would have made, if he could; or could have made, if he would.'*[1]

Exceptions to the morality of the Bible have been taken by some, who profess to find the inculcation of as pure a morality in books written by heathen sages. Confucius, Zoroaster, Socrates, Epictetus, and Seneca are very often in the mouths of such men. These ancient sages of the heathen world are, in the estimation of these objectors, immeasurably above the prophets and apostles of the Old and New Testaments. The character of these wise men should be reversed. An attempt to injure their just reputation would be ungenerous and unchristian. But no candid mind, after a comparison of their moral teaching with that of the sacred writers, would pronounce them authorities equal to the latter. Compared with Moses, David,

---

[1] *The Superhuman Origin of the Bible inferred from itself.* By Henry Rogers. London. Pp. 3-53.

Solomon, Isaiah, the Evangelists, and Paul, they resemble stars compared with the sun. Their glimmering light is lost in the dazzling effulgence of the greater orb. The proper reply to those who refer to them as of equal authority with the Bible is: Prove their equality by a careful and minute comparison of their teachings with those of the Scriptures. You have made an affirmation which very few believe; the burden of proof falls upon you.

It is generally admitted, even by some celebrated infidels, that the morality of the New Testament is of the highest and purest type. Christ's Sermon on the Mount is quoted as a model of perfect moral teaching. Nothing can be added to it, and nothing can be taken from it. It stands unique among all discourses on morality. It is the Old Testament that is at fault. It comes far short of the perfection of the New. But Christ, in the very sermon referred to, says: 'Think not that I am come to destroy the law or the prophets: I am not come to destroy, but to fulfil' (Matt. v. 17). The Saviour, in this sermon, endorses the Old Testament, as He does in many other places, and gives a spiritual depth and extent to its meaning which the Jews had never apprehended, or entirely distorted.

We hear much of the originality of Christ's teachings. In His manner of teaching He certainly was original. But if it is meant that Christ taught many original or new truths, it is very doubtful whether He was original to the extent that some imagine. He expounded and enforced the law, the scriptures of the Old Testament. The germ of all His teaching is found in 'Moses, and in the Prophets, and in the Psalms' (Luke xxiv. 44).

The moral law, called the Ten Commandments, given in the Old Testament, is perfect. We have the authority of Christ, that on the two principles involved in it 'hang all the law and the prophets' (Matt. xxii. 37–40).

Solutions of alleged moral difficulties require an examination of particular texts, which the reader can find in the excellent work of Mr. Haley, on the *Discrepancies of the Bible*.[1]

A few general directions for the treatment of them will close this chapter.

(1) It should be borne in mind that the Old Testament, in which it is alleged these difficulties exist, is inchoate and progressive; that its teachings were not so full at an early period as they were at a later; that they were completed in the New.

(2) The time and existing relations when a thing was said should be considered.

(3) It should be kept in mind that God in some instances forebore a perfection of discipline, as in the cases of polygamy and divorce, though there was no imperfection of teaching on these matters.

(4) That a record of human opinions is often given, as in the case of Job's friends and others, without any approval of these opinions; and that bad actions of good men are recorded in the same way.

(5) That it is, therefore, important to ascertain who the speaker is.

(6) That a commission to execute a divine command does not necessarily justify the spirit and manner of its execution. This, if kept in mind, may help to remove difficulties, which some find in connection with the wars of the Israelites.

(7) Objections against the imprecatory Psalms and other comminatory portions of Scripture, on the ground of morality, generally proceed from the subjective condition of the objector, and can only be removed by a

---

[1] *An Examination of the Alleged Discrepancies of the Bible*. By John W. Haley, M.A. Andover: Warren F. Draper. 1874. Pp. 219–311.

change of that condition. The writer is of the opinion that in proportion as a man loves holiness, in that proportion will these portions become less offensive to him. Such objections are the offspring of a mawkish sentimentality, which affects a refinement of feeling alien to Him who is just and true as well as merciful.

CHAPTER II.

DIVERSITY AND UNITY OF THE BIBLE.

THE reader of the Bible cannot fail to notice its diversified character. It contains nearly all the forms of literary composition. In the books of Moses, we find history, statistics, biography, prophecy, and poetry, with a style adapted to each. Of the other books, some are strictly historical; others combine history and prophecy; some are entirely poetical; and others are epistolary and doctrinal. Notwithstanding this great diversity, the Bible constitutes a unit. Its poetry takes its themes from its history; its biography is history in the concrete; and its history is the setting of its prophecy. They all unite to make one perfect book, in which we have unity in the midst of diversity —a characteristic of all the works of God. They all exhibit unity of plan with diversity of parts and of progress.

Of this unity combined with diversity, Dr. Barrows gives some appropriate and striking illustrations. 'The history of a plant of wheat,' says that author, 'from the time when the kernel is sown in the earth to the harvest has perfect unity of plan. But how unlike in outward form are the tender blade, the green stalk, and the ripened ear! The ear constitutes a self-consistent whole. But can anything be more dissimilar in form than spring and autumn? Yet no one thinks of finding a want of harmony between the fragrant blossoms of the former and the ripened fruit of the latter. The path of the harvest lies through the blossoms. Geologists dwell at great length on the varied conditions through which our planet has passed, and the wonderfully diversified forms of vegetable and animal life corresponding to these several conditions. Yet in this endless diversity of outward form they recognise from first to last a deep, underlying unity of plan. We might, then, reasonably infer beforehand, that if God should make a revelation of Himself to men, it would have not only unity, but *diversity of outward form*, especially *diversity of progress*. The fact that the revelation contained in the Bible has such diversity is one of the seals of its genuineness."[1]

The diversity of the Bible is patent to every reader of it: the unity underlying that diversity can be perceived only by the careful and diligent student of it. To the casual observer, the universe presents an endless variety of objects, without any principle of harmony. But to him who classifies these objects according to their constitutive and governing laws it appears harmonious in all its parts: it constitutes a cosmos. All living creatures have organic relations. Plants and animals are related; these again are related to the earth, the earth to the solar system, and the solar system to the universe, which is a unit made up of innumerable parts, exhibiting endless variety, yet bound together by all-pervading and controlling laws.

The Bible consists of sixty-six separate books, as already stated, the works of different authors. The number of these authors cannot be absolutely determined, for some of the books are anonymous. Some make their number about forty. They did not all write in the same language. The Old Testament, with the exception of a few portions in Chaldee, was written

---

[1] *Companion to the Bible.* By Rev. E. P. Barrows, D.D. Published by the American Tract Society, 158 Nassau Street, New York.

in Hebrew, and the New Testament in Greek. The composition of the various books extended through a period of sixteen hundred years, from the time of Moses until the death of the Apostle John. They were written in different countries, under various forms and conditions of national life and of civilisation. Their writers belonged to different grades of social position and of intellectual culture. Moses 'was learned in all the wisdom of the Egyptians' (Acts vii. 22); David was a king; Amos 'was among the herdmen of Tekoa' (Amos i. 1); Peter and John were fishermen (Matt. iv. 18, 21).

A book written under such circumstances, and by men so different in position and culture, could scarcely be expected, if of merely human origin, to agree in all its parts. We would naturally expect the same differences of opinion that characterize the literary productions of all ages and of all countries. Scarcely any two writers can be found to agree. If they are of the same school, one expounds and elucidates another, or modifies and supplements him. If they are of different schools, one endeavours to demolish what another has endeavoured to establish. Nothing of this kind is found in the Bible. All the writers are in perfect accord with each other. They attach themselves to no school of philosophy. They acknowledge no human authority. They all speak in the name of God. They begin, continue, and end all things in Him. The revelation and accomplishment of His purposes of grace form their great theme.

The central idea of the Bible is God as Creator, Preserver, and Redeemer. All its other ideas revolve round this, the sun of the system of revelation, and shine with reflected light. The Bible idea of God constitutes its grand unity. It represents Him as active, by His providence, in the affairs of men, directing all the events of history to one great end, the manifestation of His glory in the salvation of men. History is the development of His purposes with reference to this world. All its lights blend into one—the luminous path of His providence.

The Bible doctrine of God has been exhibited in the preceding chapter. We refer to it again under another aspect—the unity of its presentation throughout the Holy Scriptures. In them God is revealed as a Spirit, having life in Himself; as a personal Being, the Creator, Upholder, and Ruler of heaven and earth. He exists apart from the world and above it, yet He acts in it. He is the Eternal God, the author of all life; invisible to His creatures, but revealing Himself in His Son and by His Spirit. He is the God of all nations; the God of love, of grace, and of redemption. His oneness is assumed and recognised by all the writers of the Bible. At the same time, God the Son, begotten of the Father from all eternity, is declared to be the image of the invisible God, and the brightness of His glory, to whom the Father has given to have life in Himself. According to the personal distinction, He is God who appears and is manifested; the face of God, through whom the Father creates, sustains, and preserves all things. God the Holy Spirit, eternally proceeding from the Father and the Son, is God who communicates, in whom the Father and the Son meet in perfect and living unity and communion, through whom the Deity gives and distributes divine power, life, and grace, and through whom the union between the Deity and the creature is completed.[1]

This biblical idea of God is entirely consistent with itself throughout both Testaments. In the New Testament the revelation of it is fuller, but it is not contradictory to that of the Old. It is thus

[1] See Kurtz' *Sacred History*, Introduction, p. 24.

distinguished from the heathen idea of God, from all pure, abstract monotheism, post-Christian Judaism, and Mohammedanism.[1]

Monotheism was not an original discovery of the Hebrew mind. Comparative mythology points to it, under some crude conception, as the original religion. The sun was perhaps its earliest symbol, from which radiated at length the manifold forms of a symbol worship, which degenerated into idolatry. But the peculiarity of the monotheism of the Bible is the singleness and pureness of its conception of God as a spirit, and the ascription to Him of the attributes of a spirit in their infinity. He is styled Jehovah, the I Am, the Eternal, the Unchangeable, the Almighty, the Creator of all things, and the Universal Lord. While other systems, beginning in monotheism, terminate in pantheism, or in the personification of nature, the Bible rigidly maintains His personality. It represents Him as sustaining personal relations to other spirits by means of His moral government, His holy law, and His paternal love; and by the word holiness, which as applied to Him has no synonym, it ascribes a peculiarity of character unknown in every other system of religion.

In perfect conformity with the Bible idea and doctrine of God is its teaching respecting His government and providence. The latter, indeed, grows out of the former. It is only such a God as the Bible reveals who can exercise such a government and providence as it ascribes to Him. Such a God, from His very nature, must act as the Scriptures represent Him.

The books of ancient philosophy and religion, and all books on the subject that do not view it from a biblical standpoint, contain vague notions and barren speculations, which bewilder the mind, and leave it in

---

[1] Lange, *Introduction to the Old Testament*, p. 4, sec. 2.

suspense and doubt respecting the government of the world. According to some, it is governed by fate; according to others, by a multiplicity of deities, sometimes at variance among themselves. Some subject everything to fixed and invariable laws, and others leave all things to chance. But the Bible furnishes us with the idea of the personal government of God, extending to all parts of the creation. He upholds all things by the word of His power; He feeds all creatures by His bounty; He marks the fall of a sparrow, and numbers the hairs of our heads; 'His tender mercies are over all His works' (Ps. cxlv. 9).

This government the Bible, with a distinctness found in no other book, represents as moral as well as providential and physical. Moral government consists in rewarding and punishing intelligent and moral creatures according to their merits and demerits. They are rewarded as righteous, and punished as vicious. The Bible teaches us that God exercises such a government over our entire race, both as individuals and as nations. His moral law promises reward and threatens punishment to the former hereafter, according to their respective characters; for the latter it contains sanctions of good and evil in this life, according to their conduct. In this government God is represented as personally active, and the whole course of His providence is described as subservient to it. This idea of the Moral Ruler of the world is unique. The Bible form of it is found in no other book, unless it is derived from the Holy Scriptures. Yet it is the only idea of moral government which takes hold upon the conscience, gives ground to the penal sanctions of human law, and furnishes hope of the final triumph of justice and righteousness in the world. How this idea of the government of God comes to be found in the Bible alone it is difficult to explain, unless God revealed it.

This revelation of the nature, government, and providence of God is in keeping with what the Bible teaches of the nature, condition, and necessities of man, the subject of God's moral government in this world. It is such a revelation as his moral and spiritual wants require—one that makes known to him his true origin, his actual condition, his need as a spiritual being, and the destiny, conditioned on his character, that awaits him. If there were no such being as man in the world, there would be no revelation of God of the precise character of that which we possess; for God, the Redeemer, Ruler, and avenging Judge, and man, the sinner, the subject of government, and accountable for his actions, are correlated. The Bible revelation and doctrine of God require, to render them intelligible, just such an account as the sacred record gives of man. This account is clear, and consistent from beginning to end, constituting a complete unity of doctrine in relation to his origin, fall, condition, and redemption. God formed him of the dust of the ground, and breathed into his nostrils the breath of life, and he became a living soul. He was endowed with the faculties of speech and reason, and invested by his Creator with dominion over the lower animals and over the earth. The Bible nowhere favours the doctrine that he was developed from a lower species. It says that he was created—created in the image of God; and all the circumstances of the case incline us to believe that he was brought into existence in the full maturity of all his powers of body and soul. Endowed with freedom of will, he could have maintained his original state of integrity; but his power of free determination rendered it possible for him to fall from his happy condition into sin, and consequent misery and ruin. The opportunity of trial was afforded to him by the prohibition to eat of the tree of the knowledge of good and evil, connected with the warning that disobedience would be punished by death. He disobeyed the prohibition, and brought sin and death into the world. He and all his posterity were condemned to die. Death reigns. But he was not left in the ruined and helpless condition into which he had brought himself. Deliverance was promised through the seed of the woman. The promise was from time to time renewed with more fullness, clearness, and particularity, until the Deliverer came, vanquished the destroyer, and laid the foundations of a spiritual kingdom, which shall fill the earth. The character and glories of this kingdom formed the theme of the prophets, and constituted the visions of the Apocalypse.

In order to enter into this spiritual kingdom, both the Old and New Testaments teach that we 'must be born again;' that faith is a necessary condition to obtain the blessings of salvation. On this important subject the New Testament is fuller and more explicit than the Old; but they never contradict each other. The Old Testament teaches that men are saved, not by the merit of their good works, but by God's mercy. The New Testament reveals the ground of this mercy in Jesus Christ. The reality of this harmony may be exhibited in a clear light by taking a passage of the New Testament, which comprehends the way of salvation, and comparing it with the declarations of the Old Testament. Such a passage is Tit. iii. 5: 'Not by works of righteousness which we have done, but according to His mercy He saved us, by the washing of regeneration, and the renewing of the Holy Ghost.' Compare with this Deut. vii. 7, 8; Ps. xxv. 11; Ezek. xxxvi. 22, 25–27; Jer. xxxi. 33; Dan. ix. 18; Ps. li. 1, 6, 7, 10, 11.

The same harmony of teaching obtains in regard to

the rewards of the righteous and the punishment of the wicked. 'Say ye to the righteous, that it shall be well with him; for they shall eat the fruit of their doings. Woe unto the wicked! it shall be ill with him; for the reward of his hands shall be given him' (Isa. iii. 10, 11). Compare Ps. ix. 17; Rom. ii. 6–10; Gal. vi. 7, 8.

The doctrines of redemption and final retribution, as taught in the Scriptures, exhibit a progressive development, unfolding rudimental ideas, and unveiling more and more a unity of plan, which is perfected in the universal dominion of Christ. This plan is the purpose of Divine Providence to 'gather together in one all things in Christ, both which are in heaven and which are on earth.' For this grand consummation creation travails in birth; to it history marches forward with varying, yet with constant progress.

Can we account for this unity of the Holy Scriptures, written by so many different authors, in so many different ages, and in different countries, on any other hypothesis than that they were guided by a Divine Intelligence, who connects the end with the beginning, fitting all the intermediate links by a predetermined harmony?

CHAPTER III.

THE ORGANIC CHARACTER OF THE BIBLE.

A VERY striking characteristic of the Bible is its organic character. All its parts constitute a complete organism. This implies more than a unity arising from the harmony of its teachings. It is a unity resulting from the unfolding of a primordial germ. Such a unity is the rose, such is the oak, such is the human body.

The whole universe, when its several parts are viewed as reciprocally means and ends, is an organism. It is the evolution of a creative idea dwelling in the mind of God, manifesting itself in endless diversity, yet one and changeless. Every thing is so fitted to every other thing, that a change in the one would involve a change in the other. A storm of wind would imply a change in the state of the atmosphere, and that a change in the degree of temperature, and that some other antecedent change, affecting, it might be, the fertility or barrenness of countries and the duration of human life.

This organism of the general system of nature is concealed from the careless and unscientific observer. He may, in some of its individual parts, as a flower or a tree, be able to perceive an organism, and understand the effect of destroying any one of its parts; but the relation of this individual organism to a greater does not enter his mind. The case is similar with the careless reader of the Bible. He may understand the unity of a single book, and the effect of transposing or changing its parts; but he does not understand its organic connection with the whole system of revealed truth. It is different with the careful and devout student of Scripture. He observes a plan of progressive development, into which every part of the sacred volume fits with the utmost exactness. To him the Bible is an organism; it is not a collection of books without any connection except that of juxtaposition.

By organism is understood a 'structure consisting of parts mutually dependent,—a whole of which the parts are reciprocally means and ends.'

Botanists, for example, divide a flower into the root, the stem, the receptacle, the pistil, the stamens, the calyx, and the corolla. Each of these constituent portions is reciprocally a means and an end. There is among them a reciprocity of parts that constitutes an organic connection. The idea of an organism includes that of development, or unfolding motion from a given point, which is the beginning of the development, to another, which is its end. In this unfolding there is no isolation of parts, but a necessary and natural connection of them. There is a rational coherence, a mutual adaptation of one to the other.

If one examines the Bible carefully, he will find that it possesses such a connection of parts as to constitute it a development terminating in a perfect organic structure.

Consider, first, the intimate connection of the two great parts, the Old Testament and the New, into which the Scriptures are divided. One of the pregnant sayings of Augustine is: 'In Vetere Testamento novum latet, et in Novo vetus patet.'[1] The symbolical institutions of the Old Testament were prophetic symbols of the realities of the gospel; they were

[1] In the Old Testament the New is contained in germ, and in the New the Old is unfolded.

'shadows of good things to come' (Heb. x. 1). 'The body is of Christ' (Col. ii. 17). The ordinances of Judaism are called 'the rudiments of the world' (Col. ii. 20). The Church, while under these ordinances, is said to have been 'in bondage under the elements of the world' (Gal. iv. 3). 'The law was our schoolmaster to bring us unto Christ' (Gal. iii. 24). Such are the general descriptions of the symbolical institutions and services of the Old Testament in their relation to the gospel. The former dispensation is represented as a preparation for the latter and present. An essential unity subsists between them, a unity recognised in the predictions of the Old Testament and in the teachings of the New. In the Old we have the types and predictions; in the New, the fulfilment: in the Old we have the shadow; in the New, the substance. 'In the Old Testament we see a fiducial resting in Jehovah; in the New Testament, an unspeakable fulness of spiritual and heavenly blessings from the opened fountain of His mercy. In the Old Testament, a confidence that the Lord would not abandon His people; in the New Testament, the Lord Himself assuming our nature, the God-man connecting Himself in organic union with humanity, and sending forth streams of life through its members. In the Old Testament, in the background, night, only relieved by the stars of the word of promise, and operations of grace in suitable accordance with it; in the New Testament, in the background, day, still clouded indeed by our human nature, which is not yet completely penetrated by the Holy Spirit, and which is ever anew manifesting its sinfulness, but yet such a day as gives assurance of the cloudless sunshine of eternity, of which God Himself is the light.'[1] The New Testament is the completion of the Old.

[1] Fairbairn's *Typology*, vol. i. p. 75. Philadelphia, 1859.

An organic connection subsists not only between the Old and New Testaments, but also between the several parts of each.

The Pentateuch is the groundwork of the Old Testament—indeed of both Testaments. Destroy it, and the Scriptures lose their intelligibility. It contains an announcement of the new covenant, to which the history, the symbolical institutions, the moral teaching and predictions of the Old Testament are preparatory. The outlines of the patriarchal religion are exhibited in the first eleven chapters of Genesis and in Job; the subsequent chapters of Genesis give us the history of the transition from that religion to the temporary and typical dispensation of the Law. The other books of the Pentateuch exhibit to us the *moral* law, which is an impress of the divine character, and a compendium of human duty; the *ceremonial* law, foreshadowing the great atonement; and the *civil* law, intended to preserve the other two. With the book of Joshua commences the 'actual typical development of the old covenant, until the decline of its typical glory.' The history of this development is contained in the historical books of Judges, Ruth, Samuel, Kings, Chronicles, Ezra, Nehemiah, and Esther. The moral and spiritual life of the old dispensation finds its expression in the Psalms, Proverbs, Song of Solomon, and Ecclesiastes, which occupy an intermediate position between the law and the gospel. The greater prophets furnish us with prophetic images or representations of the new dispensation. They represent to us Christ as prophet, priest, and king. Daniel is apocalyptic: he sees in vision the Messianic kingdom in its antagonism to the world monarchies. The twelve minor prophets predict judgments upon Edom, Nineveh, and Babylon, as the types of antichrist and of the apostate world-power, and announce the approach of the everlasting kingdom, with some of its special relations. The last of them brings the canon of the Old Testament to a fitting close by the announcement of the Sun of Righteousness, and of the mission of His forerunner 'to turn the heart of the fathers to their children, and the heart of the children to their fathers.' Thus the Old Testament ends, as it begins, with a prophecy of the Messiah; and the light of this prophecy increases gradually from the first streaks of the dawn until it reaches the brightness of the rising sun.[1]

The New Testament exhibits on its first page its organic connection with the Old. It presents to us the life of Jesus as forming part of the history and life of the Jewish nation, and hence as the fulfilment of the hereditary blessing of Abraham. 'The book of the generation of Jesus Christ, the son of David, the son of Abraham' (Matt. i. 1). Jesus Christ is here set before us as the new-born King of the Jews, as the promised Messiah, and the aim and goal of every progressive stage of the theocracy. He is the great antitype of the Old Testament history, in whom it has been fulfilled. Its legal types, its worship, its typical historical events, and its gracious interpositions, had their fulfilment in Christ. The same may be said of the theocracy. When Shiloh came, the sceptre of Judah and the throne of David gave place to their antitypical ideal.

The books of the New Testament are divided into historical, didactic, and apocalyptic. The great idea that pervades the historical books is the manifestation of the kingdom of heaven by the advent of the Godman, and by the planting of the Church through the power of the Holy Spirit. This evangelical history

[1] On the organism of the Old Testament, see Lange's *Introduction to the Old Testament*. Vol. on Genesis, pp. 66–68. New York: Charles Scribner & Co. 1868.

forms the centre of all history, by terminating that of the old, and commencing that of the new world. The didactic portion of the New Testament consists of epistles, some of which are addressed to particular Churches and individuals, and others to the Church Catholic. These epistles 'are intended to serve as a directory for the development of Christian and ecclesiastical life in the kingdom of heaven, or of the kingdom of heaven as manifest in ecclesiastical and Christian life, in all its relations to the world, whether hostile or peaceable. This development is ever based upon, and traced to, the first coming of Christ for the redemption of man.' The Book of Revelation contains a prophetic description of the triumph of Christ over antichrist, of the transformation of the world, and of the second advent of our Lord. 'The foundation of the kingdom of heaven, its unfolding, its future conquests and ultimate completion; such are the three parts which constitute the kingdom of heaven.'[1]

The question now naturally arises, Can a book, the greater part of which is evolved from a single prophecy (the *Protevangelium*, Gen. iii. 15), which forms the germ of all subsequent prophecy,—a book, every part of which is connected with a grand scheme of development, culminating in the redemption of the world,—can such a book be the work of men unaided by Him who devised the scheme, and whose providence from the beginning of the world until now has been employed for its execution? Is not such a book from God?

[1] *Unity and Organic Arrangement of the New Testament: Matthew.* By J. P. Lange, D.D. Introd. pp. 23-27. New York: Charles Scribner. 1865.

CHAPTER IV.

THE UNIVERSALITY OF THE BIBLE.

THE Bible is in some of its features a national book. It was written by Jewish authors, and much of it is occupied with the details of Jewish history. It narrates the origin of the Jewish nation, the establishment of their ecclesiastical and civil polity, their conquest of Canaan, their wars and vicissitudes. The poetical portions of it, while breathing the most elevated devotion, abound in allusions to national history, manners, and customs. Not only was it written by Jewish authors, but it was also written principally in the land of Canaan,—a small country separated from the rest of the world by its peculiar laws and institutions; it contains frequent references to the natural history and physical characteristics of that country, and thus renders a knowledge of these necessary to a proper understanding of its contents.

Notwithstanding its national and local character, no book touches the universal chords of the human soul as it does. It evokes the common music of humanity in every age, in every nation, and in every clime. It is suited to every period and condition of life—to the child, the youth, the man of middle age, the hoary head; to the peasant and the king, to the rude and the uncultivated, to the learned and the refined. It speaks to all, and in language adapted to all.

This is not bare assertion, unsupported by facts. The Bible has been translated into all the principal languages of our globe, and proved its wonderful adaptation to every diversity of mind and to every condition of life. Different portions of the world have different peculiarities, arising from moral and political as well as from natural causes. These peculiarities are seen in their philosophy, in their laws, in their arts and sciences. Notwithstanding this, the Bible is suited to all men in every part of the earth alike. It seizes upon and purifies the permanent and universal, and moulds the local and temporary into harmony with its quickening and progressive spirit. Of this the history of Christian nations furnishes ample proof. Their progress — and among them alone progress exists — is the result of Christianity. But Christianity exists nowhere without the Bible. The Bible is the objective form of Christianity.

Some talk much and ignorantly about the Hindoo writings. But what meaning and life have these out of India? Elsewhere they are valued chiefly as matters of literary curiosity, or as furnishing materials for philological investigation. The productions of Grecian genius, which are justly so much admired as models of taste, and which contain much that is of universal interest, do not stir the human soul and move it to its depths as does the Bible. Socrates, Plato, and Aristotle thought profoundly on morals, on metaphysics, and on science generally; but they have not moved the world as Moses, David, the prophets, and the apostles have done. Only the learned few can appreciate the philosophers of Greece; the child and the philosopher, the illiterate and the learned, appreciate alike the beauty, the sublimity, the simplicity of the Bible, and feel alike its power. Compared with the greatest works of literary genius of every age, the Bible stands out as the book of books; it is the sun in whose light all their glories fade. When that light shines into the mind, the human soul, like the fabled statue of Memnon, which emitted a harp-like sound when touched by the rising ray, breathes the music of a new and higher existence.

'The Bible as the book of books,' says Lange (*Introduction to the Old Testament*, p. 7), 'is the sun in the centre of all other religious records,—the Kings of the Chinese, the Vedas of India, the Zendavesta of the Persians, the Eddas of the Germans [Scandinavians], the Jewish Talmud, and the Mohammedan Koran,—judging all that is hostile in them, reconciling and bringing into liberty whatever elements of truth they may contain.

'It stands also, with a like repelling and attracting force, in the centre of all literature, as well as all theology. In the same power and dignity it exercises its critical authority upon all historical traditions.

'As the ideal cosmos of the revelation of salvation, it forms, with the cosmos of the general revelation of God, an organic unity (Ps. viii., xix., civ.). It is the key of the world cosmos, while this again is the living illustration of the cosmos of Scripture.'

What is the ground of this universality of the Bible —of its adaptability to all men, in all conditions, and in all ages?

'If,' says Dr. Chalmers, 'in the system of external nature we can recognise the evidence of God being its author, in the adaptation, wherewith it teems, to the moral and intellectual constitution of man, there is room and opportunity for this very evidence in the book of an external revelation. What appears in the construction of a world might be made to appear as manifestly in the construction of a volume, whose objective truth may present as obvious and skilful an accommodation to our mental economy as do the objective things of the created universe. And it is not less favourable for an indication of its divine original, that whereas nature, as being the original system, abounds with those fitnesses which harmonize with the mental constitution in a state of health, Christianity, as being a restorative system, abounds in fitnesses to the same constitution in a state of disease. Certain it is that the same wisdom, and goodness, and even power of a moral architect may be as strikingly evinced in the reparation as in the primeval establishment of a moral nature.'

The Bible has this fitness which Dr. Chalmers, in the passage quoted, intimates. It has an 'obvious and skilful accommodation to our mental' and moral 'economy.' It reveals 'a restorative system,' and 'abounds in fitnesses to our constitution in a state of disease.' It tells us of a fall and of a redemption. It answers those questions which have baffled the attempts of the unaided human intellect to solve; it reveals a plan by which the conscience can be pacified, the affections gained, and the will renewed.

In all ages of the world there have been speculative minds that have wearied themselves in their vain endeavours to solve those profound problems of the universe, some of which lie beyond the reach of unassisted reason. The relation of matter to thought, and of thought to matter; the origin and duration of mind; the relation of the finite to the infinite; the possible production of the finite from the infinite, or of matter from thought; the creation of the world and the creation of man,—these and kindred topics were debated by the Grecian thinkers, without any one of them reaching a satisfactory solution; and they are debated at the present day by metaphysicians with a similar result. Without a revelation, or with a revelation disregarded, such speculations have generally led to pantheism, atheism, or materialism; or they have left the mind in doubt or suspense, waiting for the guidance of a heavenly messenger to lead it through the dark mazes of uncertainty into the regions of knowledge and faith. The Bible reveals such a messenger, and gives us his message. It makes known to us the existence and personality of God, and the possibility of union and fellowship with Him, as a distinct intelligence, and especially as a father and a friend. It reveals to us the origin and final cause of all things, brings life and immortality to light; and where 'the cloud sits deep,' it requires us to exercise faith in the divine wisdom, telling us that the time is coming when we shall 'know as we are known.'

It is here that the mind finds rest; it is in faith. Reason begins in faith and ends in faith. The first principles of all science are received on faith, and its loftiest demonstrations are believed on the faith that our senses and faculties do not deceive us. As we cannot demonstrate everything, but must assume some truths as ultimate and indemonstrable, faith must be the rest of the mind. To this repose the Bible has led many who wearied themselves in the endless mazes of speculation. It furnishes us with a sword to slay the Minotaur of scepticism, and with a clew to find our way out of its labyrinth.

Man feels himself guilty, and acknowledges his guilt by shedding the blood of innocent victims to atone for his sin. The streaming altars of paganism attest man's feeling of ill desert and disquiet of conscience. How can guilt be removed and conscience pacified? The Bible alone gives the answer. 'God was in Christ, reconciling the world unto Himself, not imputing their trespasses unto them' (2 Cor. v. 19). 'We were reconciled to God by the death of His Son' (Rom. v. 10).

The Bible, moreover, presents us with an object to win our affections. It tells us to look to Jesus, the pure and the lovely. It delineates His character in such a way that it is impossible for the soul reconciled

K

to God not to love Him. It tells us that while we were yet sinners 'Christ died for us' (Rom. v. 8); that though ascended into heaven, He still sympathizes with us, and watches over us with unceasing care and tender regard. In view of His loveliness and grace, the soul is drawn toward Him with devout and holy affection.

The Bible furnishes the highest motives to sway the will, and bring it into harmony with the will of Him who is our Maker and Lord; and reveals to us One whose office it is to convince, instruct, and guide.

The Bible, therefore, is adapted to the whole man, as an intellectual, moral, and spiritual being. It reveals to the troubled mind the rest of faith; to the soul oppressed by guilt, atonement for sin; to him who is longing after holiness, a sanctifier, and a perfect model for imitation. It also directs us how to promote our physical and temporal well-being. If its precepts were carefully followed, they would secure for us health and prosperity.

Man is subject to many trials and vicissitudes in life, and in all these the Bible speaks to him words of comfort. A Greek poet sings:

> 'One only healing hour remains,
> When Death, man's comforter and friend,
> Appears, his weary course to end:
> Of all the dreams of bliss there are,
> Not to be born is best by far;
> Next best, by far the best for man,
> To speed as fast as speed he can.'

The Bible says that God 'doth not willingly afflict nor grieve the children of men; that like as a father pitieth his children, so the Lord pitieth them that fear Him.' It tells us of a great High Priest who is 'touched with the feeling of our infirmities, who knoweth our frame, and remembereth that we are dust' (Lam. iii. 33; Ps. ciii. 13, 14; Heb. iv. 15). It speaks to us of One 'who is our refuge and strength, a very present help in trouble;' of 'the God of all comfort, who comforteth us in all our tribulation' (Ps. xlvi. 1; 1 Cor. i. 3, 4). However severe our trials are, it tells us that they 'are but for a moment,' and 'work out for us a far more exceeding and eternal weight of glory.'

To the mind weary in its search after the infinite, and longing for communion with One who can satisfy its aspirations, it presents 'God manifest in the flesh,' in whom all seeming contradictions are reconciled, and in the faith of whom the mind finds rest. To the lover of beauty, it speaks of the beauty of holiness, and of realms of glory far surpassing anything that the mind can conceive. To the philosopher, it propounds the profoundest problems of the universe. To him who is dissatisfied with the finite, it offers the infinite as his everlasting inheritance.

The Bible is also adapted to man in his social and domestic relations. It enjoins love to our neighbour, and such treatment of others as we would wish to receive from them. It enjoins mutual affection between husband and wife; love on the part of parents to their children, and reverence from children to their parents. There is no social and domestic duty which it does not command; no social and domestic relation which its influence does not beautify and exalt.

The question now naturally arises: How comes it that the Bible is so exactly suited to the character of man, individually and socially? How comes it that no work of the most transcendent genius has such universality, an adaptation so large and extensive, so minute and particular? Why is it as universal in its influence as the air and the sunlight of heaven? Is it not a proof that it is from Him who created man and who knows what is in man?

CHAPTER V.

THE BENEFICIAL EFFECTS OF THE BIBLE UPON THE WORLD.

WE might infer the beneficial effects of the Bible upon the world from the universality of its character, exhibited in its adaptation to the intellectual, moral, and spiritual nature of man. But we are not left to inference; facts of observation and experience abound on every hand to confirm its benign influence.

The evidence henceforth is of an objective, or external, kind. It is drawn from the influence of the Bible, from the fulfilment of prophecy, and from direct testimony.

One of the plainest lessons of history is, that man, left to his unaided powers, does not advance in morals and in the elements of a true civilisation, but degenerates. The evidence is so abundant, that it is unnecessary to do anything more than merely to refer to the great historical nations of heathendom, and to the early monuments of all nations destitute of the Bible. Retrogression is written upon every one of them, unless it be in cases in which we find the influence of Bible ideas acting as a regenerating element.

Philosophy has made large pretensions; but with all her profound research, she has never solved the problem of man's recovery, nor pointed out the means to accomplish it. She has never directed his aim to the true end of his being, nor revealed to him the heavenly agency on which he must rely to attain it.

She had a fair trial of her powers before the birth of Christ, but utterly failed. Greece admired the sublime speculations of Plato, but found in them no element of regeneration. Her philosophy left in the minds of men, exhausted by doubt, a vague feeling of want, which Oriental speculations attempted to satisfy. These proved equally fruitless. The Sun of Righteousness then arose, shedding His light amidst the darkness. To that light some of the most earnest inquirers after truth turned their eyes, and their doubts were dispelled.

In modern times, philosophy has boasted of the sufficiency of the light of nature to guide mankind in the path of duty, and to bring him at last to that happy immortality for which he sighs. France listened to her fair professions, abolished Christianity, and then set up the goddess of Reason, in the person of a courtezan, as an object of worship. That was at a time when men had become so wise by the light of nature, that they denied the existence of God, pronounced the Bible a fable, and proclaimed death an eternal sleep. Germany lent her ear to this so-called philosophy and her nonsensical prating about human reason, and soon evinced an insane rationalism, incurable by all the hellebore of Anticyra.

Philosophy, divorced from the religion of the Bible, instead of guiding men aright, has invariably led them astray. Its path has been as tortuous as that of the fabled labyrinth, in which those who entered roamed for ever, 'in wandering mazes lost.' The light of nature, under the most favourable circumstances, has never proved sufficient for man. It always shines brightest where the Bible is read and understood; and much of the light claimed for it has been derived from that very book, which the advocates of natural religion affect to despise. They have as much of the light of nature in China, India, New Zealand, and the Fiji Islands, as we have; and why are the inhabitants of those places not as enlightened and civilised as we are?

If history shows that man everywhere, without the true religion, has sunk into degradation, and if philosophy has failed to discover the means of his elevation, where then is hope? On what shall he rely for the purification of his nature, the amelioration of his woes, the establishment of liberty, justice, political stability, and social happiness? In other words, what will secure that true and highest civilisation, which consists in the regeneration and progress of both the individual and society?

When Asaph stumbled at the prosperity of the wicked, he went into the sanctuary, and there—in its teachings—he understood their end. We must go into the same place, and there we will learn the healing remedy for all human ills, and the result of its application. The Church—the kingdom of heaven upon earth—anticipates the time when by her agency the earth shall be filled with knowledge, when violence shall cease, and peace dwell on earth. This anticipation is based upon the teachings of the Bible, of which she is the depositary, and the truths of which she is commissioned to disseminate throughout the whole world, as the means of man's restoration to prosperity and happiness.

The prophet Isaiah, looking forward to the results of the universal promulgation of the gospel, says: 'It shall come to pass in the last days, that the mountain of the Lord's house shall be established in the top of the mountains, and shall be exalted above the hills; and all nations shall flow unto it. And many people shall say, Come ye, and let us go up to the mountain of the Lord, to the house of the God of Jacob; and

He will teach us of His ways, and we will walk in His paths: for out of Zion shall go forth the law, and the word of the Lord from Jerusalem. And He shall judge among the nations, and shall rebuke many people; and they shall beat their swords into ploughshares, and their spears into pruning-hooks: nation shall not lift up sword against nation, neither shall they learn war any more' (Isa. ii. 2-4).

It is evident from the teaching of Scripture that the salvation of the earth depends upon the universal establishment of the kingdom of heaven in it, and that the establishment of this kingdom depends upon the universal diffusion of the knowledge of the Lord. When this fills the earth, it shall be restored to peace and happiness.

The doctrines and precepts of the Bible have been briefly considered in a previous chapter; but it is pertinent to the object of the present one to consider more particularly the nature of some of its doctrines, and their potency to effect the regeneration of the world. These doctrines are comprised in the phrase, 'the knowledge of the Lord.' This is the highest knowledge to which man can attain. But as the Bible reveals God in His character of Creator, Preserver, Redeemer, Moral Governor, and Judge, it teaches much knowledge beside that, which pertains to His existence and attributes. It includes, together with this, a knowledge of ourselves as the subjects of His government, and of our duties in all our relations, as dependent creatures, and as members of a social body, in which Divine Providence has placed us. 'The knowledge of the Lord,' which shall fill the earth 'as the waters cover the sea,' and which will form the most distinguishing feature of the future age of the Church, includes a knowledge of both God and man. This, however, is not sufficiently definite. It is necessary to advert to some of the specific truths of the Bible, by the power of which the happy results which it predicts can be accomplished.

The Bible teaches us, as has been already intimated, concerning the true nature and character of God, and the relations that we sustain to Him. Ignorance of the divine nature and character lies at the foundation of all other ignorance; and knowledge of that nature and character is the beginning of all other knowledge. This may seem a bold assertion. But when it is remembered that some philosophers, who ignored in their speculations the existence of God, went so far as to doubt their own existence, and the existence of everything else, it will be admitted to contain more truth than some would at first be willing to allow.

What do the Scriptures teach concerning God? They teach that He is a Spirit, infinite in all His attributes, unchangeable, possessed of every intellectual and moral excellence in the highest conceivable degree. They further teach us that we owe our existence to Him, that we are supported by His power, that we receive every blessing from His hand, that He is our governor and judge.

But such a revelation inspires no love in the bosoms of guilty creatures. They feel that they can have no communion with infinite purity, and they tremble before infinite justice. To win the affections of men, and bring them back to fidelity, the Bible tells us that God has been pleased to reveal Himself in the person of His Son, who has made an atonement for us, and thus removed every obstacle to reconciliation. In this way He has placed Himself in the most amiable relations to us. He has manifested Himself as a Being of infinite mercy, by 'forgiving iniquity, transgression, and sin.' By the assumption of our nature, He has shown the utmost condescension, and exhibited a perfect model for our imitation.

The Bible also makes known to us our own true character and condition. Without a knowledge of these, we would lack an element essential to our moral and spiritual improvement. It teaches us that we are sinful creatures, subjects of a perfect moral government, accountable to God for our thoughts and actions, incapable in ourselves of any good, absolutely dependent upon our Creator for our preservation, and upon the aid of His Holy Spirit for every good thought, pure desire, and holy affection. This comprises the self-knowledge taught in the Bible,—a self-knowledge comprising more than ever entered into the mind of the Grecian sage, whose maxim, 'Know thyself,' has given him a reputation for wisdom among all succeeding generations. To have a clear understanding of this knowledge, and to act upon it, are essential to the Christian; to admit it, and embody it in practice, must always be a necessary element in every moral reform. Without self-knowledge all other knowledge is comparatively useless; for each individual being the subject of reformation cannot know his moral wants unless he knows himself.

The truths comprehended under these two branches —the knowledge of God and the knowledge of ourselves —are the forces which, when combined and rendered effective, keep the moral universe in harmony and order. They keep every moral and intelligent being who is under their control in the sphere allotted to him by his Creator.

The teachings of the Bible are as explicit in regard to duties as they are in regard to doctrines. Our duties to God, to ourselves, and to our fellow-men, are most distinctly set forth in the great text-book of our most holy religion. We are required to 'love God with all the heart, and with all the soul, and with all the mind;' and as an evidence of this love, we are required to keep His commandments. Each individual is forbidden to do harm to himself; and from various directions he is left to infer that he ought to cultivate all his powers, physical, intellectual, and moral, in such a way as will best enable him to accomplish the end of his being, and secure his happiness. We are commanded to love our neighbour as ourselves (Matt. xxii. 39), to 'be kindly affectioned one to another, in brotherly love, in honour preferring one another' (Rom. xii. 10). And that we may be under no uncertainty as to the persons whom we are required to regard as our neighbour, our Saviour has taught us in the beautiful parable of the Good Samaritan (Luke x. 29-37) that every man is our neighbour.

Governments or states, which are regarded in the Bible as moral and accountable individuals, whose deliberations and acts should be conformed, in all things, to the rule of right, have also their objects and duties defined in the word of God. It is a great and dangerous mistake to consider the State as an institution entirely divorced from religion. No state can exist without religion; and the religion of the Bible being, in the judgment of its enemies, the purest and best, should be acknowledged, wherever practicable, by every government. This religion forms the ground and sanction of law, the stability of states. It is in the Bible that we find most clearly set forth the fundamental principles of all just legislation, learn the ends of government, the duties and character of rulers. It teaches us that laws have their authority from God; that government is His ordinance, intended to be a terror to wrong-doers, to execute wrath upon him that doeth evil (Rom. xiii. 1-4); that rulers are to be men fearing God and hating covetousness (Ex. xviii. 21). 'He that ruleth over men must be just, ruling in the fear of God. And he shall be as the light of the morning, when the sun riseth, even as a morning without clouds; as the tender grass springing out of the earth by clear shining after rain' (2 Sam. xxiii. 3, 4).

These various duties, which have been briefly noticed, rest upon the highest sanction, and are enforced by the strongest motives. God commands them. The frown or the smile of Heaven, misery and woe in this life and in the life to come, or prosperity and happiness here and eternal felicity hereafter, are promised and threatened to the obedient and disobedient respectively.

This brief exhibition of the teachings of the Bible, and of the motives by which they are enforced, brings us to consider their power to effect the regeneration of man, both individually and socially. Their power under the agency of the Divine Spirit arises from their adaptation to meet our moral and spiritual wants. The remedy is precisely such as is suited to the nature of the disease. From mistaken ideas of man's moral condition have arisen all the chimerical schemes of human improvement; but where a true knowledge of that condition, and of the appointed cure, exists, no such schemes can find place. There can be nothing fanciful, nothing ideal; all is certain knowledge, all is fact.

All men acknowledge that they are not what they ought to be. All their schemes and longings for improvement, and their efforts to attain it, are a confession that there is something wrong. There are much ignorance, immorality, and many social evils in the world. The cause of all these is departure from God. Impiety is the root of all immorality. In confirmation of this statement, we have the testimony of the Apostle Paul. In the first chapter of his Epistle to the Romans, he says: 'Because that, when they knew God, they glorified Him not as God, neither were thankful; but became vain in their imaginations, and their foolish heart was darkened. Professing themselves to be wise, they became fools, and changed the glory of the incorruptible God into an image made like to corruptible man, and to birds, and four-footed beasts, and creeping things. Wherefore God also gave them up to uncleanness, through the lusts of their own hearts, to dishonour their bodies between themselves: who changed the truth of God into a lie, and worshipped and served the creature more than the Creator, who is blessed for ever. Amen. For this cause God gave them up to vile affections.' This passage teaches very clearly that immorality is the natural result of impiety. When men forsake God, they abandon their only protection against wicked practices.

Now any effectual method of restoration must consist of two corresponding steps,—corresponding to those of our departure from God, and of our consequent evil course. We must return to Him whom we have forsaken, and then seek the purification of our polluted nature. Our relations to God must be changed, and we must be sanctified. No other system of reform except that taught in the Bible makes provision for these two things. It teaches us that God is reconciled to us through the atonement of Jesus Christ; that on the ground of that atonement we can be justified. This is a most important change, and absolutely necessary to our purification. Having our relations to God changed by means of the atonement, we become partakers of divine grace; we receive the gift of the Holy Spirit, whose office it is to sanctify all that are justified, and make them meet for heaven. This He does by leading us into an understanding and appreciation of the truth, by opening our eyes to see the beauty and excellence of the divine character. Assimilation to this character constitutes holiness.

A certain one has remarked that the character of men will generally be as the character of the god that they worship. If this be true, where can we find a foundation for such grandeur and elevation of thought, feeling, and action as we find in the worship of the God of the Bible? Majesty and beauty are in all His works; goodness, justice, and mercy are manifested in all His actions; and holiness invests Him with all that is lovely. We are commanded to be like Him; and were we to obey the command, what manner of persons would we be!

In mental and moral culture, we attach, perhaps, too little importance to that power of assimilation by which we are made like those with whom we associate, and whom we admire. To be improved by meditating upon transcendently pure and holy objects is a law of our moral and spiritual nature. Just as we cultivate our taste, or our capacity to discern the beautiful, by exercising its discriminating power upon the most perfect specimens of art, so our moral nature is improved by meditating upon the character of a pure and holy God. The power of this law or principle is acknowledged by the apostle, when he says: 'We all, with open face beholding as in a glass the glory of the Lord, are changed into the same image, from glory to glory, even as by the Spirit of the Lord' (2 Cor. iii. 18).

It is in this way that the religion of the Bible makes a full and complete provision for the purification and perfection of our nature; and it gives us a pledge of that perfection in the person of the God-man Jesus Christ. He has united humanity to divinity, and raised it to the throne of the heavens. There He sits, and there He will for ever sit, both God and man. Made members of His body by a spiritual union with Him, we, too, will become pure, 'even as He is pure.' Let men talk as they may about the progress and perfection of humanity, all progress and all perfection are conditioned by the belief and imitation of the God-man. It is 'God manifest in the flesh' who is the only hope of the world. Before the light of this truth, superstition forsakes his dim temples, carrying with him his gods of wood and stone.

> 'Nor is Osiris seen
> In Memphian grove or green,
> Trampling the unshowered grass with lowings loud;
> Nor can he be at rest
> Within his sacred chest—
> Nought but profoundest hell can be his shroud!
> In vain, with timbrelled anthems dark,
> The sable-stoled sorcerers bear his worshipp'd ark.
> He feels from Judah's land
> The dreaded Infant's hand,
> The rays of Bethlehem blind his dusky eyne;
> Nor all the gods beside
> Longer dare abide.'[1]

From the purifying influence of the religion of the Bible upon the minds and hearts of individuals, it is natural to turn to its influence upon society in general. Society being composed of individuals, its character must be determined by that of its component elements. If the latter be pure, it will itself be pure. When every one acts upon the principle of doing unto others what he wishes them to do to himself, and cultivates a charitable and conciliatory spirit in all things, then society becomes what it ought to be, a collection of individuals, each stimulating one another to zeal in good works. Such a condition of society, at least in any great degree, has never yet existed; but, nevertheless, none can deny that the tendency of Christian principles is to produce such a state; and if these principles were faithfully applied in each individual case, it would necessarily result. The laws of chemical affinity do not act with more unvarying certainty than do the laws of man's spiritual being. Let his relations

---

[1] Milton's *Hymn on the Nativity*.

to God be right, then his relations to everything else will be right. There will be neither jar nor discord throughout his whole sphere of action.

From society in general, we may ascend to the State, —a society of men united for the purpose of promoting their mutual safety and happiness, and exhibited visibly in some form of government. The objects of the State ought to be the highest objects of humanity, with reference to this world; it should aim to secure, consistently with the general welfare, the greatest amount of temporal good to each individual; but it can accomplish this only in connection with Christianity.

Where the religion of Christ does not prevail, government generally becomes a system of organized oppression. This is in some degree rendered necessary; for where public morals are corrupt, where men do not feel the sanctions of a holy religion, that forbids all sin and commands righteousness, force must be employed to repress injustice and rebellion, and prevent the outburst of malignant passions; and this force, being under the direction of men destitute of moral principle, is frequently exercised to gratify their caprice, ambition, or revenge.

Power can only be salutary when it is justly exercised. It can only be justly exercised when it proceeds from proper authority, and when it is used in accordance with the laws, and for the ends for which that authority has been established. All legitimate authority is from God. No other authority can bind the conscience. Government, therefore, can only be legitimate when it represents the authority of God among men; in other words, when it acts as His ordinance. It cannot do this unless it act in obedience to His laws, revealed either in nature or in the Bible. But even the laws of nature are more clearly revealed in the Bible than in nature itself. They are supplemented in the Bible, and constantly exhibited in its teachings. The religion of the Bible, then, either acknowledged and openly avowed, or assumed and interwoven into the very texture of the body politic, is essential to the legitimate constitution, well-being, and permanent security of the State.

This is not mere theory; it is confirmed by history. Every nation that has abandoned idolatry and become Christian, has changed its laws to correspond to its religion; and the change has always been from cruel to humane, from oppressive and unjust to equitable and just, from sanguinary and brutal to mild and merciful; and just as the government has conformed to Christian ideas, in that proportion have the people become contented, and disposed to acknowledge the justice and benignity of the authority exercised over them. Here we find the theory of progress in Christian countries, and they are the only countries in which we find any progress; it is the embodiment of Christian ideas in their legislation, and the endeavour to realize these ideas in practice. If any one is sceptical in regard to these statements, let him examine the history of the European nations, and that of the Sandwich Islanders in more recent times, and he will find ample confirmation of their truth. Let him compare the condition of those countries in which the Bible is known, read, and believed, with the condition of those in which it is unknown, and the difference will furnish a proof of its civilising and humanizing influence.

But the blessings conferred by the Bible on the world are not confined to the amelioration of the moral, civil, and religious condition of mankind. The most polished nations now in existence are indebted to it for the preservation and diffusion of literature and of the fine arts. It is interwoven with the finest productions of the human mind; it forms the inspiration of the loftiest poetry, and pervades the highest productions of genius. Its spirit breathes in Milton's song, which soars 'with no middle flight above the Aonian mount.' Raphael, Michael Angelo, and Leonardo da Vinci drew from it the subjects of their greatest works.

The enlightening and civilising influences of the Bible are well illustrated by the late Rev. Gardiner Spring, D.D.[1] 'That martyr of the missionary cause,' says Dr. S., 'the Rev. John Williams, of the London Missionary Society, relates a circumstance which took place among the South Sea Islands, which those who have read the biography of this remarkable man will remember. The officers of the British ship *Seringapatam*, after intercourse with a number of the natives who had been converted to Christianity, expressed their doubts whether the views which these ignorant people had uttered on the subject of religion were their own views; and even asserted that both the missionary and these professed converts were practising deception upon their visitors. In order to decide this question, Mr. Williams invited Captain Waldegrave, the Rev. Mr. Watson, the ship's chaplain, and other gentlemen, to an interview with fifteen of the natives, for the purpose of free conversation on religious subjects.

'On their being assembled, Captain Waldegrave proposed the question to them, "*Do you believe the Bible is the word of God, and that Christianity is of divine origin?*" The natives were rather startled at the question, having never entertained a doubt upon that point. At length one replied, "*Most certainly we do.*" "And why do you believe it?" After some reflection one of them said, "*We look at the power with which it has been attended in effecting the entire overthrow of idolatry among us; and which, we believe, no human means could have induced us to abandon.*"

[1] *Bible not of Man*, pp. 227–229.

'The same question being proposed to a second, he replied, "*I believe the Scriptures to be of divine origin on account of the system of salvation they reveal. We had a religion before, transmitted to us by our ancestors, whom we considered the wisest of men; but how dark and black a system that was compared with the bright scheme of salvation presented in the Bible! Here we learn that we are sinners; that God gave His Son Jesus Christ to die for us; and that through believing the salvation procured becomes ours. Now, what but the wisdom of God could have devised such a system as this?*"

'The question being repeated to an old and shrewd pagan priest, then a devoted Christian, instead of replying at once, he held up his hands, and rapidly moved the joints of his wrists and fingers; he then opened and shut his mouth, and closed these singular actions by raising his leg and moving it in various directions. Having done this, he said: "*See, I have hinges all over me; if the thought grows in my heart that I wish to handle anything, the hinges in my hands enable me to do so. If I want to utter anything, the hinges of my jaws enable me to say it; and if I desire to go anywhere, here are hinges to my legs to enable me to walk. Now, I perceive great wisdom in the adaptation of my body to the various wants of my mind; and when I look into the Bible, and see there the proofs of wisdom which correspond exactly with those which appear in my frame, I conclude that the Maker of my body is the Author of that book.*"'

This is the substance of the argument from adaptation, which has been briefly presented in Chapter Fourth, on the Universality of the Bible.

The universality of the Bible, and its beneficial effects, give it an exceptional position in the world. This position is illustrated with great ability by Mr. Rogers. 'We are struck,' says Mr. R., 'with another anomaly, or rather knot of anomalies, when we come to consider the various modes and the extraordinary degree in which the Bible, as compared with any other book, sacred or profane, has stimulated the intellect and energy, and attracted the love and veneration of men. It will be seen, I think, as we follow the argument into its details, that on the supposition that this book is a fortuitous collection of tracts, composed by men who belonged to a nation in many respects among the most insignificant, and certainly among the most despised, on the face of the earth,—a nation that is chiefly distinguished by the degree in which these writings have extorted the homage of mankind,—their prodigious influence is not a little curious. It adds to the difficulty that all subsequent literary productions of this nation have been characterized by no special excellence; in fact, are rather below than above the average merit of other literatures. Indeed, the productions of Jewish rabbis are generally such as to engender a natural suspicion that, since they did no better even with such models for imitation before them, no such powers as theirs unaided could have produced books which have so arrested the attention of an alien world. Nearly all else that the Jews have written, men willingly leave in obscurity. On these books alone they concentrate their regards.'[1]

NOTE.—The facts which Mr. Rogers adduces, and illustrates with great force and beauty, to show the exceptional position which the Bible occupies among other books, are:

(1) The welcome given to the Bible is wonderfully independent of race. It has been received by men of far more various races and nations than any other religious books ever have been.

[1] *The Superhuman Origin of the Bible inferred from itself.* By Henry Rogers. New York: Scribner, Armstrong, & Co. 1874. Lecture VIII.

(2) The prodigious literature which it has evoked.

(3) There is no other book, no other ten books, that have left so many or so deep traces on human literature; none that are so often cited or alluded to; none which have supplied so much matter for apt illustration, or been so often resorted to for its vivid imagery and energetic diction.

(4) Its influence on the imaginations of men, especially as seen in poetry, sculpture, painting, and music.

(5) On the supposition of the human origin of the Bible, it might fairly have been anticipated that some *quasi-sacred* books, or *other* works of human genius, would have been produced within the last eighteen hundred years, which might, in general estimate, have vied with the Bible, if they had not supplanted it. But none such have been produced.

CHAPTER VI.

PROPHECY.

THE beneficial effects of the religion of the Bible, considered in the preceding chapter, were foretold by the holy prophets, whose foresight of the future is a proof of their inspiration. For prophecy, in the sense of prediction, is a miracle of knowledge, and belongs as really to the supernatural as miracles of power. If, therefore, we find in the Bible predictions of future events, which have been fulfilled in every particular, we have clear evidence that its writers possessed supernatural intelligence.

That the writers of the Holy Scriptures did predict future events, which have been accurately fulfilled, can be satisfactorily proved. The instances in the sequel selected for this purpose by no means cover the whole field of fulfilled prophecy; they are only some of the most prominent.

I. *Prophecies relating to the Jews.*

Prosperity and happiness were promised to the Jews on condition of obedience to their God and King; but in case of disobedience, they were to become the subjects of manifold calamities. They rebelled against Jehovah, and they still continue in rebellion against Him. Their history, during the whole career of their apostasy, was graphically and accurately delineated by Moses more than three thousand years ago. Shortly after they were formed into a nation, and before they entered into the possession of Canaan, their lawgiver foretold the vicissitudes of their national fortunes. They were to be scattered among the heathen (Lev. xxvi. 33, 36-39; Deut. iv. 27); a nation that they knew not should eat up the fruit of their land and all their labours; they were to be oppressed and crushed always; and they were to become an astonishment, a proverb, and a by-word among all nations (Deut. xxviii. 28, 29, 32, 33, 36, 37); and the Lord would make their plagues wonderful, and the plagues of their seed, even great plagues and of great continuance (Deut. xxviii. 45-48, 59, 63-67).

Similar predictions are found in the writings of all the succeeding prophets. 'I will cause them to be removed into all kingdoms of the earth. I will cast them out into a land that they knew not, where I will show them no favour. I will feed them with wormwood, and give them water of gall to drink. I will scatter them also among the heathen, whom neither they nor their fathers have known. The children of Israel shall abide many days without a king, and without a prince, and without a sacrifice, and without an image, and without an ephod, and without a teraphim' (Jer. xv. 4, xvi. 13, ix. 15, 16; Hos. iii. 4. See also Jer. xv. 7, xxix. 18, xxiv. 9, 10; Ezek. v. 10, xii. 15, vii. 19; Amos ix. 4, 9; Isa. vi. 10–12; Jer. viii. 3, xxxi. 10, xlvi. 27, 28; Hos. ix. 17).

These predictions respecting the Jews are delivered with great explicitness and particularity. Every one of them has been fulfilled. In proof of this, it is necessary to refer only to the history of that people since their dispersion until the present time. In that we find a complete verification.

II. *Prophecies respecting the Kingdoms of Judah and Samaria.*

(1) Samaria was to be overthrown; but Judah was to be preserved (Isa. vii. 6-8; Hos. i. 6, 7; 1 Kings xiv. 15).

(2) Judah and Jerusalem, though rescued from the Assyrians, were to fall into the hands of the Babylonians (Isa. xxxix. 6; Jer. xxv. 9-12).

(3) The catastrophe was to be hopeless to Samaria (Micah i. 6-9).

(4) It was not to be hopeless to Judah; a restoration was to ensue (Jer. xxix. 10-14).

(5) The person appointed to be the restorer of Judah was foretold by name—Cyrus (Isa. xliv. 28, xlv. 1).

(6) The medium of their restoration—the capture of Babylon—was predicted (Isa. xlv. 1-3, 13).

(7) The Medes and Persians were to be the powers engaged in the siege (Isa. xxi. 2; Dan. v. 28).

(8) The city of Jerusalem and the temple were to be rebuilt (Isa. xliv. 28).

The most cursory perusal of the history of these two kingdoms will enable the reader to verify all these predictions to the very letter. Not one thing failed of all that God had spoken concerning them by His prophets.

III. *Prophecies concerning Jerusalem.*

While the children of Israel were wandering in the wilderness, they were threatened with the destruction of their cities. 'The Lord shall bring a nation against thee from far, from the end of the earth, as swift as the eagle flieth; a nation whose tongue thou shalt not understand; a nation of fierce countenance, which shall not regard the person of the old, nor show favour to the young. . . . And thou shalt eat the fruit of thine own body, the flesh of thy sons and of thy daughters, in the siege, and in the straitness, wherewith thine enemies shall distress thee: so that the man that is tender among you, and very delicate, his eyes shall be evil toward his brother, and toward the wife of his bosom, and toward the remnant of his children which he shall leave: so that he will not give to any of them of the flesh of his children whom he shall eat; because he hath nothing left him in the siege, and in the straitness, wherewith thine enemies shall distress thee in all thy gates. The tender and delicate woman among you, which would not adventure to set the sole of her foot upon the ground for delicateness and tenderness, her eye shall be evil toward the husband of her bosom, and toward her son, and toward her daughter, and toward her young one that cometh out from between her feet, and toward her children which she shall bear: for she shall eat them for want of all things secretly in the siege and straitness, wherewith thine enemy shall distress thee in thy gates' (Deut. xxviii. 49-57).

Other prophecies foretold that 'Jerusalem was to be encamped round about, to be besieged with a mount, to have forts raised against it, to be ploughed over as a field, and to become heaps; that the end was to come upon it; and that the Lord would judge them according to their ways, and recompense them for all their abominations; the sword without, and the famine and pestilence within: he that is in the field shall die with the sword; and he that is in the city, famine and pestilence shall devour him' (Lev. xxvi. 30, etc.; Micah iii. 12; Jer. xxvi. 18; Ezek. vii. 7-15; compare with these, Matt. xxiv. 2-21).

The reader of Josephus can find the fulfilment of these predictions recorded by that historian. The ill-fated city suffered all that had been foretold. The Chaldeans took Jerusalem, and destroyed the temple. The Romans, after a protracted siege, laid both the city and the second temple in ruins. The sufferings of the Jews on the latter occasion were unparalleled in the history of war. 'The famine was too powerful for all other passions, for what was otherwise reverenced was in this case despised. Children snatched the food out of the very mouths of their fathers; and even mothers, overcoming the tenderest feelings of nature, took from their perishing infants the last morsels that could sustain their lives. In every house where there was the least shadow of food, a contest arose; and the nearest relations struggled with each other for the miserable means of subsistence. While in all these cases the eye of man was evil towards his brother, in the siege and in the straitness wherewith their enemies distressed them, the unparalleled human compact between the two women of Samaria; the bitter lamentation of Jeremiah over the miseries of the siege which he witnessed,—"The hands of the pitiful women have sodden their own children, they were their meat in the destruction of the daughter of my people;" and the harrowing recital by Josephus of the noble lady killing with her own hands, and eating secretly, her own suckling (the discovery of which struck even the whole suffering city with horror), —which are all recorded as facts, without the least allusion to the prediction, too faithfully realized, to the very letter, the dread denunciations of the prophet. When any well authenticated facts of so singular and appalling a nature were predicted for ages, they could not possibly have been revealed but by inspiration from that Omniscience which alone can foresee the termination of the iniquities of nations' (Keith on the *Prophecies*, pp. 53, 54).

IV. *Prophecies concerning Nineveh, Babylon, Tyre, Egypt, Ammon, Moab, Edom, and Philistia.*

The citation of all the prophecies relating to these cities and countries, and the notice of their fulfilment, would fill a volume. It is unnecessary to do more than to refer the reader to the works of Newton and Keith on the prophecies, in which he will find them collected, together with the proofs of their fulfilment in history.

No one can fail to see that all these prophecies are of such a character as to elude the keenest human foresight; for at the time that they were delivered, many of them seemed very improbable, and names and circumstances are mentioned which could not have been foretold without an absolute knowledge of the future. What uninspired man could have foretold the name of the conqueror of Babylon, and the name of the nation whose forces he led to the siege,—a nation that had not yet risen to power? Yet this Isaiah did, more than a hundred years before Cyrus destroyed the proud city of the Chaldeans.

V. *Prophecies concerning Christ.*

The coming of a great Deliverer was the prominent theme of Old Testament prophecy. It was the common belief of the Jews. We find it at the very beginning of the history of our race. Immediately after the fall, our first parents were consoled by the promise that the seed of the woman should bruise the serpent's head. The same promise was conveyed in a more definite form to Abraham. Jacob spoke of the coming of Shiloh; and Moses, of a Prophet like unto himself, whom the Lord would raise up.

(1) The time of the coming of this Deliverer is fixed by a number of circumstances that concur in the date of Christ's advent. 'The sceptre shall not depart from Judah, nor a lawgiver from between his feet, until Shiloh come; and unto Him shall the gathering of the people be' (Gen. xlix. 10). 'Know therefore and understand, that from the going forth of the commandment to restore and rebuild Jerusalem, unto Messiah the Prince, shall be seven weeks and threescore and two weeks' (Dan. ix. 25). 'And I will shake all nations, and the Desire of all nations shall come: and I will fill this house with glory, saith the Lord of hosts' (Haggai ii. 7; compare v. 9). 'Behold, I will send my Messenger, and He shall prepare the way before me; and the Lord, whom ye seek, shall suddenly come to His temple, even the Messenger of the covenant, whom ye delight in: behold He shall come, saith the Lord of hosts' (Mal. iii. 1).

(2) The place of His nativity was foretold (Micah v. 2; compare Matt. ii. 5; Luke ii. 4).

(3) It was predicted that He should spring from the tribe of Judah, and from the family of David (Gen. xlix. 10; Isa. xi. 1; Ps. lxxxix. 3, 4; Jer. xxiii. 5, 6; compare Matt. i. 1, and Luke iii. 23–31).

(4) Prophecy foretells the facts of His life, and delineates, with a precision that cannot be misunderstood, the features of His character (Isa. xlii. 1–4, chap. liii.; Zech. ix. 9).

(5) It was predicted that this Deliverer, the Messiah, would establish a spiritual kingdom co-extensive with the earth (Ps. ii. 8; Isa. ii. 2–4, lx. 1-16; Dan. ii. 35, 44, vii. 18, 27).

In view of these manifold prophecies,—prophecies pertaining to particulars entirely beyond the reach of human sagacity and foresight,—which have been so marvellously fulfilled, the reader will naturally conclude that the men who uttered them possessed something more than human intelligence, that they had more than the inspiration of genius, that they were under the teaching and guidance of the Divine Spirit.

CHAPTER VII.

TESTIMONY OF THE SCRIPTURES THEMSELVES.

THE canon of Scripture furnishes the testimony of the Church to its inspiration. Its immemorial doctrine is, that the sixty-six books that compose the sacred canon are plenarily inspired. When we consider that so many apocryphal books have been written, it is a remarkable fact that only these, and no more, have been transmitted to us as possessing divine authority. It is a remarkable fact, too, that the composition of these books should be limited to two periods,—the first from Moses to Malachi, the second from Christ to the death of the Apostle John. There must have been some good reason for this limitation, a reason founded upon the most indubitable historical proofs. Such a reason existed. We learn not only from the Scriptures, but also from Josephus, that the Jewish system had a miraculous introduction by Moses; and that the reign of prophecy extended from him, with a slight interruption, until the time of Malachi. With this prophet the gift of prophecy ceased until the time of Christ, the great Prophet 'like unto Moses,' when the present dispensation was miraculously introduced by Him and His chosen apostles; 'God also bearing the latter witness, both with signs and wonders, and with divers miracles, and gifts of the Holy Ghost' (Heb. ii. 4). This period of miracles closed, according to the best authorities, with the death of the Apostle John. The periods during which the Bible was written, therefore, coincide with those of miraculous gifts; and it is believed, on the ground of competent authority, that it was written by men who possessed those gifts. This explains the fact of the exclusion of all books from the canon that were known to be the productions of uninspired men. It does not follow from this that every writing of every inspired man was admitted into the canon; for some inspired men may have written things that were never intended to have a place among canonical writings, but merely to subserve some particular interest, or to accomplish some specific object, forming no part of God's revelation to His Church. It is only such books, we have reason to believe, as constitute a part of divine revelation to the Church that were admitted into the canon, by men whom God appointed to communicate His will to mankind. As soon as any such book was written, it became canonical, without any vote on the matter. The authority of its author or of its editor—an authority sanctioned by God—was enough.

With this reference to the testimony of the Church contained in the sacred canon, we now proceed to consider the testimony of the Scriptures themselves.

It may seem strange, at first sight, to include the testimony of Scripture in the external evidence of inspiration. But it seems to belong there; for the Scriptures are brought upon the stand and interrogated as witnesses. This, it will be perceived, is a very different kind of evidence from that which is derived from a perception of their unity, organism, and adaptation to our intellectual, moral, and spiritual nature. The latter is derived from what we discover in them; the former from what they tell us.

The Scriptures bear witness of themselves that they are the word of God. This alone would not furnish sufficient proof, unless their character and influence were conformable to their testimony, and unless they were confirmed by proofs of supernatural agency. But having been thus confirmed, and their character and influence being thus conformable, their own testimony becomes the strongest possible. It cannot be resisted, unless we can prove that the sacred writers were deceivers, and that God lent His power to support imposture.

We believe that the Holy Scriptures were confirmed by supernatural proofs; that their character and influence are in harmony with their divine claims; that the analogy of nature illustrates their teachings; and that historical, antiquarian, and grammatical criticism has established their genuineness, authenticity, and historical credibility. Their character, and the mass of evidence in their favour, raise them above the suspicion of forgery. This every unprejudiced mind that reads them attentively must admit. Their candour, honesty, truthfulness, and historical character render the very idea of forgery impossible. If they are a forgery, they are the most unparalleled forgery ever palmed off upon the human race, and utterly inexplicable on any principles of human reason.

An objection is made against an appeal to the testimony of Scripture, on the ground that it is a begging of the question. 'You require us,' it is said, 'to receive the Bible as true, because it is inspired, and you then undertake to prove its inspiration from its own pages.' The objection is not fair. We have presented an array of evidence from which we are entitled to assume the genuineness, the authenticity, the perfect truthfulness, and supernatural character of the books of Holy Scripture. 'To examine, therefore, the nature of the influence under which these books have been drawn up, by the light which they themselves afford, can never be justly charged with logical fallacy. As well might we reject the personal statements of an ambassador, with respect to the nature of his powers and the source of his instructions, after we had verified his credentials, and satisfied ourselves as to his veracity. And thus the adducing of arguments from Scripture itself, in proof of its own inspiration, is no *petitio principii*. It would only become so were we to assume the fact of its inspiration in order to infer therefrom the *credibility* of its contents. The credibility we establish by independent proofs.'[1]

The Scriptures state expressly that they were 'given by inspiration of God' (2 Tim. iii. 16). 'Prophecy came not in old time by the will of man: but holy men of God spake as they were moved by the Holy Ghost' (2 Peter i. 21).

These statements refer chiefly, if not entirely, to the Old Testament, and furnish the testimony of Paul and Peter to its inspiration. It was written by prophets; and a prophet, in the scriptural sense of the term, was one who spoke for another, in his name, and by his authority. This idea of a prophet is derived from Exodus vii. 1, compared with Exodus iv. 14–16: ' And the Lord said unto Moses, See, I have made thee a god to Pharaoh; and Aaron thy brother shall be thy prophet. And the anger of the Lord was kindled against Moses, and he said, Is not Aaron the Levite thy brother? I know that he can speak well. And also, behold, he cometh forth to meet thee: and when he seeth thee, he will be glad in his heart. And thou shalt speak unto him, and put words in his mouth: and I will be with thy mouth, and with his mouth, and will teach you what ye shall do. And he shall be thy spokesman unto the people: and he shall be, even he shall be to thee instead of a mouth, and thou shalt be to him instead of God.' A prophet,

---

[1] *The Inspiration of Holy Scripture.* By William Lee, M.A. New York Robert Carter & Brothers. 1860. Pp. 97, 98.

then, is a spokesman who speaks in the name of another, who is responsible for the prophet's words (comp. Jer. xxxvi. 4-6, 17, 18). This the prophets of the Old Testament professed to be and do. They were the mouth of God: through them God spoke to the people; so that what the prophet said, God said.

Moses spoke to the children of Israel in the name of the Lord. Many of his laws and instructions are prefaced by the formula: 'And the Lord spake unto Moses, saying.' He was also commanded to 'write what God said in a book' (Ex. xvii. 14, xxxiv. 27; comp. Deut. iv. 13, xxxi. 9).

In all the prophets, we find language bearing witness to their inspiration. Referring to their own statements, they say: 'The mouth of the Lord hath spoken;' 'Thus saith the Lord;' 'Hear the word of the Lord;' 'The word that Isaiah the son of Amos saw concerning Judah and Jerusalem;' 'The word that came to Jeremiah from the Lord, saying;' 'The word of the Lord came expressly to Ezekiel;' 'The beginning of the word of the Lord by Hosea;' 'Now the word of the Lord came unto Jonah the son of Amittai, saying;' 'The word of the Lord that came to Micah;' 'The book of the vision of Nahum;' 'The burden which Habakkuk the prophet did see;' 'The word of the Lord which came to Zephaniah;' 'In the first day of the month came the word of the Lord by Haggai the prophet;' 'In the eighth month came the word of the Lord unto Zechariah;' 'The burden of the word of the Lord to Israel by Malachi.'

Such language has only one meaning, namely, that the prophets believed themselves to be supernaturally inspired, and commissioned to record the revelations given to them. They were conscious of their call to the prophetic office, of the prophetic visions which they saw, and of their inspiration, when 'the word of

M

the Lord came unto' them; and were therefore reliable witnesses, for there is no testimony so strong as that of consciousness.

The testimony which has been adduced is that of direct assertion from the Old Testament itself. There is another class of evidence, consisting of quotations from it, and allusions to it, in the New Testament. These are conclusive, and the more so the more minutely they are examined; for they embrace the testimony of our Lord, and that of the New Testament writers.

The full amount of this evidence cannot be understood without an induction of all its particulars; and its force cannot be apprehended unless it is followed out in its minute applications. But instead of doing this, we shall give a few passages from the Old Testament, with their citations in the New, leaving the examination of them to the reader.[1] These passages are the following, and all found in the Gospel of Matthew:—Isa. vii. 14, cited Matt. i. 20; Mic. v. 2, cited Matt. ii. 5; Hos. xi. 1, cited Matt. ii. 14, 15; Jer. xxxi. 15, cited Matt. ii. 17, 18; Isa. xl. 3, cited Matt. iii. 3, Mark i. 3, Luke iii. 4; Mal. iii. 1, cited Matt. xi. 10, Mark i. 2, Luke vii. 27; Deut. viii. 3, cited Matt. iv. 4; Ps. xci. 11, 12, cited Matt. iv. 6; Deut. vi. 16, cited Matt. iv. 7; Isa. ix. 1, 2, cited Matt. iv. 14–16; Lev. xiv. 34–57, referred to Matt. viii. 4, Mark i. 44, Luke v. 14; Isa. liii. 4, cited Matt. viii. 17; 1 Sam. xxi. 6, cited Matt. xii. 3, 4, Mark ii. 26, Luke vi. 4; Isa. xlii. 1–4, cited Matt. xii. 17–21; Jonah i. 17, cited Matt. xii. 40; Isa. vi. 9, 10, cited Matt. xiii. 14, 15, Mark iv. 12, John xii. 39, 40, Acts

---

[1] An examination of many of those passages can be found in Dr. Bannerman's work on *Inspiration*, pp. 311-351. The selection of passages that I have made is taken from his work.—*Inspiration of the Holy Scriptures.* By James Bannerman, D.D. Edinburgh: T. & T. Clark. 1865.

xxviii. 25-27; Gen. i. 27, cited Matt. xix. 4, 5, Mark x. 7, 8, 1 Cor. vi. 16, Eph. v. 31; Zech. ix. 9, cited Matt. xxi. 4, 5, John xii. 14, 15; Isa. lvi. 7, Jer. vii. 11, cited Matt. xxi. 13, Mark xi. 17, Luke xix. 46; Ps. viii. 2, cited Matt. xxi. 16; Ps. cxviii. 22, 23, Isa. viii. 14, 15, cited Matt. xxi. 42, Mark xii. 10, Luke xx. 17, Acts iv. 11, Eph. ii. 20, 1 Pet. ii. 4-8; Ex. iii. 6, cited Matt. xxii. 32, Luke xx. 37; Ps. cx. 1, cited Matt. xxii. 44, Mark xii. 36, Luke xx. 42, 43, Acts ii. 34, 35; Ps. lxix. 21, cited Matt. xxvii. 34, 48, Mark xv. 23, 36, Luke xxiii. 36, John xix. 28-30; Ps. xxii. 18, cited Matt. xxvii. 35, Mark xv. 24, John xix. 24; Ps. xxii. 7, cited Matt. xxvii. 39, 43, Mark xv. 29, Luke xxiii. 35; Ps. xxii. 1, cited Matt. xxvii. 46, Mark xv. 34.

The citations from the Old Testament given above are all found in the Gospel of Matthew, together with the other books specified. We might now proceed with Mark, and go through the books of the New Testament in their order; but instead of making so extensive a comparison, we will limit it to the Epistle to the Hebrews:—Ps. ii. 7, 2 Sam. vii. 14, Ps. xcvii. 7, civ. 4, xlv. 6, 7, cii. 25-27, cx. 1, all cited Heb. i. 5-13; Ps. xxii. 22, Isa. viii. 18, cited Heb. ii. 12, 13; Ps. xcv. 7-11, cited Heb. iii. 7-11, iv. 3, 7; Gen. xiv. 18-20, Ps. cx. 4, cited Heb. v. 6, 10, vi. 20, vii. 1-21; Jer. xxxi. 31-34, cited Heb. viii. 7-13, x. 14-17; Ex. xxx. 10, Lev. xvi. 18, Num. xix. 9, cited Heb. ix. 7 sqq.; Ps. xl. 6-8, cited Heb. x. 5-9; Haggai ii. 6, 7, cited Heb. xii. 25-27.

In some of these passages the writers of the New Testament ascribe what was written by the writers of the Old directly to God. David, in the ninety-fifth Psalm, said, 'To-day, if ye will hear his voice, harden not your heart;' but the apostle (Heb. iii. 7) says that these were the words of the Holy Ghost. Again, in Heb. x. 15, the same apostle says: 'Whereof the Holy Ghost also is a witness to us: for after that He had said before, This is the covenant that I will make with them after those days, saith the Lord;' quoting the language of Jer. xxxi. 33 as the language of the Holy Ghost. In Acts iv. 24, 25, the assembled apostles 'lifted up their voice to God with one accord, and said, Lord, thou art God . . . who by the mouth of Thy servant David hast said, Why did the heathen rage?' In Acts xxviii. 25, Paul said to the Jews: 'Well spake the Holy Ghost by Esaias the prophet unto our fathers.' And Christ said that David by the Spirit called the Messiah Lord (Matt. xxii. 43).

In addition to the particular passages of the Old Testament cited in the New, it is important to consider the general names or titles applied to it by our Lord and His apostles. Those names or titles are not used to designate a part, but the whole of the Old Testament, and furnish evidence of its inspiration as a volume.

The name most frequently used in the New Testament, when the sacred volume of the Old is spoken of, is 'Scripture,' or 'the Scriptures,'—the term being used both in the singular and the plural.

'Ye do err,' says our Lord, when declaring the truth of the resurrection, 'not knowing the Scriptures nor the power of God' (Matt. xxii. 29). 'The Scriptures must be fulfilled' (Mark xiv. 49). 'The Scripture was fulfilled' (Mark xv. 28). 'In all the Scriptures the things concerning himself' (Luke xxiv. 27). 'That they might understand the Scriptures' (Luke xxiv. 25). 'Believed the Scripture' (John ii. 22). 'Search the Scriptures' (John v. 39). 'As the Scripture hath said' (John vii. 38). 'The Scripture cannot be broken' (John x. 35). 'That the Scripture may be fulfilled'

(John xiii. 18). 'That the Scripture might be fulfilled' (John xvii. 12, xix. 28). 'All Scripture is given by inspiration of God' (2 Tim. iii. 16). 'No prophecy of the Scripture is of any private interpretation' (2 Pet. i. 20).

This list of references may be greatly extended; for the word occurs more than fifty times in the New Testament, and uniformly denotes, with perhaps the exception of 2 Pet. iii. 16, the books known to the Jews as belonging to the Old Testament canon.

Another title employed to designate the Old Testament arose out of the threefold division of its books into Moses, the Prophets, and the Psalms, which was adopted by our Lord (Luke xxiv. 44). Probably the earliest notice of this division is found in the apocryphal book of Ecclesiasticus. It is mentioned in the writings of Philo; and it is recognised as a well-known division by Josephus, through whom it can be identified with the writings, neither more nor fewer, which are found in the Old Testament canon at the present day. 'Sometimes one or more of the three divisions gave a general title, under which were included all. It was occasionally the Law and the Prophets, or sometimes the Prophets, or the Law, that represented the whole of the Old Testament volume. The varied use of the general title, however, was too well known to give rise to any ambiguity; and there is no room for any doubt as to the meaning of the names employed in the New Testament to express the ancient Scriptures.'[1]

Under the twofold designation of the Law and the Prophets, our Lord explains His own relations to the Old Testament Scriptures, and affirms that He came not 'to destroy,' but 'to fulfil' them (Matt. v. 17). He then assigns as a reason for this the unchangeable certainty of every one of their declarations (ver. 18).

[1] Bannerman on *Inspiration*, p. 352.

Under the same general title of the Law and the Prophets, He recognises the divine and absolute obligation of the moral precepts of the Old Testament as on the same level of authority with the plainest commandment of the moral law (Matt. vii. 12).

The New Testament occasionally uses the complex terms, 'Word of God' and 'Oracles of God,' to designate the Old Testament writings (Mark vii. 13; Rom. iii. 2; Heb. v. 12; 1 Pet. iv. 11). These terms are the very strongest that can be used to express the divine authority of the volume.

The employment in the New Testament of the general titles which have been specified, and which recognise the Hebrew canonical books as a whole, is of a twofold service in the argument for their inspiration. In the first place, the testimony in such a form to the inspiration of the Old Testament is an addition to the evidence derived from what the New Testament writers have said of the inspiration of particular passages of it; and, in the second place, it puts upon the same level, as to authority and inspiration, the whole of the writings included under the general names applicable to the Old Testament, whether they be quoted in the New Testament and referred to or not, and whether we know or do not know the authorship of the particular books, or indeed know anything at all beyond the fact that they truly belong to the collection of writings which are included under the various names of 'the Scripture,' 'the Law and the Prophets,' 'the Word of God,' 'the Oracles of God.'[1]

The testimony of the New Testament has been appealed to in proof of the inspiration of the Old. It is a lawful witness in case it is itself inspired. The proofs of its inspiration will now be briefly presented.

Any one will admit that, if the writings of the Old

[1] Bannerman on *Inspiration*, p. 359.

Testament were given by inspiration of God, much more were the writings of the New so given. 'If the ministration of death, written and engraven in stones, was glorious, . . . how shall not the ministration of the Spirit be rather glorious?' (2 Cor. iii. 7, 8.) Though the New Testament is more glorious, yet its religion does not differ from that of the Old. The prophets of the Old declared beforehand the coming salvation; the evangelists of the New announced its accomplishment. It was not a different revelation that Moses and John were commanded to write. It was the same from beginning to end; and it was the same God who gave it. Moses wrote its beginning, and John its close. We cannot understand Christianity, except in connection with its preparatory stages; nor Judaism, except in connection with the Christian dispensation, which makes it intelligible. The New Testament revelation, in its doctrines and facts, is the reality of the Old Testament history, prophecy, and type. 'The law was given by Moses, but grace and truth came by Jesus Christ' (John i. 17). By 'truth' we are to understand the reality of the legal types. The law had 'a shadow of good things to come,' but 'not the very image of the things' (Heb. x. 1). In the Old and New Testaments there is a divine unity, constituted by the progressive revelation of the truth of the same God.

With this view of the connection between the Old Testament and the New, it is impossible to separate between the inspiration of the one and that of the other. But apart from this connection, the New Testament furnishes independent evidence of its own inspiration.

(1) Christ promised to His apostles, by whom much the greater part of it was written, the Holy Spirit, who should bring all things to their remembrance, and

render them infallible in teaching. It is not you, He said, that speak, but the Spirit of my Father speaketh in you. He that heareth you, heareth me. He forbade them to enter upon their office as teachers until they were endued with power from on high (John xiv. 26; Matt. x. 20; Mark xiii. 11; Luke xxi. 15; John xvi. 13; Luke xxiv. 49).

(2) This promise was fulfilled on the day of Pentecost, when the Spirit descended upon the apostles as a mighty rushing wind, and they were filled with the Holy Ghost, and began to speak as the Spirit gave them utterance (Acts ii. 1-4).

(3) After the day of Pentecost, the apostles claimed to be infallible organs of God in all their teachings. Men were required to receive what they taught as the word of God (1 Thess. ii. 13). The things which they wrote were the commandments of God (1 Cor. xiv. 37). The salvation of men was made to depend on faith in the doctrines which they taught (Gal. i. 8). John says that whoever did not receive the testimony which he bore concerning Christ made God a liar, because John's testimony was God's testimony (1 John v. 10). 'He that knoweth God, heareth us; he that is not of God, heareth not us' (1 John iv. 6). Paul, writing to the Corinthians, declares that he 'came not among them with excellency of speech or of wisdom;' that his 'speech and his preaching were not with enticing words of man's wisdom, but in demonstration of the Spirit and of power, that their faith should not stand in the wisdom of men, but in the power of God' (1 Cor. ii. 1-5). The things which he taught, which he calls 'the wisdom of God,' 'the things of the Spirit,'—*i.e.* the gospel, the system of doctrine taught in the Bible,—he says had never entered into the mind of man. God had revealed these truths by His Spirit, for the Spirit is the only competent source of such knowledge. 'For

what man knoweth the things of a man, save the spirit of man which is in him? even so the things of God knoweth no man, but the Spirit of God' (vers. 7-11).

It is evident, therefore, from the statements of the New Testament, that our Saviour promised to His apostles the Spirit of truth; that this Spirit was 'to bring to their remembrance all things that He had said to them;' that, in addition to this, the Spirit was 'to guide them into all truth;' that He was to 'show them things to come,' thereby filling up the measure of the prophetic office, which had to do with revelations of future things as well as of present truth, and comprehended both predictive and declarative prophecy; and that the apostles claimed that these promises had been fulfilled in them.

(4) This claim to infallibility on the part of the apostles was duly authenticated, not only by the nature of the truths which they communicated, and by the power which those truths exerted over the minds and hearts of men, but also by the inward witness of the Spirit of which John speaks when he says: 'He that believeth on the Son of God hath the witness in himself' (1 John v. 10). It was confirmed also by miraculous gifts. As soon as the apostles were endued with power from on high, they spake in 'other tongues,' they healed the sick, restored the lame and blind. 'God also bore them witness, both with signs and wonders, and with divers miracles and gifts of the Holy Ghost, according to His own will' (Heb. ii. 4). And Paul tells the Corinthians that the signs of an apostle had been wrought among them 'in all patience, in signs, and wonders, and mighty deeds' (2 Cor. xii. 12).[1]

It may be said that the testimony adduced refers mainly, if not exclusively, to the writings of the apostles. But Mark and Luke were not apostles. That

---
[1] Hodge's *Systematic Theology*, Vol. I. pp. 161, 162.

being the case, are their Gospels equal in authority to those of Matthew and John? It was universally believed in the ancient Church, that Mark's Gospel was written under the influence, and almost by the dictation, of Peter; and that Luke's was written largely under the direction of Paul. Whatever truth there may be in regard to the influence which Peter and Paul exercised in the composition of them, one thing is firmly established, and must be received as an undoubted fact. They were immediately and universally received by the Church as possessing divine authority. They were never placed in the same category with the spurious documents, which soon made their appearance after them. In both external history and in internal character they differ entirely from the apocryphal gospels. The Church must have had satisfactory reasons for putting them on a level with the other two gospels,—reasons which justify the same claims to inspiration accorded to the other books of the New Testament. The Gospel of Luke was written before the death of Paul, and that of Mark before the death of John: both, therefore, may be considered as having received apostolical sanction, and infallibility is claimed for them as well as for the others.

The claim for the divine authority of its teachings, and the assertion of infallibility, are characteristic of the whole Bible. The sacred writers everywhere disclaim personal authority. They do not rest the obligation to faith in their teachings on their own knowledge or wisdom. They do not rest it on the truth of what they taught as manifest to reason, or as capable of being proved by argument. They speak as messengers, as witnesses, as organs. They declare that what they said God said; and that on His authority it was to be received and obeyed.[1]

[1] Hodge's *Systematic Theology*, Vol. I. p. 161.

NOTE.—Inspiration, in the strict sense of the term, as has been already stated, chap. iv. p. 64, is claimed only for the autographs of the sacred writers, or to exact copies made from them in the same language. We find no promise in Scripture that transcribers should be preserved from mistakes. The Scriptures were miraculously given; but they are not miraculously preserved. God has put them in the care of fallible men; and for their preservation men are responsible. Yet no one would deny the great advantages of an original, inspired copy, from which all editions and translations derive their authority. We do not reject, as destitute of value, the *Corpus Juris Civilis* because it has passed through transcriptions and various editions.

PART III.

DEFINITIONS, THEORIES, DISTINCTIONS, NATURE, AND EXTENT OF THE INSPIRATION OF THE HOLY SCRIPTURES.

CHAPTER I.

MEANING OF THE TERM INSPIRATION.

THE English word inspiration comes from the Latin noun *inspiratio*, derived from the verb *inspiro*, which signifies to blow or breathe in or upon. The corresponding Greek word is ἐμπνέω, which has the same signification.

The word is sometimes used to denote the excitement and action of the imagination of the poet or orator. Milton, though he does not use the word, alludes to this meaning, when he invokes the Spirit:

'What in me is dark,
Illumine; what is low, raise and support.' [1]

In this case there is a reference to a supposed divine influence, to which the illumination and elevation of the poet are due. In Job xxxii. 8 (comp. Gen. ii. 7), the word is used to denote that divine agency by which man is endued with the faculties of an intelligent being. The meaning now under consideration is that of the word as employed by the Apostle Paul in 2 Tim. iii. 16.

[1] *Paradise Lost*, Book I. lines 22, 23.

The word used in that passage is θεόπνευστος, inspired of God, literally, God-breathed. The Scripture itself is called θεόπνευστος; but that can only mean that the writers were subject to a divine influence, or under a divine afflatus, when they penned the sacred writings. The same word is used by Phocylides and Plutarch, in the expressions θεόπνευστος σοφίη (wisdom inspired of God) and θεόπνευστοι ὄνειροι (dreams inspired of God). 'The neutral form, in the sense of God-inspired,' is used by Nonnus (*Paraphr. Ev. Jo.* i. 27), and applied to Scripture by Origen (*Hom.* xxi. *in Jerem.* vol. ii. de la Rue: ' Sacra volumina spiritus plenitudinem spirant ').[1]

The Apostle Peter says: ' Prophecy came not in old time by the will of man : but holy men of God spake as they were moved by the Holy Ghost' (2 Pet. i. 21). The word rendered 'moved' means borne along, carried onward, as a ship by the wind.

These passages would seem to describe the state of inspiration as purely passive; and so some of the Greek Fathers described it. We will not, however, at present, attempt to define the relation of the divine agency in inspiration to human spontaneity. Whatever was revealed to the sacred writers by God must have been passively received; but revelation and inspiration are not synonymous. Until we understand the distinction between them, we are not prepared to define clearly the relation of the divine agency to the human in the composition of the Scriptures.

Orthodox believers are generally agreed in any one of the following definitions, which are merely stated, their acceptance being held in abeyance until the close of our investigation.

Knapp defines inspiration to be '*an extraordinary divine agency upon teachers while giving instruction, whether*

[1] M'Clintock & Strong's *Bib. Theol. and Eccles. Cyclop.*, s. v. *Inspiration.*

oral or written, by which they were taught what and how they should write or speak.'

Lee: '*That actuating energy of the Holy Spirit, in whatever degree or manner it may have been exercised, guided by which the human agents chosen of God have officially proclaimed His will by word of mouth, or have committed to writing the several portions of the Bible.*'

Bannerman: '*As an act, inspiration is the supernatural operation of the Spirit of God upon a man, by which he is enabled to speak or write with infallible accuracy the objective truth revealed to him by God for that purpose. Or, as the result of that act, inspiration is a statement, in speech or writing, made with infallible accuracy, through the supernatural operation of the Spirit, of objective truth revealed to man by God to be so stated.*'

CHAPTER II.

OPINIONS AND THEORIES ON THE SUBJECT OF INSPIRATION.

WHILE there has been great unanimity in the Church in all ages in regard to the fact of the inspiration of the Holy Scriptures, various opinions have been held about the nature of it. An exhibition of these opinions is the object of the present chapter.

The earliest testimony of any profane Jewish writer to the inspiration of the Holy Scriptures is found in the apocryphal books, which throughout make mention of that long series of divine revelations which had been given in the line of Abraham, and of the prophetic character of Moses and the other prophets under the Old Testament dispensation. Absolute certainty and truth are ascribed to their writings, and God Himself is represented as speaking through their lips.

Josephus, who nowhere discusses the question of inspiration as a dogma or theory, furnishes unmistakeable evidence in his works of the belief of his countrymen in the great truth of the divine authority and infallibility of the Bible. In his writings we find no notice of any more than one kind and degree of inspiration attaching to the books of the Old Testament. 'Every one,' says Josephus (*contra Apion*, Book I. chap. 7, 8), 'is not permitted of his own accord to be a writer, nor is there any disagreement in what is written; they being only prophets that have written the original and earliest accounts of things, as they have learned them of God Himself by inspiration; and others have written what hath happened in their own times, and that in a very distinct manner also.

'For we have not an innumerable multitude of books among us, disagreeing from and contradicting one another [as the Greeks have], but only twenty-two books, which contain the record of the past times, which are justly believed to be divine.'

Philo Judæus, who was nearly contemporary with Josephus, coincides with him in his testimony to the universal belief of his countrymen in the plenary inspiration of the Old Testament books. Philo was a native, and throughout life an inhabitant, of Alexandria. Writing from that centre of Greek philosophy at that time, and deeply imbued with its style of thinking, he theorizes more than Josephus in his statement of the doctrine, but he is not less decisive in his testimony to the prevalence of it among the Jewish people. Speculating on the kind of influence exerted upon the sacred writers, and on their state of mind during the continuance of it, Philo was accustomed to transfer the ideas of the ancients respecting the μαντική, or divine possessions, under which the oracles were uttered, to the case of the prophets of the former economy. In this way Philo sought to give a heathen explanation to a Jewish fact. Under the influence of inspiration, the person inspired was, in harmony with the prevalent views of ancient times, reduced to a state of unconsciousness, and became the unintelligent instrument of giving utterance to the thoughts and words of another: under the higher degree of the divine afflatus (ἑρμηνεία, interpretation), the party subjected to it became one with the divine power that moved and spoke within him; under the lower degree of the same power (προφητεία, prophecy), he was taught by God in answer to his inquiries, and received the ability to predict future events. But while the explanations given by Philo of the theory of inspiration are entirely speculative, and even to a large degree unintelligible, yet nothing can be more certain than his belief of the fact in connection with the writings of the Old Testament. While assigning to Moses the first place in rank and nearness of communion with God among the authors of the sacred volume, he asserts his own belief, shared by the Jews, that God inspired and spake by them all. Indeed, his own system of allegorical interpretation is to a large extent founded on his conviction of the divine truth and significance of the slightest statement, or even word, of Scripture, and of the fulness of spiritual truth embodied within the letter. However little we may value his theories of inspiration, or his methods of interpretation, they both go to add to the strength of the evidence he furnishes for the universal belief of his countrymen in the infallibility of the Old Testament Scriptures.[1]

The fable about the origin of the Septuagint version shows that the Jews believed in a verbal inspiration. This theory may have been, in its external form, mixed up to some extent with the heathen notions concerning the μαντική (art of soothsaying), but it did not spring from them.

The Jews made three divisions, as already stated, — Moses, the Prophets, and the Psalms, — of their sacred books; but there is no intimation, before the advent of Christ, that they attributed to these divisions different degrees of inspiration.

' After the Christian era, the Jews felt themselves constrained to assume a position as distinctly antagonistic to that of the Christians as they possibly could. And as the Christians made frequent, direct, and very

---

[1] Bannerman, *Inspiration of the Scriptures*, pp. 120, 121. Hagenbach's *History of Doctrines*, Vol. I. pp. 86, 87. New York: Sheldon & Co. 1868. Lee, Appendix F, pp. 418–423.

earnest reference to the Holy Spirit, and to those passages of the Hebrew Scriptures which speak of the " Spirit," the " Spirit of Elohim," the " Spirit of Jehovah," they set about devising a theory by which this might be set aside, or at least neutralized. This theory ripened into the theory of *degrees of inspiration;* and according to it, the Jews then and since ascribe to their sacred books *three degrees of inspiration,*—the Mosaic, the prophetical, and that of the Holy Spirit, which latter they regarded as the lowest of all. The Mosaic degree of inspiration, under which the law was written, was the most exalted; in it no other man of God was thought to share. Prophecy, properly so called, or the foreseeing of what should afterwards come to pass, was regarded as the next degree. The third and lowest degree was that of the Holy Spirit, which consisted chiefly in revelations by dreams and by symbolical visions, so that those who enjoyed only this kind and degree of inspiration knew only a part of the truth; and their writings, though entitled to be included in the canon, must be placed in that portion of it called merely the Hagiographa.'[1]

The allusions to inspiration in the writings of the subapostolic Fathers are incidental. These writings are practical rather than doctrinal, and we must endeavour to discover the teaching which they involve, rather than merely that which they express. *Barnabas* uses such phrases as the following, when quoting Scripture: 'The Lord saith in the Prophet' (Ps. xvii. 45); 'The Spirit of the Lord prophesieth' (Ps. xxxiii. 13). Again, he tells us that 'the prophets received their gift from Christ, and spake of Him,' and that 'Moses spake in the Spirit.' Consistently with this view, he asserts the presence of a spiritual meaning in the law and history

---

[1] Hetherington's *Apologetics of the Christian Faith*, pp. 460, 461. Edinburgh: T. & T. Clark. 1867.

of the Jews, and discovers types of the cross in the ancient Scriptures (Ex. xvii. 11, 12; Isa. lxv. 2; Num. xxi. 9).

Clement of Rome quotes many passages from Scripture with the words: 'For the Scripture saith;' 'By the testimony of Scripture;' 'The Holy Spirit saith;' 'Ye know, beloved, ye know well the sacred Scriptures, and have looked carefully into the oracles of God.'

Polycarp tells us, with touching humility, that 'neither he nor any like him is able to attain perfectly to the wisdom of the blessed and glorious Paul;' and seems for once to burn with the zeal of his master, when he declares that 'he is the first-born of Satan whoever perverts the oracles of the Lord to suit his own passions, and says that there is neither resurrection nor judgment.'

Ignatius, in one of his letters, expresses a trust 'to attain to that lot to which he has been mercifully called, having fled to the gospel as to the flesh of Jesus, and to the apostles as to the presbytery of the Church;' and 'yet more,' he adds, 'let us love the prophets, because they were the heralds of the gospel, and by belief in it were saved; for the divinest prophets lived according to Jesus Christ, being inspired by His grace. He was the subject of their preaching, and the gospel is the perfection of immortality.'

Papias, who was a contemporary of Polycarp, styles the Synoptic Gospels, in an exposition of them, 'the oracles of the Lord.'

'The *Shepherd of Hermas* evinces, by its form and reception, the belief of the primitive age in the nature and possibility of inspiration; and its existence is a distinct proof of the early recognition of a prophetic power somewhere existent in the Church.'[1]

---

[1] Westcott's *Introduction to the Study of the Gospels*, Appendix B, pp. 403–407.

The writings of the earliest apologists, *Quadratus* and *Aristides*, have perished. *Justin Martyr* quotes largely from the Holy Scriptures, and his mode of citation is singularly expressive. He tells us of the 'history which Moses wrote by divine inspiration, which the Holy Spirit of prophecy taught through him.' Again, he quotes the language of David, 'who spake thus (Ps. xix. 2–5) through the Spirit of prophecy;' and of Isaiah, who was moved by the same Spirit (Isa. lxv. 2, lviii. 2). He says that, 'as Abraham believed on the voice of God, and it was reckoned to him for righteousness, so do the Christians too believe on the voice of God, which has been addressed again to them by the apostles of Christ, and proclaimed by the prophets, . . . whose writings—the memoirs of the apostles or the books of the prophets—were read each Sunday in the public assembly;' for 'we have been commanded by Christ Himself to obey, not the teaching of men, but that which hath been proclaimed by the blessed prophets and taught by Him.'

Speaking of the prophet's office, *Justin* says: 'We must not suppose that the language proceeds from the men who are inspired, but from the divine Word which moves them. Their work is to announce that which the Holy Spirit, descending upon them, purposes, through them, to teach those who wish to learn the true religion. For neither by nature nor human thought can men recognise such great and divine truths, but by the gift which came down from above upon the holy men [under the Jewish dispensation], who needed no art of words, nor skill in captious and contentious speaking, but only to offer themselves in purity to the operation of the Divine Spirit, in order that the divine power of itself might reveal to us the knowledge of divine and heavenly things, acting on just men as a plectrum on a lyre.'

Tatian, drawing a contrast between the positions of the heathen and of the Christian, says: 'The Spirit of God is not with all men, but abiding with some, whose conversation is just, and being united with their soul, it proclaimed to all other souls, by prophetic teaching, that which had been hidden; and those who obeyed wisdom attracted to themselves a kindred spirit, while those who did not obey were found to fight against their God.' In another place he notices the great antiquity of Scripture, and says that its prophetic power was one of the grounds on which he was led to believe in its doctrine.

Athenagoras expresses himself in language which has been regarded with good reason as teaching the doctrine of Montanism. He says that, while entranced and deprived of their natural powers of reason by the influence of the Divine Spirit, they uttered that which was wrought in them, the Spirit using them as its instruments, as a flute-player might blow a flute. And again, under another image, he describes 'the Holy Spirit, which works in those who speak prophetically, as an emanation issuing from God, and carried back to Him, like a ray from the sun.' Thus the Christian 'gives no heed to the doctrines of men, but those uttered and taught by God; for he has prophets as witnesses of his creed, who, inspired by the Spirit, have spoken of God and the things of God.'

According to *Theophilus of Antioch*, the inspired writers were not mere mechanical organs, but men who, coincidently with the divine influence, displayed a personal and moral fitness for their work. 'The men of God, being filled with the Holy Spirit and gifted with prophecy, having inspiration and wisdom from God, were taught of Him, and became holy and just. Wherefore, also, they were deemed worthy to obtain this recompence, to be made the instruments of God, and receive the wisdom which cometh from Him, by which wisdom they spoke of the creation of the world, and all other things .... which happened before their birth, and during their own time, and which are now being accomplished in our days; and so we are convinced that in things to come the event will be as they say.' Again, he adds that 'the Christians alone have received the truth, inasmuch as they are taught by the Holy Spirit, who spake by the holy prophets, and [still] announces all things to them beforehand:' who is 'the Beginning and Wisdom and the Power of the Most High,' so that 'the words of the prophets are the words of God.' Moreover, 'the contents of the Prophets and of the Gospels are found to be consistent, because all the writers spake by the inspiration of the one Spirit of God.'[1]

The fragments of *Hegesippus* contain little or nothing which bears on our inquiry; yet in one sentence, preserved in Eusebius, he seems to recognise Christian documents, when he says that in 'each city all is ordered according to the preaching of the Law, of the Prophets, and of the Lord.' Among the works of *Melito*, Bishop of Sardis, we find discourses 'On [Christian] Conversation and Prophets,' 'On Prophecy,' 'On the Revelation of St. John,' and 'The Key.' The last-mentioned book necessarily suggests to us an anticipation of the Alexandrian school; and some examples of Melito's exegesis, probably borrowed from it, sufficiently indicate the extent to which he carried the typical significance of each word and detail of Scripture.

A fragment of *Claudius Apollinaris* furnishes another instance of the typical interpretation of Scripture; but the fullest and most comprehensive treatment of in-

[1] Westcott's *Introduction to the Study of the Gospels*, Appendix B, pp. 407–411.

spiration is by *Irenæus*, the pupil of Polycarp, and Bishop of Lyons. According to him, the successive dispensations of God wrought together to one great end by the operation of one power, as 'men were accustomed to bear (*portare*) God's Spirit and hold communion with Him.' Thus 'the prophet spake of the advent of the Word in the flesh, as acted on by His influence;' and 'all who foretold the coming of Christ received their inspiration from the Son;' for 'how could Scripture testify, as it does, of Him alone, unless all things had been revealed by one and the same God, through the Word, to believers?' Yet till His advent 'Christ was, as it were, the hidden treasure in the field of Scripture, since He was [only] indicated by types and parables; for all prophecy, till its accomplishment, is full of riddles and ambiguities to men.' To us, however, 'the apostles, by the will of God, have consigned the gospel in the Scriptures to be the ground and pillar of our faith, and by them we have learned the truth, that is, the doctrine of the Son of God. . . . For after that our Lord rose from the dead, and they were clothed with the Spirit from on high, they were filled with a perfect knowledge in all things.' Consequently, 'they are beyond all falsehood.'

Irenæus sees a mystical fulness and meaning in the four evangelists: 'As God made all things in fair order and connection, so was it needful that the [outward] form of the gospel should be well framed and fitted together;' and 'as there are four regions of the world in which we are, and four general winds,—as the Church is scattered over the whole earth, and the gospel is the pillar and support of the Church,—we might expect it should have four pillars [and four winds as it were], breathing on all sides immortality, and kindling [the divine spark] in men.' Again, as in 'the ancient Church the visible form of God rested on the four-faced cherubim, so Christ, when manifested to men, gave us His gospel under a fourfold form, though held together by one Spirit, and on these Gospels he rests.'

In many of his general views, *Irenæus* anticipates the thoughts and language of *Origen*. He tells us that 'the Scriptures are perfect, inasmuch as they were uttered by the word of God and His Spirit, though we want the knowledge of their mysteries;' 'and how much,' he adds, 'is unexplained to us in the operations of nature—the rising of the Nile, the migration of birds, the ebb and flow of the tide; is it, then, a hard case that—as in the outward world some truths are, as it were, sacred to God, while some have come under our knowledge—some of the difficulties in the Scriptures, which are all full of spiritual meaning, should be explicable by the grace of God, while the solution of others must rest with Him, and that not only in this world, but also in the world to come, that God may still teach, and man still ever learn from God?" The revelations of the Bible may seem too meagre to satisfy our curiosity; yet 'no small punishment will be his who adds to, or takes from, the Scripture.' The details may seem insignificant; yet 'nothing is empty or without meaning in the dealings of God.' The connection of its parts may seem perplexing; yet 'all Scripture, as it has been given to us by God, will be found to be harmonious.' The interpretation of its teaching may be difficult; yet 'we guard our faith, which has been admitted by the Church, and which, like a precious gift stored up in a fair vessel, is ever renewed by the Spirit of God, and gives new life to the vessel in which it is. For this gift of God is entrusted to the Church to give life to the world as the soul to the body, and in it [the gifts of faith entrusted to the Church] lies the enjoyment of the

Holy Spirit sent by Christ, which is the earnest of our immortality, the confirmation of our faith, the ladder by which we ascend to God. For where the Church is, there is also the Spirit of God; and where the Spirit of God is, there is the Church and all grace; but the Spirit is truth, and truth is one; for we acknowledge as one the God of creation and the God of redemption, the author of the old dispensation and the author of the new;' 'we follow Him alone as our teacher, and regard His words as the rule of truth.'[1]

In a fragment preserved in *Eusebius*, *Caius* seems to regard 'revelations' as a mark of an apostle, and in the same place uses the striking phrase, 'the Scriptures of God.' In another fragment, which is attributed by some to *Caius*, the writer speaks of the followers of Artemon, 'who fearlessly laid their hands on the divine Scriptures, saying that they corrected them. . . . How great is the daring of their error,' he adds, 'cannot be unknown even to themselves; for either they do not believe that the divine Scriptures were spoken by the Holy Spirit, and are unbelievers; or they hold themselves wiser than the Holy Spirit, and we must say they rave.'

The writings of *Novatian* are full of quotations from the Old and New Testaments, and his view of their authority is clear and wide. He regards the whole law as spiritual, for 'divine ordinances must be received in a divine sense;' and traces the symbolic meaning of the Mosaic restrictions on food. The books of the prophets furnish him with a clear proof of God's providence, 'which not only extends at all times over individuals, but also over cities and states, whose issues God declared by the words of His servants, yea, even the whole world.' And the forms of the prophetic

---

[1] Westcott's *Introduction to the Study of the Gospels*, Appendix B, pp. 412-416.

language prove the certainty of their predictions; for they use the past tense in speaking of the future, since 'divine Scripture regards as accomplished that which will, beyond all doubt, come to pass.' Yet more grace was given to the writers of the New Covenant, for though 'the prophets and apostles were inspired by one and the self-same Spirit, but still on the former He came but for a time, while He abode with the latter always. To the one, some degree of His influence was vouchsafed; on the other, His whole energy was poured. In the one case, it was a scanty gift; in the other, a bounteous loan, not set forth before the resurrection, but conferred by it, according to Christ's promise (John xiv. 26) of a Comforter, . . . who strengthened the hearts and minds of the apostles, who made clear to them the mysteries of the gospel, who dwelt within them and enlightened their minds on divine things.'

According to tradition, *Hippolytus of Portus* was a disciple of Irenæus. He forms a link between the Asiatic and Alexandrian schools. His writings exhibit the same deep sense of the spiritual meaning of Scripture as we have already traced in his immediate teacher and in earlier writers. He regards that which has been once revealed by God to man as still full of instruction and wisdom after the primary application is gone. 'The Law and the Prophets were from God, who, in giving them, compelled His messenger to speak by the Holy Spirit, that, receiving the inspiration of the Father's power, they may announce the Father's counsel and will. In these men, therefore, the Word found a fitting abode, and spoke of Himself; for even then He came as His own herald, showing the Word, who was about to appear in the world.' 'These blessed men . . . spake not only of the past, but also of the present and of the future, that they might be shown not to be for a time merely, but heralds of the things to come to all generations. For these fathers, having been perfected by the Spirit of prophecy, and worthily honoured by the Word Himself, were brought to an inner harmony, like instruments, and having the Word within them, as it were, to strike the notes (like a plectrum), by Him they were moved, and announced that which God wished. For they did not speak of their own power (be well assured), nor proclaim that which they wished themselves; but first they were rightly endowed with wisdom by the Word, and afterwards well foretaught of the future by visions, and then, when thus assured, they spake that which was [revealed] to them alone by God.'

It will be readily seen how widely this view is removed from that of *Athenagoras*, though conveyed under a similar metaphor; differing from it, indeed, just as the analogous description of Justin. The instrument here is first tuned to express the divine strain; the moving power dwells within as a vivifying principle, and does not act from without on an involuntary subject. The reason is cleared, and not clouded; the melodies of heaven are fitted to the words of men, not by an arbitrary power, but by an inward affinity. 'The blessed prophets,' to use another image, 'are eyes of Christ.' They ministered 'the oracles of God for all generations.' So, then, it is our duty to listen to the faintest voice of the Bible, to trace its relation to ourselves and its source from above us: 'As the divine Scriptures proclaimed the truth, so let us view it; all they teach, let us acknowledge by the growth of faith; as the Father pleaseth to be believed, let us believe Him; as the Son pleaseth to be glorified, let us glorify Him; as the Holy Spirit pleaseth to be given, let us receive Him,—not according to our own choice or our own mind, forcing to our own tastes that which has been given by God, but as He chose to show the truth through the Holy Scriptures, so let us view it.'[1]

The preceding extracts exhibit the doctrine of inspiration as unfolded in the Greek and Roman Churches. There are yet two other Churches, and two other forms of mental development,—those of North Africa and Egypt,—in relation to which it remains to consider our subject. 'In the writers of North Africa, whether at Carthage or Hippo, we find an intensity of zeal, a depth of feeling, a power of intuition, but little modified by cautious criticism or severe logic. The aspirations of Tertullian after a stricter life led him into Montanism; and the craving for a clearer knowledge at first united Augustine with the Manichees. We shall thus see how the doctrine of inspiration was regarded by men of a warmer temperament and a more restless faith, who sought out the truth with earnestness, and embraced whatever conclusion they obtained without reserve. Indeed, the whole character of the African Church is emotional, if we would distinguish it from the doctrinal and practical types of Asia and Rome.' On one point, it has been well observed, Tertullian never doubted; whether Catholic or Montanist, he still maintained alike the inspiration of the Old and New Testament Scriptures. Whether he be writing to the heathen, the heretics, or the orthodox, he expresses the same belief in the same unwavering language. He tells us in his *Apology* that ' God sent forth from the first men who, by their justice and innocency, were worthy to know God and to make Him known, and filled them to overflowing with the Divine Spirit ;'. . . and so 'gave us a written Testament, that we might more fully and more deeply learn of Him, and of His counsels, and of His will.' Nor does he scruple to

[1] Westcott's *Introduction to the Study of the Gospels*, Appendix B, pp. 416-41

call these books the 'writings and the words of God,' which the Christian studies for warning or remembrance, and to which he looks ' as the food of his faith, the spring of his hope, and the bulwark of his trust.'

Tertullian, like all the other Fathers who have been quoted, sees a profound unity in the dispensations of God. ' The same divine power was preached in the gospel which had ever been known in the Law, though the discipline was not the same.' ' The Law, indeed, is the root of the Gospels;' and ' in succession all the prophets utter the words of the same God, enforcing the same law by an iteration of the same precepts.'

Prophets, evangelists, and apostles are placed by Tertullian in one rank as God's ministering servants. Christ spoke by Moses, for ' He was the Spirit of the Creator;' and 'the prophecies are the voice of the Lord.' . . . ' The four Gospels,' he tells us, ' are reared on the certain basis of apostolical authority, and so are inspired in a far different sense from the writings of the spiritual Christian.' ' All the faithful, it is true, have the Spirit of God, but all are not apostles.' . . . ' The apostles have the Holy Spirit in a peculiar sense; they have it in the works of prophecy, and in the operation of mighty powers, and in the gift of tongues, not as possessing the influence in part as the rest.' . . . The revelation of the apostles is the revelation of Christ; and ' happy is that Church which combines the Law and the Prophets with the writings of the evangelists and apostles, and draws her faith from them.'

Cyprian considers the books of the Old and New Testaments as 'the foundations of divine fulness, from which the Christian must draw strength and wisdom;' the source of those ' divine commands by which God has vouchsafed to train and instruct us, that, enlightened by His pure and bright radiance, we may hold the way of life through their saving mysteries.' They are 'the foundation of our hope, the bulwark of our faith, the support of our hearts, the guide of our path, the safeguard of our salvation.' In the Scripture the Christian must find ' the torch which shall kindle his faith' in the hour of danger; the 'arms with which he shall face the terrors of persecution and the coming of Antichrist;' and 'the trumpet which shall rouse him to battle.' We read in his writings, again and again, that the Holy Spirit spake in the Law and in the Gospel, by prophets, apostles, and evangelists. ' By Him the prophets were quickened to a knowledge of the future.' By Him the apostles teach us ' what they learnt from the precepts of the Lord and heavenly revelations,' being 'full of the grace of the inspiration of their Master.' By Him, too, according to the promise, the Christian answers his accusers in the hour of death; for 'we do not speak, but the Spirit of the Father, who departeth not from His confessors, and Himself speaketh in us, and shareth our crown.' And thus it is that the power of God lives in the Church, 'which, like Paradise, includes within her walls all fruit-bearing trees, which she waters with four rivers, even the four Gospels, and on which she pours, with a heavenly stream, the grace of a saving baptism.'

' Yet more, the teaching of Scripture, whether by history or prophecy, by laws or psalms, is full of deep meaning, and its spiritual import is perfect — " the gospel cannot stand in part and fall in part," nor is it limited in its application like the doctrine of man.'[1]

The aim of the Alexandrian school of theology was to reconcile the existing culture with Christianity, and to imbue it with a Christian spirit. Clement, a

[1] Westcott's *Introduction to the Study of the Gospels*, Appendix B, pp. 419–424.

catechist of that school, traced, in the progressive steps of the Greek philosophy, the working of a divine system for the education of mankind, a sort of preparation for Christianity, suited to the peculiar character of the Greeks. It was a favourite idea of his, that the divine plan for the education of mankind constituted ;a great whole, the end of which he considered to be Christianity, and within which he included not merely the providential dealings of God with the heathen world. He traces the origin of pagan philosophy to the same God who was the author of the Mosaic and Christian covenants, and compares the Jewish prophets with those among the heathen, ' whom He raised up as prophets in their own dialect, and separated from common men, as they were able to receive divine favour;' while in another place he does not hesitate to call philosophy ' a peculiar covenant given to the Greeks, on which might be built the philosophy of Christ.' But it was by 'the masters of Israel' that God led men properly to the Messiah, 'speaking to them in the Law, the Psalms, and the Prophets; for, disregarding the lifeless instruments, lyre and harp, the Word of God reduced to harmony by the Holy Spirit not only this world, but man the microcosm, both body and soul, and so makes melody to God through that many-voiced instrument, and says to man: Thou art my harp, my flute, my temple: my harp, from the harmony [of many notes]; my flute, from the Spirit that breatheth through thee; my temple, from the Word that dwelleth in thee.' . . . 'Truly of man the Lord wrought a glorious living instrument after the fashion of His own image; one which might give every harmony of God, tuneful and holy.' Thus the foundations of our faith rest on no insecure basis, ' for we have received them from God through the Scriptures, . . . of which not one tittle shall pass away without being accomplished; for the mouth of the Lord, the Holy Spirit, spoke it; and we have believed on Him through His voice; and he that believeth on the Word, knoweth that the thing is true, for the Word is truth; but he that believeth not on him that speaketh, disbelieveth God:' for he disbelieveth 'that which hath been spoken by the Holy Spirit for our salvation.'

'The Gospel dispensation is still more glorious than the Law: the prophets were perfect in prophecy, the just perfect in righteousness, . . . but the apostles were filled in all things.' Yet 'there is no discord between the Law and the Gospel, but harmony, for they both proceed from the same Author, differing in name and time to suit the age and culture of their hearers, by a wise economy, but not potentially, since the faith in Christ and the knowledge of the Gospel are the explanation and fulfilment of the Law.' In all the Scriptures, 'in the Law, in the Prophets, and in the Gospel, which are ratified by the authority of Almighty power, we have the Lord as the spring of our teaching, who, by the various ministrations of His servants, *in sundry times and in divers manners*, from beginning to end, guides the course of knowledge.'

The method of interpretation adopted by the Alexandrine Fathers serves to place their view of inspiration in the clearest light; for it was not to them, as it might seem now, a mere exercise of ingenuity, but an earnest search after a wider and more certain knowledge. *Clement* maintains the existence of an allegorical meaning throughout the whole of the Bible, whose deeper mysteries are only seen 'by the light which dawns on those who are truly initiated in knowledge, and seek the truth in love. Moses,' he tells us, 'was a living law guided by the gracious Word,' so that his writings are still full of instruction, though their literal acceptation has passed away. The details of patriarchal history and the proportions of the Jewish tabernacle are significant to the Christian philosopher. Even the admission of Psalms into the sacred canon suggests the idea 'of the harmony of the Law and the Prophets, of the Gospel and the apostles in the Church, and of that undercurrent of melody which flows on through all the changes of persons.'

Origen's work on *Principles* exhibits the most complete view of his theory of inspiration. At the commencement of the first book he assumes the doctrine as acknowledged by all Christians, and in the last he supports it by a profound and independent proof, which in later times suggested the *Analogy* of Butler. 'Truly,' he says, 'it is most evidently preached in the churches that the Holy Spirit inspired each of the saints, prophets, and apostles, and that the same Spirit was present in those of old time as in those who were inspired at the coming of Christ; for Christ, the Word of God, was in Moses and the Prophets, and by His Holy Spirit they spake and did all things. By the help of this illuminating power the ministers of truth explained the hidden mysteries in the life and actions of man; unfolded the workings of God's providence in creation and redemption; and, at the same time, edified the simple and unlearned by instructive narratives. The true God acted on the prophets to enlighten and strengthen them, and not to cloud or confuse their natural powers, like the Pythian deity, who was akin to those demons which Christians are wont to drive out by prayers and adjurations; for the divine messengers, by the contact of the Holy Spirit with their soul, so to speak, gained a keener and a clearer intuition of spiritual truth.'

The details of the cosmogony and the records of the chosen people were, in *Origen's* judgment, as truly written by the inspiration of divine wisdom as the works of the prophets. He assumes that 'the records of the Gospels are *oracles of the Lord, pure oracles, as silver purified in the fire* (Ps. xii. 6), and that there is a meaning in their minutest details; while they are without error, inasmuch as we believe that they were accurately written by the co-operation of the Holy Spirit.' The opening words of St. Luke's Gospel seem to him to prove and illustrate this doctrine of inspiration: they 'attempted' to write histories who did so without the gift of God's grace; our Evangelists did not 'attempt' that which they did by the motion of the Holy Spirit, and their books only we receive on the authority of the Church of God. *Origen* does not hesitate to say that the Christian receives the words of Paul as the words of God, for he was made fit to be a minister of the New Covenant, not of the letter, but of the spirit. They only, he elsewhere tells us, will find contradictions in the apostle's writings who sever the one doctrine of faith into the diverse opinions of sects, and examine only those testimonies of Scripture which support their peculiar view, regardless of the full and perfect meaning of such passages as exhibit the opposite side of the truth. But, again, he notices that St. Paul speaks some things in his own person which do not possess the same authority; and he seems to consider that the inspiration of the Epistles generally is derived from the Gospels, for they are the gospel in another form. Yet still they are not less pregnant in meaning than the other parts of Scripture, though to some they may seem more plain than the historic and prophetic books, but are full of the elements of the mightiest and most manifold thoughts. Such is the variety which we find in the Bible, yet all parts combine into one harmonious whole. 'There are many sacred writings, yet there is but one Book: there are four Evangelists, yet their histories form but one Gospel: they all conspire to one end, and move by one way. All the sacred volumes breathe the spirit of fulness, and there is nothing, whether in the Law or in the Prophets, in the Evangelists or in the Apostles, which does not descend from the fulness of the Divine Majesty. Even at the present time the words of fulness speak in Holy Scripture to those who have eyes to see the mysteries of heaven, and ears to hear the voice of God.'

'We may call the gospel "the first-fruits of the Scriptures;" we may believe that the divinity of the prophetic revelations, and the spiritual meaning of the Law, shone forth by the dwelling of Jesus on earth, and that there were no clear proofs of the inspiration of the writings of the Old Covenant before that time; yet the Christian—who has recognised in his own faith the fulfilment of prophecy, and received the substance which the Law shadowed—will prize equally all the words of God. We cannot say of the writings of the Holy Spirit that anything in them is otiose or superfluous, even if they seem to be obscure. We cannot believe that there is one jot or tittle written in the Scriptures which does not work its own work, when men know how to employ it. The fault is our own if the rock of stumbling remain, for we shall indeed find connection and use in all that has been written, if we give heed to our reading, and pass over no letter without examination and inquiry. As in the natural world the skill of the Creator is not only seen in the stars of heaven, but in the organization and life of the meanest insect, and in the structure of the smallest plant, so too we conceive of all that has been recorded by the inspiration of the Holy Ghost, believing that the divine foreknowledge which supplies superhuman wisdom to the race of man by the Scriptures, has placed, so to speak, the seeds of saving truths in each letter as far as possible; . . . at least, whoever has once received these Scriptures as inspired by the Creator of the world must expect to find in them all difficulties which meet those who investigate the system of the universe.'

Origen rests his proof of inspiration on the influence of the Sacred Books and the fulfilment of prophecy; and answers objections against its being plenary, by analogies from life, from nature, and from providence. The anthropomorphic language of Scripture he compares with our own mode of addressing children suitably to their understanding, to secure their benefit and not to exhibit our own capacity.[1]

These opinions of the Fathers of the first three centuries, on the nature of inspiration, are some of them fanciful; but we learn from them what these early luminaries of the Church thought of the Bible. While they had no definite theory of inspiration, they held, in the most decided manner, the divine origin, authority, and perfection of the Holy Scriptures.

Eusebius of Cæsarea says that it is bold and rash to assert that the sacred writers could have substituted one name for another, *e.g.* Abimelech for Achish. *Chrysostom* designates the words of the apostle, not as his, but as the words of the Holy Spirit, or of God. *Jerome* says, that the prophets did not, as Montanus, together with some foolish women, vainly imagines, speak in a state of ecstasy, so that they did not know what they were saying; neither, when they taught others, were they ignorant of what they taught. He admits that human (*e.g.* grammatical) faults might have occurred; yet he guards himself against any dangerous inferences which might have been drawn from his premises. *Epiphanius* opposed very decidedly

[1] Westcott's *Introduction to the Study of the Gospels*, Appendix B, pp. 425–440.

the same notion that the sacred writers were entirely passive, and supposed that they enjoyed a clear perception of the divine, a calm disposition of mind.

Theodore of Mopsuestia assumed different degrees of inspiration. He ascribed to Solomon, not the gift of prophecy, but only that of wisdom, and judged of the Book of Job and the Song of Solomon only from the human point of view. Hence the fifth Œcumenical Council found fault with him on this account.

Augustine compares the apostles to the hands which noted down that which Christ, the head, dictated. He calls the Sacred Scriptures *venerabilem stilum Spiritus Sancti* [the style, to be regarded with reverence, of the Holy Spirit]. He communicates to Jerome his theory of inspiration in the following manner:—'I most firmly believe that none of the authors of the canonical books committed any error in writing. If I meet with anything in these writings that seems contrary to truth, I do not hesitate to affirm that the manuscript is faulty, or that the translator has not caught the sense, or that I do not understand it.' His opinion concerning the miraculous origin of the Septuagint version accords with that of the earlier Fathers. He attributes, as many of the ultra-Lutherans afterward did in reference to the Lutheran translation, the defects of that translation to a kind of inspiration, which had regard to the circumstances of the times. But behind this fantastic notion lies the grand idea of a revelation, which continues to manifest itself in a living way,— an idea which is above the narrow adherence to the letter, and is expressed in the belief of tradition.

Gregory the Great was probably induced by similar views to say in reference to the researches of learned men relative to the author of the Book of Job, that it was not necessary to know the pen with which the King of kings had written His royal letter, but that it sufficed to have a full conviction of its divine contents. Thus he assigns, on the one hand, the authorship of this book to the Holy Spirit, while, on the other, he leaves open all discussions concerning the human instruments.[1]

One or two writers, in the period between the Fathers and the Schoolmen, adopted the theory of verbal inspiration; but there was no generally received theory of the kind. Agobard, archbishop of Lyons, in answer to Fradegis, abbot of Tours, who held that the Holy Spirit formed the words in the mouths of the sacred writers, and who extended infallibility even to translators and commentators, showed, with sound mother wit, that great absurdity would follow from such a view.[2]

'By the Schoolmen, and subsequently by the doctors of the Church generally, a distinction was made in inspiration between *revelatio* and *assistentia* (*revelation* and *assistance*).'[3]

All the great Reformers spoke in the strongest possible language of the divinity, credibility, and infallibility of the sacred writings.

'Luther had experienced, in his own case, the practical blessings of the Scripture, and everywhere shows the profoundest reverence for the Bible, and the most lively sense of its divine blessedness, and of its peculiar worth as distinguished from other writings. So that he does not scruple to say, that we must look upon the Scripture "as if God had spoken therein;" and he calls the Holy Spirit the most clear and simple writer there is in heaven and earth.' Once he terms the holy word of Scripture 'God Himself.' 'To sum up all, the Holy

---

[1] Hagenbach's *History of Doctrines*, Vol. I. pp. 320–323. New York: Sheldon & Co. 1868.
[2] *Ibid.* p. 425.
[3] M'Clintock & Strong's *Bib. Theol. and Eccles. Cyclop.* Vol. IV., *s.v.* 'Inspiration.'

Bible is the most excellent and best book of God, full of comfort in all temptations; concerning faith, hope, and love, it teaches very different things from those which reason can see and feel, comprehend and experience; and in adversities, it teaches how Christian virtues are to shine forth, and that there is another and eternal life *beyond* this poor and miserable one.' Along with this profound reverence for Scripture, he also expressed himself very freely about individual writers. He called the Epistle of James *epistola straminea*—an epistle of straw; and he expressed himself with similar freedom about the Epistle of Jude and the Apocalypse. It seems that Luther admitted the existence of historical contradictions in the Scriptures; and Melancthon only claimed freedom from error in the apostles as to doctrine, but not in the application of doctrine, as in the difference between Paul and Barnabas, and between the former and Peter at Antioch. Heppe says that there is no trace in Melancthon of a proper theory of inspiration. Calvin held very strict views on inspiration, though he granted a difference in Scripture in respect to form.[1]

After the Reformation the idea of inspiration was more precisely defined. At first it was identified with revelation, but afterward treated of by itself. Along with the critical treatment of the Holy Scriptures, various theories were propounded, which still have their advocates in different parts of the Christian world.

In the seventeenth century, the notion of verbal inspiration, which had before only floated about from one individual to another, took the shape of a definite theory, and received a proper ecclesiastical sanction. The subject was treated at length by Calovius (the

---

[1] Hagenbach's *History of Doctrines*, Vol. II. pp. 241-243. New York: Sheldon & Co. 1868.

bitter opponent of Grotius and Calixtus), who set forth the verbal theory very fully; and later writers, both Lutheran and reformed, carried it so far as to extend inspiration to the vowel-points and the punctuation. The *Formula Consensus Helvetici* declares that the Old Testament is θεόπνευστος, equally as regards the consonants, the vowels, or at least their force.[1]

The theory of verbal inspiration has been defended, in very recent times, by many English and American divines; and also by some of the orthodox school of French Protestantism. Among the latter was the late Rev. S. R. L. Gaussen, Professor of Theology in Geneva, Switzerland, who states the theory thus: 'Such is, then, the word of God. It is God speaking in man, God speaking by man, God speaking as man, God speaking for man.' Quoting 2 Tim. iii. 16, Professor Gaussen says: 'It admits of no restriction; it is *the whole Scripture*, all that *is written* (πᾶσῃ γραφή)—that is to say, the thoughts that have already put on the clothing of language. It admits of no restriction; all Scripture is so far a work of God, that it is represented to us as given by the breath of God, in the same manner as the word of a man is given by the breath of his mouth. The prophet is the mouth of the Most High.' Again: 'Now the entire Bible is not only named the 'Word of God' (ὁ λόγος τοῦ Θεοῦ), it is called without distinction, *The Oracles of God* (τά λόγια τοῦ Θεοῦ). Who does not know what the oracles were, in the opinions of the ancients? Was there, then, a single word which could express more absolutely a complete and verbal inspiration?'[2]

Whatever theory of inspiration we adopt, it is neces-

---

[1] Hagenbach's *History of Doctrines*, Vol. II. p. 244. M'Clintock & Strong's *Bib. Theol. and Eccles. Cyclop.*, *s.v.* 'Inspiration.'
[2] Gaussen on *Inspiration*, pp. 42, 345, 355. New York: Baker & Scribner. 1846.

sary to admit as a fact that the Bible presents to us two distinct elements—the human and divine. God has given to us a revelation, chosen men as agents to record it, and made human language the channel to convey it. All the varieties of opinion respecting inspiration have sprung from the manner in which the fact referred to has been taken into account. Some ignore the human element, by the prominence which they attach to the divine; and others exclude the divine, by unduly exalting the human. It is impossible to separate these two elements, and to point out where the one begins and the other ends. The two are combined and work together for the production of an infallible record. The Holy Spirit did not employ the sacred writers as mere amanuenses, or as pens, but as penmen.

The assumption on the part of those who advocate the verbal theory in its boldest form, that we cannot think without words, is contradicted by our consciousness. We do think without words. Children have thoughts long before they have words; and some of the lower animals pursue trains of thought without words.

Some hold the opinion that words, strictly speaking, are incapable of inspiration. They are either oral, consisting of certain sounds, or written, consisting of certain marks on some writing material. In both these cases they are simply material signs. The spiritual element is the thought which they embody; and this only, they say, can be properly said to be inspired.

It is, perhaps, pushing the language of the Scriptures too far, to quote in proof of the strict verbal theory, such passages as 'Wherefore as the Holy Ghost saith' (Heb. iii. 7); '*Whereof* the Holy Ghost also is a witness to us: for after that He had said before, This is the covenant that I will make with them after those days, saith the Lord,' etc. (Heb. x. 15, 16); 'Thou by the mouth of Thy servant David hast said,' etc. (Acts iv. 25); 'Well spake the Holy Ghost by Esaias the prophet unto our fathers,' etc. (Acts xxviii. 25); 'Which things also we speak, not in the words which man's wisdom teacheth, but which the Holy Ghost teacheth' (1 Cor. ii. 13). It is true that the Holy Ghost said these things; and yet we can say with equal truth that David, Jeremiah, Isaiah, and Paul said them.

This, which has of late years been termed the *mechanical* theory of inspiration, cannot be satisfactorily reconciled with the individuality of the sacred writers. We observe in the Scriptures differences of language, of conception, and of style. These differences prove the personal action of the sacred writers in the composition of the Bible. No intelligent reader would confound Isaiah with Jeremiah, Ezekiel with Daniel, Amos with Hosea, Zephaniah with Nahum, Paul with John, or Peter with James. The genius, the habits, the condition, the education, and circumstances of each of these exercised an influence over his reasoning, and over his language.

An advocate of this theory has remarked: 'The Holy Ghost inspired His amanuenses with those expressions which they would have employed had they been left to themselves.' This hypothetical statement assumes an exercise of the divine agency for which no motive can be assigned or pointed out.[1]

This theory, in the form that the Holy Spirit dictated the words to the sacred writers, cannot be maintained, and must, therefore, be abandoned. At the same time, it must be admitted that in matters of pure revelation, the words were probably given, yea, in some instances doubtless were given. But this was not the normal method. If we may judge from the statements and

[1] See Lee on *Inspiration*, p. 36. London, 1860.

facts of Scripture, the action of the Holy Spirit and the action of the minds of the sacred writers—each maintaining his distinct individuality—were so combined and so wrought in unison as to produce an infallible book for the religious instruction and guidance of mankind. The Holy Spirit inspired it: men wrote it. The treasure was committed to earthen vessels. The mode of union between the divine and human cannot be explained.

The *mystical* theory, which may be regarded as an exaggerated form of the verbal, regards the sacred writers as passive, wholly possessed by the Spirit, and uttering His words in a species of frenzy. This theory is supposed to have been held by Philo, Josephus, and some of the primitive Christian Fathers; but it was condemned by the early councils as savouring of the heathen μαντεία. It is strictly mechanical. The Holy Spirit, according to it, used the sacred writers just as a flute-player blows a flute.

This theory has no support in Scripture, and it is opposed to the common judgment of the Church in every age. The pretended prophets and diviners of the heathen world exhibited outward signs of violent excitement, often amounting to insanity, during their simulated afflatus; and that abnormal, or more properly feigned excitement, was not regarded as an accidental circumstance, but as a necessary sign of inspiration. This we gather from the etymological affinity between the Greek words μάντις (a prophet), and μανία or μαίνομαι (madness, or to be mad, prophetic frenzy). But the inspiration of the sacred writers was distinguished by the opposite peculiarities of calmness, self-possession, and active intelligence. Their mental condition was not a morbid one. Whatever might be the mode of receiving their communications, they were as fully in possession of their faculties, and in the exercise of self-control, as at any other time. They were not in what the Greeks called ἔκστασις—a state of passive subjection to a higher power, holding their own faculties in temporary but complete abeyance.[1]

Another theory, propounding different degrees of inspiration, was wrought out by Maimonides, and having been skilfully introduced by Spinoza, Le Clerc, and others, entered unfortunately into the minds of Christian writers, and soon largely influenced all their speculations on the subject of inspiration, instead of being set aside, as it ought to have been, as the mere theory of Jewish philosophical writers.

Some English writers directed their attention to the Bible, to learn what information it seemed to furnish on the matter. They saw that God had been pleased to communicate supernatural information to man in a variety of different ways. They perceived instances of articulate voices uttered by God — angelic or supernatural visions—symbolic visions of a prophetic character—typical or prophetic dreams; and they admitted these as intimations that there must have been different modes, and probably also different degrees of inspiration. The next step in the process was to inquire into the *kinds* of inspiration given in Scripture; and here also they descried great and numerous diversities, such as instances of direct revelations of the divine will, in the form of law, commandment, covenant, and precept; then practical instructions, admonitions, exhortations, censures; then predictions of events still future; then lofty spiritual odes and hymns fitted for the subject of divine worship; and finally, a great number of historical or family records, or personal incidents which might have been known to or collected by the writers from other sources of information, or from their own know-

[1] Alexander's *Introduction to Isaiah*, Vol. I. pp. 5, 6. New York: Charles Scribner. 1865.

ledge as relating to themselves. These great diversities of subject seemed to them, in their practical and systematic way of thinking, to imply corresponding diversities of inspiration; and they set about trying to conceive what kind and amount of inspiration would be needed for these respectively, and to give corresponding names to them, such as should indicate their relative degrees.

The Rev. Daniel Wilson, D.D., formerly of Islington, and subsequently bishop of Calcutta, after stating his theory, and enumerating the degrees of what he called *suggestion, direction, elevation,* and *superintendency,* says: 'By the inspiration of *suggestion* is meant such communications of the Holy Spirit as suggested and dictated minutely every part of the truths delivered. The inspiration of *direction* is meant of such assistance as left the writers to describe the matter revealed in their own way, directing only the mind in the exercise of its powers. The inspiration of *elevation* added a greater strength and vigour to the efforts of the mind than the writers could otherwise have attained. The inspiration of *superintendency* was that watchful care which preserved generally from anything being put down derogatory to the revelation with which it was connected.'

Dr. Henderson's theory is somewhat more minute, enumerating five degrees—namely, *divine excitement, invigoration, superintendence, guidance,* and *direct revelation.* He says: 'In the first place, the sacred penmen were subjects of a *divine excitement.* By this we understand both the supernatural intimation given to the writers, that it was the pleasure of the Most High they should pen any particular book or portion of Scripture; and also the influence by which they were impelled to comply with such intimation. Secondly, there was an *invigoration* experienced by the inspired writers, by which their natural faculties were elevated above the imperfections which would have incapacitated them from receiving those communications of a higher order with which they were favoured, and by which also they were enabled perfectly to recollect and infallibly reason respecting truths and facts with which they were previously unacquainted. In the third place, the influence was that of simple yet infallible *superintendence*. By this is meant the watchful care which was exercised over them, when, in performing their task, they made use of their own observation, or availed themselves of their previous knowledge of existing documents, or of other external sources to which they had access. In the fourth place, *guidance* was another of the modes in which divine inspiration operated upon the penmen of Scripture. This view of the subject is suggested by that part of our Lord's gracious promise to His apostles, that the Spirit should *lead* them into all truth. They were not left to choose their own way; they were guided in the selection, order, and combination of the facts and doctrines to be narrated. The last and highest species of inspiration is that of *direct revelation*. To this head are to be referred all those doctrines which had previously been hid in the divine mind; all knowledge of past events respecting which no record or tradition existed; all acquaintance with circumstances present in point of existence, but of which the writers could not but be totally ignorant; and all communications respecting future contingent events, the foreknowledge of which is the sole prerogative of Deity.' With this theory of Dr. Henderson, that of Dr. John Pye Smith is almost identical.[1]

Dr. Bannerman remarks: 'The origin and occasion of this theory cast no small measure of light upon the

[1] Hetherington's *Apologetics of the Christian Faith*, pp. 461–463. Edinburgh: T. & T. Clark. 1867.

character of it. It was introduced avowedly for the purpose of meeting the allegations of errors and imperfections in Scripture, and in order to reconcile the existence of real defects with the belief of a divine agency employed in the composition of it. And had there been any foundation of truth in the theory itself, it would have answered the purpose for which it was used. Wherever imperfections existed in Scripture, it was sufficient for the advocates of such a scheme to say that there the human element was present to the exclusion of the divine, and that the error was due to the former in the absence of the latter. The theory was undoubtedly based upon a compromise between the friends and the enemies of inspiration, in which the enemies were allowed to retain the errors which they alleged in the sacred volume, and the friends were enabled to account for them, while yet retaining the general doctrine of an inspiration, at least in name.'[1]

Dr. Bannerman well observes: 'But the compromise was one fatal to the character of the theory itself. It allowed of the introduction of error into the infallible text, to an indefinite and unknown extent. Inspiration, measured out as a supplement to human ability in the sacred volume, leaves much of it with no impress of divine truth or authority beyond what is partial and insufficient. The very idea of degrees of divine inspiration carries with it the implication that there is something there which is not wholly God's, and something that is not altogether His infallible truth. To the extent that inspiration, according to such a theory, is given, the word is God's; to the extent to which it is withheld, the word is man's. In that joint result of inspiration and reason which we call the Bible, there will be a line to be drawn, whether the eye can see to draw it or not, at which, on the one

[1] Bannerman on *Inspiration*, p. 250. Edinburgh: T. & T. Clark. 1865.

side, is found the product of God's wisdom, and on the other the product of man's.[1]

This theory, inasmuch as it does not distinctly tell us what is God's and what is man's, furnishes nothing on which the faith of the believer can rest with unshaken confidence, and thus leaves the mind in uncertainty. A record, part of which is God's and part of which is man's, can never, until we are able to distinguish infallibly the one from the other, rule the judgment and bind the conscience. There is certainly a great difference between a volume whose statements are some of them inspired in full, some of them partially, some of them not at all, and one that is plenarily inspired in all its parts.

The theory, moreover, is inconsistent with the declarations of Scripture, which speaks of all its books as equally inspired, and clearly intimates that inspiration extends to all their contents. It is not confined to moral and religious truth: the statements of facts, whether scientific, historical, or geographical, come equally within its sphere. It is not limited to those facts, the importance of which is obvious, or which are involved in matters of doctrine, but extends to everything which any sacred writer asserts to be true. The scriptural proof of this is manifold. It is involved in the proposition that the sacred writers were the organs of God; in the affirmation of our Lord that 'the Scriptures cannot be broken' (John x. 35), *i.e.* they cannot err. It is involved in the reference, by Christ and His apostles, to the whole volume of Scripture as the word of God. They make no distinction as to the authority of the Law, the Prophets, and the Hagiographa, but quote them all as equally the divine word. They refer to all classes of facts—doctrinal, historical, and incidental circumstances—

[1] Bannerman on *Inspiration*, p. 250. Edinburgh: T. & T. Clark. 1865.

recorded in the Old Testament, as infallibly true. It is in the very nature of the Bible that God chose some men to write history, some to indite psalms, some to predict the future, and some to teach doctrine. All were equally His organs, and each was infallible in his sphere.[1]

Many writers do not regard inspiration as supernatural at all. They do not hold it to be the miraculous agency of God, exerted for the purpose of supernaturally controlling human weakness and imperfection, and excluding human errors,—an agency with whose presence falsehood is inconsistent, and which leaves no room for anything but infallible truth. Those who adopt this view do not all belong to the same class. Some of them are pure naturalists, who believe that God having created the world, and having endowed matter with its properties and minds with their attributes, left everything to the absolute control of the laws imposed upon it. According to their view, miracles, prophecy, supernatural revelation, and even providential government, whether general or special, are impossible. The Bible must therefore be regarded as a purely human production. Others admit that God is everywhere present and everywhere active; that His providential efficiency and control are exercised in the occurrence of all events. But they maintain that He always acts according to fixed laws, and always in connection and co-operation with second causes. According to this theory, also, all miracles and all prophecy properly speaking are excluded. A revelation is admitted, or at least is possible. But it is merely providential. It consists in such an ordering of circumstances and such a combination of influences as to secure the elevation of certain men to a higher level of religious knowledge than that

[1] Dr. Hodge's *Systematic Theology*, Vol. I. p. 163.

attained by others. They may also, in a sense, be said to be inspired in so far as their inward, subjective state is purer and more devout, as well as more intelligent, than that of ordinary men. There is no specific difference, however, according to this theory, between inspired and uninspired men. It is only a matter of degrees. One is more and another less purified and enlightened. This theory also makes the Bible a purely human production. It confines revelation to the sphere of human knowledge.'[1]

With reference to this naturalistic theory, it is enough to say that one of the postulates of Christianity is that the supernatural is possible, and that the great facts on which it rests were miracles. If any one deny the possibility of miracles, the question at issue must be relegated to the province of apologetics.

There is a theory which differs little from the preceding. Its author was Schleiermacher, who adopted the same philosophy with some modification. All intervention of the immediate agency of God in the world, with the exception of the creation of man and the constitution of the person of Christ, was precluded. There was a supernatural intervention in the origin of man and in the manifestation of Christ. Everything else in the history of the world is natural. Of course there is nothing supernatural in the Bible. Human nature was adequate to produce everything in the Old Testament; and Christianity, the life of Christ—a life common to all believers—was sufficient to account for everything in the New Testament.

Schleiermacher makes revelation to consist, not in the Bible, but in Christ,—meaning by that, not in the words that He uttered, nor in the doctrines that He taught, but in His person. The New Testament, according to him, is no more a communication from

Dr. Hodge's *Systematic Theology*, Vol. I. pp. 172, 173.

God through His chosen servants, than are the writings of any other Christians, recording their religious views and sentiments. He admits, however, an advantage on the side of the sacred writers of the New Testament, in the circumstance that they stood in closer proximity than others to Christ, and came under the nearer effect of His personal influence. The disciples of Schleiermacher in England make the Bible to be the product of the spiritual life and beliefs of its authors, illuminated and taught by the gracious influences of the Spirit, in the same manner as every child of God is instructed and enlightened at the present day. According to this theory, the inspiration of the prophets and apostles is nothing but the result of the gracious and illuminating influences which maintain the Christian life of the Church in common, and are peculiar to no chosen few; and the products of inspiration in the Bible may exhibit a higher religious wisdom, or a deeper spiritual feeling than the Christian authorship of other good men, but are not raised above the risk or the reality of error by any influence different from that which keeps the lips of a Christian from falsehood, and his writings from heresy. Neander, Nitzsch, Tholuck, and others have advanced toward a stricter orthodoxy; but they have left untouched the fundamental principle of this theory, which admits of the introduction of human imperfection into the sacred text, to an unknown and indefinite extent.[1]

Mr. Morell, in expounding this theory, says: 'The essential germ of the religious life is concentrated in the absolute feeling of dependence,—a feeling which implies nothing abject, but, on the contrary, a high and hallowed sense of our being inseparably related to Deity.'

[1] Bannerman on *Inspiration*, pp. 168, 231.

'Revelation and inspiration indicate one united process, the result of which upon the human mind is to produce a state of spiritual intuition, whose phenomena are so extraordinary, that we at once separate the agency by which they are produced from any of the ordinary principles of human development. And yet this agency is applied in perfect consistency with the laws and natural operations of our spiritual nature. Inspiration does not imply anything generically new in the actual processes of the human mind; it does not involve any form of intelligence essentially different from what we already possess; it indicates rather the elevation of the religious consciousness, and with it, of course, the power of spiritual vision, to a degree of intensity peculiar to the individuals thus highly favoured of God.'

This view does not admit of any specific difference between genius and inspiration. 'Genius,' says Morell, 'consists in the possession of a remarkable power of intuition with reference to some particular object, a power which arises from the inward nature of a man being brought into unusual harmony with that object in its reality and its operations. Let there be a due purification of the moral nature, a perfect harmony of the spiritual being with the mind of God, a removal of all inward disturbances from the heart, and what is to prevent or disturb this immediate intuition of divine things?'[1]

This theory proceeds upon the assumption that religion is a feeling, a life, unconnected with any form of knowledge or any particular system of doctrine. This does not accord with the teaching of Scripture and the common conviction of Christians. According to these, 'religion, subjectively considered, is the reception of certain doctrines as true, and a state of

[1] Hodge's *Systematic Theology*, Vol. I. pp. 174-176.

heart and course of action in accordance with those doctrines. The apostles propounded a certain system of doctrines; they pronounced those to be Christians who received those doctrines so as to determine their character and life. They pronounced those who rejected those doctrines, who refused to receive their testimony, as antichristian; as having no part or lot with the people of God. Christ's command was to teach; to convert the world by teaching. On this principle the apostles acted, and the Church has ever acted from that day to this. Those who deny theism as a doctrine are atheists. Those who reject Christianity as a system of doctrines are unbelievers. They are not Christians. The Bible everywhere assumes that without truth there can be no holiness; that all conscious exercises of spiritual life are in view of truth objectively revealed in the Scriptures. And hence the importance everywhere attributed to knowledge, to truth, to sound doctrine in the Word of God.'

'This theory is inconsistent with the scriptural doctrine of revelation. According to the Bible, God presents truth objectively to the mind, whether by audible words, by visions, or by the immediate operations of His Spirit. According to this theory, revelation is merely the providential ordering of circumstances which awaken and exalt the religious feelings, and which thus enable the mind intuitively to apprehend the things of God.' There is a specific difference between genius and revelation: 'genius consists in a remarkable power of intuition;' revelation 'presents truth objectively to the mind.' There is also a specific difference between genius and inspiration: in the former, there is only a single factor—the human —at work; in the latter, there are two factors, the human and divine.

This theory confines the intuitions of the sacred

writers to what are called 'eternal verities.' But the great body of truths revealed in Scripture—such as the fall of man; that all men are sinners; that the Redeemer from sin was to be of the seed of Abraham, and of the house of David; that He was to be born of a virgin, to be a man of sorrows; that He was crucified and buried; that He rose again the third day; that He ascended to heaven, and that He will come again to judge the world— are not 'eternal verities,' or intuitive truths. They are not truths which the religious consciousness, however exalted, would enable any man to discover.

This theory divests the Bible of normal authority as a rule of faith. The Scriptures, according to it, contain no doctrines revealed by God, and to be received as true on His testimony. They contain only the thoughts of holy men; the forms in which their understandings, without supernatural aid, clothed the intuitions due to their religious feelings. But the Bible makes revelation to be the communication of doctrines to the understanding by the Holy Spirit. It makes those truths or doctrines the immediate source of all right feeling. The feelings come from spiritual apprehension of the truth, and not the knowledge of truth from the feelings. Knowledge is necessary to all conscious holy exercises. Hence the Bible makes truth of the greatest importance. It pronounces those blessed who receive the doctrines which it teaches, and those accursed who reject them. It makes the salvation of men to depend upon their faith. The creed of man, according to this theory, is of comparatively little consequence.[1]

This subjective theory of inspiration found an advocate in Coleridge, who had a more intimate knowledge of German philosophy than of Christian theology. His dictum was: 'The Bible is the word of God because we have found it to be true.' We would reverse it, and

[1] Hodge's *Systematic Theology*, Vol. I. pp. 177, 178.

say, 'The Bible is true, because we have found it to be the word of God.'

'In the case of Coleridge himself, the principle of a subjective inspiration, identical with that "grace and communion with the Spirit which the Church, under all circumstances, and every regenerate member of the Church of Christ, are permitted to hope and instructed to pray for," is not carried out with the same consistency in reference to the whole of Scripture as is seen in the theology of Germany. He admits an exception in favour of the "Law and the Prophets, no jot or tittle of which can pass away," as having been inspired by supernatural agency, while the remainder of the sacred volume has been written under the impulse and guidance of that gracious influence common to all Christian men. But this inconsistency of Coleridge's views is not seen in the writings of his more advanced disciples.'[1] This theory, as expounded by Coleridge, has been termed 'partial.'

The theory of partial inspiration has assumed other forms,—some limiting the inspiration of the sacred writers to their doctrinal teaching; others to the thoughts, as distinguished from the words of Scripture; and some, as we have already noticed, making different degrees of inspiration. All these views are opposed to the teaching of the Bible, which claims a plenary inspiration. It matters not how plausible some of them may appear; the question is, What does the Bible teach on the subject?

Some theologians regard inspiration as one of the ordinary fruits of the Spirit, who renews, sanctifies, illuminates, guides, and teaches all the people of God. They do not distinguish inspired and uninspired men by any specific difference. The sacred writers were merely holy men under the guidance of the ordinary

[1] Bannerman on *Inspiration*, pp. 108, 145.

influence of the Spirit. Some of those who adopt this theory extend it to revelation as well as to inspiration. Others admit a strictly supernatural revelation, but deny that the sacred writers in communicating the truths revealed were under any influence not common to ordinary believers. And as to those parts of the Bible which contain no special revelations, they are to be regarded as the devotional writings or historical narratives of devout but fallible men.[1]

The theories of Schleiermacher and Coleridge do not differ essentially from this. They are all modifications of the false assumption that inspiration is not to be regarded as supernatural, but as the gracious agency of God illuminating the rational or the spiritual consciousness of a man. They are all inconsistent with the authority claimed by the sacred writers. They spoke in the name of God, asserting that God spoke by them. They preface their declarations by the emphatic announcement, 'Thus saith the Lord.'

The doctrine that inspiration is common to all believers is inconsistent with the whole nature of the Bible, which professes to be, and which is, a revelation of truths not only undiscoverable by human reason, but which no amount of holiness could enable the mind of man to perceive. This is true not only of the strictly prophetic revelations relating to the future, but also of all things concerning the mind and will of God. The doctrines of the Bible are called *mysteries*, unknown and unknowable, except as revealed to the holy apostles and prophets by the Spirit (Eph. iii. 5).

Of these theories which have passed under review, it will be perceived that there are two leading ones,—the one assigning such prominence to the divine element that the human is practically ignored, and the other exalting the human to such a degree as to overlook the

[1] Hodge's *Systematic Theology*, Vol. I. p. 179.

divine. The latter theory takes three forms: (1) 'The Bible *contains* the word of God,' instead of the orthodox formula, 'The Bible *is* the word of God;' (2) there are different degrees of inspiration; and (3) the awakening and elevation of our Christian consciousness. Both these theories, in all their forms, do not furnish a satisfactory explanation of the doctrine of inspiration.

There remains another theory, which has been termed the *dynamical*. This theory sets out with the assumption of two elements—the divine and the human—in the Bible. This assumption is warranted by the facts of Scripture—facts patent to every reader, who cannot fail, even on the most superficial survey, to recognise varieties of diction and personal peculiarities of the writers of both Testaments. At the same time, he must, if unbiased, acknowledge the presence of a supernatural element, for which the possession of the highest genius cannot account. It is impossible to show how these two elements are combined, for inspiration belongs to the sphere of the miraculous. But of the reality of their union the facts of Scripture leave us in no doubt. Without the divine element, the Bible would cease to be a revelation; without the human, the communication from God would have been confined to the individual to whom it was originally made. The two co-exist and work together; and through their co-existence and co-operation we have received the divine record of infallible truth, the Holy Scriptures.

According to this theory, the Holy Spirit employed the faculties of the sacred writers in accordance with their natural laws. These writers are not to be considered as being in any sense the source or the originators of the revelation given to us in the Bible. Of this God alone is the source; but human agency is regarded as the condition under which He made His revelation known to mankind. In short, the divine and human elements, mutually interpenetrating and combined, formed one organic whole, called the Bible, or the Holy Scriptures.

For the full understanding of this theory, it is necessary to distinguish between revelation and inspiration, the neglect of which has led to mistakes and errors, which are particularly manifest in the theory of degrees. After the consideration of this distinction, the present theory will be developed and illustrated in connection with the nature of inspiration.

The theories that have been specified are all of any importance that have ever been advanced in relation to the subject of inspiration. Indeed, they are all that can be advanced; for the Scriptures are either human or divine, or both: they are either partially or plenarily inspired; they were written under either a gracious or a supernatural influence and guidance. The only other theory possible—if it can be properly called a theory, for it refers to the continuance, not to the nature of inspiration—is that inspiration is perpetuated in the Church. This, I believe, is the doctrine of the Roman Catholic Church, which understands the promise of the Holy Spirit and of miraculous powers, which Christ gave to His apostles, as given to the whole Church for all time. According to the Romanists, 'Christianity is, or includes, a system of doctrine, and those doctrines are in the Scriptures; but many of them are there only in their rudiments. Under the constant guidance and tuition of the Spirit, the Church comes to understand all that these rudiments contain, and to expand them in their fulness.' To the Church, they affirm, 'Christ imparted His unity. Thus, the ideas of Christ become the ideas of the Church, and of every member of the Church; and the truth of these ideas, as it lies in the mind of Christ, lies in the mind of the Church and in the mind of its members. The infallibility of the Church is a privilege received by her from Christ, in virtue of which she cannot be deceived, nor deceive others, in proposing to the world doctrines of faith and morals. Hence, whatever she proposes to be believed and practised, is infallibly true, whether she proposes these truths from the Bible or from tradition.'[1]

This view of inspiration is in harmony with the doctrine that the Pope is the successor of the Apostle Peter, and with that of the Roman Catholic doctrine of apostolical succession in general.

All that is necessary to be said in reference to it is:

(1) The Pope is not the successor of the Apostle Peter in any official sense.

(2) The doctrine of apostolical succession as held by the Roman Catholic Church is a mere figment. The apostles, who were chosen to be witnesses of Christ's resurrection, could, strictly speaking, have no official successors.

(3) Christ and the Church are not personally and numerically one, so that the ideas of Christ become the ideas of the Church. He has revealed His ideas to the Church in the Holy Scriptures.

(4) The Church, which is composed of members uninspired individually, cannot be inspired as a body.

(5) The New Testament being, as Protestants believe, a final and complete revelation, there is no need, as there was under the progressive revelation of the Old Testament, of a class of inspired men like the Hebrew prophets, to instruct the Church by new revelation, or by the declaration of new doctrines. The gracious guidance of the Holy Spirit, enlightening the minds of God's people in the knowledge of the truth revealed, is all that is needed under the present dispensation.

---

[1] *Points of Controversy.* By Rev. C. F. Smarius. New York: John Gilmary Shea. 1869. Pp. 109–169.

CHAPTER III.

DISTINCTION BETWEEN INSPIRATION AND REVELATION.

THE duty of the sacred writers was to express accurately, in human language, the thoughts which they were officially directed to communicate to men. They were divinely commissioned to write what has been transmitted to us in the Holy Scriptures. This is evident from the claims of the writers themselves, from the fact that the Church has received, as of divine authority, the writings of both the Old and New Testaments to the exclusion of others, some of which claimed like authority with those composing the sacred canon. The writers of the Scriptures may have written many things which were not inspired, and which consequently were never received by the Church as a part of the revelation of God, and hence not transmitted to us. But those writings which have come down to us as inspired, were known to be such by their authors, and received as such on sufficient testimony by the Church. Their authors had a divine commission to write them, and they furnished satisfactory credentials of that commission, otherwise we cannot account for the fact that such and such writings only were received, and others rejected.

The sacred writings exhibit great diversity of style, and treat of different subjects. The range of these subjects is God and man, the infinite and the finite, the eternal and the temporal.

Two questions naturally arise: How did the sacred writers acquire a knowledge of what they wrote? and under what guidance or influence did they commit their knowledge to writing?

It is evident that, in regard to those subjects that lie beyond the range of human intelligence, they must have received them by revelation. But how was it with the facts of history, which they could have learned by human testimony, and with things with which they were themselves conversant? Did they need revelation and inspiration to record such things? A statement of the views of some able theologians on this subject will precede an answer to the question.

Archdeacon Lee says: 'By revelation I understand a direct communication from God to man, either of such knowledge as man could not of himself attain to, because its subject-matter transcends human sagacity or human reason (such, for example, were the prophetical announcements of the future, and the peculiar doctrines of Christianity), or which (although it might have been attained in the ordinary way) was not, in point of fact, from whatever cause, known to the person who received the revelation. By inspiration, on the other hand, I understand that actuating energy of the Holy Spirit, in whatever degree or manner it may have been exercised, guided by which the human agents chosen by God have officially proclaimed His will by word of mouth, or have committed to writing the several portions of the Bible. I repeat, in whatever degree or manner this actuation by the Holy Spirit may have been exercised; for it should never be forgotten that the real question with which our inquiry is concerned is the result of this divine influence as presented to us in the Holy Scriptures, *not* the manner according to which it has pleased God that this result should be attained. Moses unquestionably received more abundant tokens of the divine favour than Ezra, or Nehemiah, or the author of the books of Chronicles; but this does not render that element of the Bible, in composing which Moses was the agent, one whit more true or more accurate in its details than the writings of the others. The disciple whom Jesus loved, and who reclined upon His bosom, enjoyed personally far higher privileges than St. Mark or St. Luke. But still this affection of his Divine Master does not render St. John's Gospel in one single feature a more trustworthy vehicle of that portion of divine truth which it conveys, than the records of those who were but the companions of the apostles.'

... 'Revelation and inspiration are also to be distinguished by the sources from which they proceed, —revelation being the peculiar function of the eternal Word; inspiration the result of the agency of the Holy Spirit. Their difference, in short, is specific, and not merely one of degree; a point which is amply confirmed by the consideration, that either of these divine influences may be exerted, although the other be not called into action. The patriarchs received revelations, but they were not inspired to record them; the writer of the Acts of the Apostles was inspired for his task, but we are not told that he ever enjoyed a revelation. But although thus specifically distinct, a fixed relation subsisting between the two ideas, as applied to the Bible, must be noticed. It is plain that, without inspiration a divine communication would have been in a measure useless as a guide and rule; for without such spiritual illumination, how could we be assured that the revelation would be correctly transmitted to others, or even rightly apprehended by the recipients themselves? Consider a single case, which exhibits the relation of the two ideas. Certain Tyrian prophets, mentioned in the twenty-first chapter of the Acts, " said to Paul, through the Spirit, that he should not go up to Jerusalem." To them had been *revealed* what the

Holy Ghost was witnessing "in every city," namely, that bonds and afflictions awaited St. Paul in Jerusalem. These prophets, however, enjoyed no *inspiration*; they adulterated the revelation which they had received with human wishes and human feelings, and thus directly contradicted the will of God, which the guidance of the Spirit enabled St. Paul himself to understand and to obey. "And now, behold! I go bound in the Spirit unto Jerusalem, not knowing the things that shall befall me there, save that the Holy Ghost witnesseth in every city that bonds and afflictions abide me."'[1]

'In affirming,' says Dr. Bannerman, 'that the Bible contains a supernatural communication of truth from God, we make no distinction between different passages of the sacred volume, or different portions of its contents, as if one were more or less of a revelation than another, or as if some were and some were not a revelation at all. The general fact of the existence of a supernatural revelation, in the proper sense of the word, may be admitted while it is limited to certain departments of Scripture, and to a certain kind of Scripture truths, and denied to others. And the question is a very important one, both generally and in its bearing upon the debate as to inspiration, whether or not we are warranted and required to recognise within the Bible itself a distinction between some of its facts and statements as, strictly speaking, constituting a revelation from God, and others of its facts and statements as not entitled to that character or appellation.'

'The Scripture use of the term revelation, and the account given of what is implied under it, justify us in asserting that it is to be taken in the sense of a supernatural communication from God, in no ways restricted

[1] *The Inspiration of Holy Scripture.* By William Lee, M.A. Pp. 40–43. London, 1860.

to any particular class of facts or truths, to the exclusion of others, but equally embracing all, of whatever character they be, that are recorded in the Bible. Looking exclusively to the language and statements of Scripture itself, there is, with a very narrow exception, no ground whatever for assigning the name or character of revelation to any one of its facts and truths, which there is not for assigning it to them all; and conversely, there is no ground whatever for excluding any of its facts and truths from the category of a revelation, which there is not for excluding them all.'

'The distinction that divides the Bible into what is revelation and what is not, according as the matters recorded are supernaturally or only naturally known to the writers, is one that has been advocated by some who yet assert that the Bible is all throughout inspired. The only right representation of Scripture, and the one that gives us a record infallibly true and divinely guarded from error, is made up of the two ideas of a supernatural communication given by God, and of that communication supernaturally inspired by God. The revelation and the inspiration are co-extensive, and belong alike and equally to every portion of the Bible; and where the one or the other is either mutilated or wholly denied, we fail to reach the true idea of Scripture infallibility. But there are some who, limiting the notion of a revelation from God to what in Scripture was not known to the penman from other sources, still maintain that all its contents, whether previously known or unknown, were alike recorded under the inspiration of the Spirit. According to such a theory there is a large portion of the sacred volume, and an extensive and important class both of its facts and truths, written from the personal knowledge of the authors, and not a revelation, but yet written under the guidance of the Spirit, and therefore an inspiration.'[1]

Dr. Hodge states the distinction between revelation and inspiration thus: 'They differ, first, as to their object. The object of revelation is the communication of knowledge. The object or design of inspiration is to secure infallibility in teaching. Consequently they differ, secondly, in their effects. The effect of revelation was to render its recipient wiser. The effect of inspiration was to preserve him from error in teaching. These two gifts were often enjoyed by the same person at the same time. That is, the Spirit often imparted knowledge, and controlled in its communication orally or in writing to others. This was no doubt the case with the psalmists and with the prophets and apostles. Often, however, the revelations were made at one time, and were subsequently under the guidance of the Spirit committed to writing. Thus the Apostle Paul tells us that he received his knowledge of the gospel not from man, but by revelation from Jesus Christ; and this knowledge he communicated from time to time in his discourses and epistles. In many cases these gifts were separated. Many of the sacred writers, although inspired, received no revelations. This was probably the fact with the authors of the historical books of the Old Testament. The Evangelist Luke does not refer his knowledge of the events which he records to revelation, but says he derived it from those "which from the beginning were eye-witnesses and ministers of the Word" (Luke i. 2). It is immaterial to us where Moses obtained his knowledge of the events recorded in the Book of Genesis; whether from early documents, from tradition, or from direct revelation. No more causes are to be assumed

---

[1] Bannerman on *Inspiration*, pp. 174, 178, 190, 191. Edinburgh: T. & T. Clark. 1865.

for any effect than are necessary. If the sacred writers had sufficient sources of knowledge in themselves, or in those about them, there is no need to assume any direct revelation. It is enough for us that they were rendered infallible as teachers.'[1]

'When God,' says Dr. Patton, 'designed His communications to serve a public purpose, He not only gave revelations to His servants, but He rendered them infallible in communicating them, through the influence of the Holy Spirit. Inspiration was the influence under which the sacred writers became infallible in the communication of truth to their fellow-men. This definition, however, though true, is not complete, and is liable to the objection that it only provides against the possibility of error on the part of the sacred writers, but does not give the character of divine authorship to their writings. It would be better to say, that we understand the inspiration under which the Scriptures were written to mean that intimate relation between the Holy Spirit and the minds of the sacred writers in virtue of which we are justified in saying the words of Scripture are the words of God.'

'But a revelation . . . means more than that a conception has originated in the mind through divine agency. It implies that truth has been *objectively* presented to the mind by dream, vision, or audible voice, and that *its reception has been attended with the consciousness that it came from God.* Take, for example, the vision of Paul (Acts xvi. 9), which influenced him to go to Macedonia. How did he know that it was not a mere subjective state? Simply because consciousness testified as clearly as to his own identity that he had been in direct communication with God.'[2]

---

[1] Hodge's *Systematic Theology*, Vol. I. p. 155.

[2] *The Inspiration of the Scriptures*, pp. 123, 129. By the Rev. Francis L. Patton. Philadelphia: Presbyterian Board of Publication.

On comparing the foregoing views, we find that Archdeacon Lee limits revelation to a direct communication from God to man, either of such knowledge as man could not of himself attain to, because its subject-matter transcends human sagacity or human reason; or of such knowledge as was not, in point of fact, from whatever cause, known to the person who received the revelation. Dr. Bannerman makes revelation and inspiration co-extensive. Dr. Hodge, though not expressly, yet impliedly, adopts the view of Archdeacon Lee in the words: 'Many of the sacred writers, although inspired, received no revelations. This was probably the fact with the authors of the historical books of the Old Testament. The Evangelist Luke does not refer his knowledge of the events which he records to revelation, but says he derived it from those which from the beginning were eye-witnesses and ministers of the Word.' Dr. Patton says that 'revelation implies that truth has been *objectively* presented to the mind by dream, vision, or audible voice, and *that its reception has been attended with the consciousness that it came from God.*' He concludes: 'We cannot affirm, with Dr. Bannerman, that revelation is co-extensive with inspiration; and, on the other hand, we cannot, with Dr. Lee, be confident that it is not.'[1]

Dr. Patton states very clearly the difference between Archdeacon Lee and Dr. Bannerman in the following extracts:—'It is evident that in this controversy two very different questions have been confounded, to wit: (1) The character in which the Bible *addresses us*, as the result of the labours of the sacred writers; and (2) The manner in which the writers themselves derived the information which is recorded in the pages of Scripture. The first is evidently in Dr. Bannerman's mind when he says:

[1] Dr. Patton on *The Inspiration of the Scriptures*, p. 131.

'"It is something startling to be told, not by the opponents but by the friends of inspiration, that the Acts of the Apostles and other such historical portions of the Bible are no part of the revelation of God."'

'Again: "Had the prophets, or the evangelists, or the apostles, the supernatural commission and gift of God to write in His name? This is the question which, if answered in the affirmative, gives to all they wrote the character of revelation."'

'Again: "If all the books, and all the parts of each book, uncorrupted and unmutilated, which are usually accounted to belong to the canon, have a right to their place there, it is impossible, without playing fast and loose with the evidence that accredits all alike, to deny one portion the character of revelation, while assigning it to the remainder." These remarks would have been just if, as Dr. Bannerman seems to have supposed, Dr. Lee had cast discredit upon the historical portions of the Scripture by denying their divine authorship. He has been led into this line of reasoning by a misapprehension of the real questions at issue. If the question be put, Is the Bible a revelation to us from God? we answer, "*Yes—in all its parts,*" since the words of Scripture are the words of God. But if we are asked whether all the contents of the Bible are the records of supernatural communications objectively presented to the minds of the writers, it will not be so easy to give an affirmative answer.'[1]

It seems to me that Archdeacon Lee covers all the ground necessary to be covered by inspiration, when he says that 'such knowledge as might have been attained in the ordinary way, but which in point of fact was not, might become the subject of revelation.' It does not seem to be a proper use of the word 'reve-

---

[1] Dr. Patton on *The Inspiration of the Scriptures*, pp. 124, 125.

lation,' to ascribe to it matters of history, with which the sacred writers were conversant, and genealogical tables, which they could consult. They were doubtless directed to employ in their writings historical documents and genealogical tables; but that the facts of such documents were revealed to them cannot be affirmed, except in a very loose way of speaking. They may have had a revelation to select such and such materials, and they were under a supernatural guidance in the use of these materials; but anything beyond this we are not authorized to affirm. To say that those facts were revealed to them which were already on record, and with which they were acquainted, assumes an exercise of the divine agency for which no motive can be assigned.

But says Dr. Bannerman: 'If inspiration be nothing else (in so far as regards written, not oral inspiration) but the supernatural transference of the facts and truths, as they are found in the mind of the writer, to the page of the record which he indites, so that the expression of them there in human language shall be unerringly the same as the conception in the mind, then a very slight consideration will be enough to convince us that inspiration alone, without revelation, cannot secure infallibility in respect either of the facts or the truths. By means of inspiration all error may be indeed excluded in the human expression of what is recorded; the imperfect ability of man to put in writing, without inaccuracy or defect, the conceptions of fact or truth he may seek to impress upon the page, may be remedied by supernatural agency, so that the copy in the record may infallibly correspond with the original in the mind. But that original itself may be erroneous, and so the copy infallibly transmit the error to the written page.'

'The conception in the mind of the sacred penmen,

both of facts and truths, may have been misconceived and inaccurate, so that the facts and truths, although recorded with infallible accuracy *as conceived*, may not yet answer to the reality. In such a case, the miracle of inspiration, without the additional and previous miracle of revelation, would secure only with supernatural certainty that the original apprehension in the mind of the writer of the facts and truths, being itself erroneous, would reproduce the error in the accurate statement of them embodied in the inspired language of the record. It is when the conception as well as the record of the conception is infallibly true, that we can expect to find infallible truth in the latter. This can be effected only by the help of supernatural revelation in addition to supernatural inspiration,— the former securing, through the instrumentality of a miraculous presentation of facts and truths to the mind of the prophet by God, that his original apprehension of them shall be perfectly free from error; the latter securing, through the instrumentality of a miraculous transference of them to the written page, that the record of them intended for others shall be equally free from imperfection. Without a revelation, in the proper sense of the word, the first idea of them in the conception of the writer may be mingled with human and involuntary misapprehension; without an inspiration, in the proper sense of the word, the copy in human speech of the idea would· fail to re-exhibit with infallible accuracy the original.'[1]

The difficulty raised by Dr. Bannerman seems to be a real one, in case we adopt Archdeacon Lee's theory. If inspiration secures only the infallibility of the record and not of the contents, then what guarantee have we against error? Some of the documents employed by the sacred writers proceeded from men of whose inspi-

[1] Bannerman on *Inspiration*, pp. 192, 193.

ration we have no evidence. Such were the proclamations of Nebuchadnezzar and Cyrus, the genealogical tables of the antediluvians and of the Jews. Might these not partake of the imperfection of all human documents, and contain error? And admitting that they contained error, have we any evidence that the Holy Spirit corrected the error before they were used by the writers of the Bible? For instance, the genealogical table of Luke inserts Cainan between Salah and Arphaxad. In the Hebrew, Salah follows Arphaxad immediately; but in the Septuagint we find, as in Luke, Cainan between them. Luke must, therefore, have copied from the Septuagint. The question naturally arises, Which is correct? the Hebrew or the Septuagint? If the name was omitted in the Hebrew, did Luke supply it by revelation? If it was inserted in the Septuagint without any authority, why should Luke have retained it? Again, there are omissions in the genealogical table given by Matthew. Did he receive a revelation to make these omissions? or did he copy them from incomplete lists, in which the omissions may have been made designedly? Take, again, the inscriptions on the cross, which vary in form. Which is the true form? We have no evidence that the Holy Spirit supplemented omissions, or corrected statements, in case of error in the documents employed by the sacred writers. On the other hand, we have no evidence that these documents originally contained errors. Different modes of statement, as long as there is no contradiction, are not errors. Omissions are not necessarily errors. Quotations which are not verbally identical with the original passages are not errors, unless we can prove that it was the intention of the writer making citations to quote verbatim. Utterances not scientifically accurate are not errors, for the Bible employs popular language, not the language of formulated science. Scientific men speak as the Bible does; they never think of using scientific language in ordinary conversation. Expressions conformed to the popular views and philosophy of the times are not errors, unless it can be shown that they were intended to endorse those views and that philosophy. We all use terms that belong to systems of philosophy exploded long ago, and yet we are not accused of sanctioning those systems. When we speak of a jovial, saturnine, or mercurial disposition, we do not declare our belief in astrology. Had the sacred writers expressed themselves otherwise than they did, they would have made themselves liable to misapprehension. They wrote to be understood. To do this they were obliged to clothe their thoughts with the changing garb of human language. The thoughts remain; but their form is subject to change.

If any positive errors are found in the Scriptures, it must be proved that they existed in the original documents, and were not introduced through the blunders of transcribers, before they can be charged upon the sacred writers. Here sacred criticism finds a field for its exercise; and it is probable that if it possessed all the appliances necessary for the purpose, it could remove every error alleged to exist in the Bible. But suppose that the appliances of criticism have been exhausted, and that the errors still remain. The objector must then show that the errors are of such a character as to vitiate the documents in which they exist, and thus render them unfit for the purpose for which they were used. A document might contain an omission, or an inaccurate statement, and yet be of infallible authority on the point intended to be proved by it. The genealogical table of Matthew omits some names in the lineage of Christ, and yet furnishes the proof that He descended from Abraham through David, the very thing which the writer intended to prove by it. It is infallible for this purpose; but it is not infallible as a list of Jewish kings. An inaccurate statement is different from an omission, yet if it is a statement in no way affecting the document in the character in which it is employed, and for the truth of which the sacred writers do not intend to vouch, the document containing it may be, notwithstanding, infallible for the purpose intended by its use. It is a true document, teaching what it was intended to teach; and so far it has inspired authority. Inspiration did not render the sacred writers omniscient: it only secured them from error in their teaching. It is easily conceivable, therefore, how a document employed by them for a certain purpose, and infallible for that purpose, might, in regard to some things having no relation to the matter on hand, contain incorrect statements. This I say is conceivable, though I do not admit that it is the case, for the reason that I do not know. In my opinion, no instance of erroneous statement, in any of the documents of Scripture, has been conclusively proved. The presumption is that they are infallible in all their statements of facts, so far as the sacred penmen intended to vouch for the truth of these facts. In some things they may not have aimed at mathematical exactness; and in others they may have expressed the popular ideas of their times. But in all cases the substantial truth was maintained.

To get rid of the difficulty raised by Dr. Bannerman, I cannot adopt his view, that revelation and inspiration are co-extensive. It is not easy to see why things with which they were personally conversant, or which they could procure from well-known documents, should be revealed to the sacred writers. All that was necessary was divine direction to use them, and divine guidance in the use of them. Moreover, the view of

Dr. Bannerman does not conform to facts. Luke says that he wrote from his own 'perfect understanding of all things from the very first.'

The author of the Book of Ecclesiastes, who was inspired, gives, like Asaph (Ps. lxxiii.), the results of his own meditations and reasonings; and in the Book of Job, the friends of that afflicted man utter many things wide of the truth. Neither Job nor his friends were inspired, so far as we know; nor had they revelations. They gave utterance to their own thoughts. All that devolved upon the sacred penman was to make an infallible record of their thoughts. It can scarcely be believed that, in addition to the document containing them, if any such existed, a revelation was made of them to the canonical writer, whoever he was.

It seems to me, in view of all the circumstances of the case, that we must rest in the following conclusions :—

(1) The sacred writers acted under plenary inspiration in the selection of materials, and in committing them to writing.

(2) The documents which they employed in their writings were rendered, by virtue of the plenary inspiration of those who employed them, infallible for the end for which they were used.

(3) We have no evidence that the sacred writers supplied omissions in these documents, unless it was necessary for the end in view.

(4) Positive errors, within the sphere of inspired teaching, were not admitted.

(5) If seeming errors exist, we ought to rest in the conclusion that if we had the means at our command to elucidate the text, they would disappear.

CHAPTER IV.

NATURE AND EXTENT OF INSPIRATION.

THE Bible contains two elements,—a divine and a human. God is its Author, and man is its author. The divine authorship has been already exhibited.[1] We have the testimony of the sacred writers to the fact, which testimony they present in a variety of forms. They expressly assert that the Holy Spirit spoke by them; that all their official writings had the character of infallible truth, and possessed absolute authority; that as prophets and apostles they spoke and acted for God; and that what they said, He said. Hence the frequently recurring formulas: 'Thus saith the Lord;' 'The Holy Ghost spake;' 'The word of the Lord;' 'It is written.' More explicit terms could not have been used had the Scriptures proceeded from God alone.

In making known His revelation to men, God might have dispensed with human instrumentality. He might have spoken as He spoke from Mount Sinai, and written as He wrote upon the tables of stone; and the words uttered or written would have been the same as we actually find them in the Bible recorded by human hands. The same formulas: 'Thus saith the Lord,' 'The Holy Ghost spake,' 'The word of the Lord,' would express the supernatural character of the message, and assert its infallible truth and divine authority. Indeed, no fitter terms could be chosen for such a purpose.

[1] Part II. chap. vii.

But what God might have done does not pertain to us to inquire: our concern is with what He has actually done. This can be easily ascertained. The same Scriptures that claim to be the word of God, claim also to be the word of man. While God chose human language as the medium of His communications, He chose also human agents to record them. These agents were not instruments like a pen in the hand of a writer. They were authors—authors as really as if they had been the only agency employed in the production of the Scriptures.

The evidence of the human authorship is as distinct and strong as it is in the case of the divine. It is of the same kind and embodied very much in the same form. We find it, just as in the case of the divine authorship, in the testimony of the sacred writers, who affirm their own agency, as if there had been no other employed; and their direct assertion is confirmed by many forms of indirect implication. The formula is changed as to the person, and instead of 'Thus saith the Lord,' we read, 'The prophet Isaiah saith' (John xii. 38, 39, 41; Rom. ix. 27, 29, x. 16, 20). 'Then was fulfilled that which was spoken by Jeremiah the prophet' (Matt. ii. 17). 'I Paul say unto you;' 'Ye see how large a letter I have written unto you with mine own hand' (Gal. v. 2, vi. 11). 'That the law of Moses should not be broken' (John vii. 23). 'Did not Moses give you the law?' (John vii. 19). 'For David speaketh concerning,' etc. (Acts ii. 25).

These, and many other testimonies to the human authorship of Scripture which might be cited, correspond in a striking manner to the evidence of its divine authorship already adduced. They are of exactly the same sort that we find in any uninspired book, when it speaks of its human origin; and in the case of the

Bible they could not have been different, had there been only human agency concerned in it.

But in addition to the direct testimonies to the human authorship of the Bible, so nearly parallel to those quoted in proof of its divine, we discover human features impressed upon its whole frame and style. These are exactly analogous to the divine features, which constitute so large a portion of the proof of inspiration. We find throughout the volume of Scripture differences of style and diversities of statement in matters of detail. Each author has his own manner of expressing his thoughts. When we read Isaiah, we say this is not the style of Jeremiah, or of Ezekiel; and when we read John, we say this is not the style of Paul.

The individuality of the sacred writers, exhibited in connection with the controlling agency of the Holy Spirit, is beautifully illustrated by Professor Gaussen, in his work on *Inspiration*. 'As a skilful musician,' says Professor Gaussen, 'who has to execute alone a long score, will avail himself by turns of the funereal flute, the shepherd's pipe, the dancer's bagpipe, or the warrior's trumpet; thus the Almighty God, to proclaim to us His eternal word, has chosen of old the instruments into which He would successfully breathe the breath of His Spirit. He chose them before the foundation of the world; He separated them from their mother's womb.'

'Have you visited the cathedral of Freyburg, and listened to that wonderful organist, who, with such enchantment, draws the tears from the traveller's eyes, while he touches, one after another, his wonderful keys, and makes you hear by turns the march of armies upon the beach, or the chaunted prayer upon the lake during the tempest, or the voices of praise after its calm? All your senses are overwhelmed, for it has all passed before you like a vivid reality. Well, thus the eternal God, powerful in harmony, touches by turns with the fingers of His Spirit the keys which He had chosen for the hour of His design, and for the unity of His celestial hymn. He had before Him, from eternity, all the human keys; His creating eyes embraced, at a glance, this key-board of sixty centuries; and when He would make this fallen world hear the eternal counsel of its redemption and the advent of the Son of God, He laid His right hand on Enoch, the seventh from Adam, and His left hand on John, the humble and sublime prisoner of Patmos. The celestial hymn, seven hundred years before the deluge, began with these words: 'Behold, the Lord cometh with ten thousand of His saints to judge the world;' but already in the thought of God, and in the eternal harmony of His work, the voice of John was responding to that of Enoch, and terminating the hymn, three thousand years after him, with these words: 'Behold, He cometh, and every eye shall see him, yea, those that pierced Him! Even so, Lord Jesus, come quickly. Amen!' And during this hymn of three thousand years, the Spirit of God did not cease to breathe upon all His ambassadors; 'the angels stooped,' says an apostle, 'to contemplate its depths; the elect of God were moved, and eternal life descended into their souls.'

These ambassadors did not all speak or write alike. 'It was,' says Professor Gaussen, 'sometimes the sublime and untutored simplicity of John; sometimes the excited, elliptical, startling, argumentative energy of Paul; sometimes the fervour and solemnity of Peter; it was the majestic poetry of Isaiah, or the lyrical poetry of David; it was the simple and majestic narrative of Moses, or the sententious and royal wisdom of Solomon. Yes, it was all that; it was Peter; it was

Isaiah; it was Matthew; it was John; it was Moses; but it was God!'[1]

'It was Matthew; it was John; it was Moses; it was God.' The Bible is all of man, and it is all of God. The fact that the sacred writers preserved their individuality is a proof that inspiration did not destroy their conscious self-control. 'The spirits of the prophets are subject to the prophets' (1 Cor. xiv. 32). Inspired men were not thrown into a state of ecstasy, in which their understandings were held in abeyance, while they gave utterance to words of which they knew not the import. They did not speak or write in spite of themselves, as was the case, according to the belief of the heathen, with the utterers of oracles. From the beginning of the Bible to its end, there is evidence of their calm, constant self-control, and dispassionate judgment. They all spoke and wrote like men in the full possession of their faculties, and just as we would expect men of their age and circumstances to speak and write. They spoke and wrote, it is true, under divine influence and guidance; but this was perfectly consistent with their conscious self-control, and their conscious self-control was perfectly consistent with supernatural direction. In the affairs of this life, we often act under the conscious direction of others, while, at the same time, we feel that we have perfect control over our own faculties, and experience no difficulty in the case. There is, therefore, no reason why any difficulty should be raised in the case of inspiration.

With this view of the matter, it is a perversion of the doctrine of inspiration to represent it as reducing the sacred writers to mere machines, as though they were carried along by an impulse, which destroyed

---

Theopneusty; or the Plenary Inspiration of the Holy Scriptures. By S. R. L. Gaussen. New York: Baker & Scribner. 1846. Pp. 64–66.

their own voluntary activity. If the Spirit of God can lead a man to repent and believe, and persevere in holiness, without interfering with his consciousness and liberty, why may He not guide the mental operations of a man, so as to enable him to speak and write, without interfering with his liberty and self-control? The difficulty, so far as it regards the understanding, or the explanation of it, is as great in the one case as in the other.

The conclusion from the testimony and the facts of Scripture, which prove a twofold authorship, is that the two agencies—the divine and the human—employed in its composition are so combined as to produce one undivided and indivisible result. Notwithstanding the exercise of human agency in writing the Bible, it is all alike divine; and notwithstanding the divine agency employed in its composition, it is all alike human. The divine and the human elements together constitute a theanthropic book.

In accepting this conclusion, we accept along with it the difficulty of understanding it, and acknowledge the impossibility of explaining it. How such a union of the divine and human agencies in the one result of an inspired book can be effected, while, on the one hand, the power of God does not supersede the faculties of man, and, on the other hand, the freedom of man is not incompatible with the operation of God, it is impossible for us to understand. But it does not follow from the impossibility of our understanding it, that it is an actual impossibility, beyond the power of God to effect it. There are many things which we cannot understand, or explain, which are not only possible, but actual facts, and which upon sufficient evidence we unhesitatingly believe. We accept the evidence in spite of the difficulty or mystery of the fact to be believed, and we do so on the reasonable ground, that

R

difficulties which are not impossibilities, and which may derive all their plausibility and force from our own ignorance, amount to a very slight presumption against the truth of facts supported by abundant and reliable testimony. Such, we believe, is the testimony in the present instance.

However inexplicable the union of the two elements in Scripture may be, it is not a fact that stands alone in the world. It has an analogue in the person of Christ.

Dr. Schaff, in his introduction to Lange's *Commentary on Matthew*, beautifully remarks: 'The Bible, like the person and work of our Saviour, is theanthropic in its character and aim. The eternal personal Word of God "was made flesh," and the whole fulness of the Godhead and of sinless humanity was united in one person for ever. So the spoken word of God may be said to have become flesh in the Bible. It is, therefore, all divine and yet all human from beginning to end. Through the veil of the letter we behold the glory of the eternal truth of God. The divine and human in the Bible sustain a similar relation to each other as in the person of Christ: they are unmixed, yet inseparably united, and constitute but one life, which kindles life in the heart of the believer.'

The analogy between the written Word and the incarnate Word is sufficiently indicated in Scripture by the application of the same term to both. They are both called the Word of God, or simply the Word (John i. 1, 14; 1 Tim. iv. 2; Jas. i. 22, 23; 1 Pet. ii. 2; Isa. xl. 8; Luke viii. 11; Rom. x. 17; 2 Cor. iv. 2; Eph. vi. 17; Heb. iv. 12, vi. 5; 1 Pet. i. 23; Rev. xix. 13).

The limits and extent of this analogy lie within the confines of a mystery which the human intellect cannot unveil. We ought, therefore, to speak with caution and modesty; but, at the same time, so far as the Scriptures warrant it, with confidence. On their authority we can confidently affirm that the person of Christ is theanthropic, and that they themselves are theanthropic. But this analogy must not be pressed so far as to extend it to the person of Christ and the persons of the sacred writers; for the incarnation of the Eternal Word is personal, and the revelation of divine wisdom in human language is impersonal. Notwithstanding this limitation, the analogy is true. Christ is God and man. The two natures—the divine and the human—exist in His person, without confusion, without absorption of the human into the divine, and without suspension of the powers of humanity by deity. His whole life exhibited the free and plenary development of divine and of human agency. The fulness of the Godhead and the perfection of humanity dwelt in Him bodily.

Notwithstanding the fulness of the Godhead and the perfection of humanity dwelt in Jesus Christ, His human nature was subject to the limitations of that nature. It was subject to human laws. He was a child and grew up to manhood. He 'increased in wisdom' (Luke ii. 52). He suffered hunger and thirst, weariness of body, and sorrow of mind. He wept. He prayed in agony. He was crucified. He was laid in the grave. In these things we see the weakness of humanity. He raised the dead. He calmed the fury of the waves by a word. He rose from the grave and ascended into heaven. Here we see divine power.

In a similar manner, we observe in the sacred writers, progress in knowledge, human limitation; but at the same time they furnish evidence of supernatural knowledge. The phenomena of their writings cannot be explained, except on the hypothesis of a divine power co-operating with them, or working in them, in such a way as to produce a book at once human and divine.

In the person of Christ we perceive the co-existence of the infinite and finite, and their co-operation. It is a great mystery, insolvable by human minds. For aught we know, it may be a mystery to angels. It is this mystery of the co-existence and co-operation of the infinite and finite that creates the difficulty, upon which the psychological objection to the twofold authorship of Scripture and to plenary inspiration in general is founded. The objection is, as already intimated, that the doctrine of a twofold authorship represents the sacred writers as mere machines. Such an authorship, say the objectors, is inconsistent with the use of men's faculties according to their natural laws. This difficulty is removed, if not explained, by the union of the infinite and the finite, and by their harmonious co-operation in the person of Christ. Whatever may be the metaphysical difficulties of the problem of the union of these two, it has been solved as a historical fact. We point to the person of Christ, and say, Behold the solution!

But we have other analogies illustrative of a twofold agency in the authorship of the Holy Scriptures.

One of these is the gracious agency of the Holy Spirit upon the mind and heart of the Christian. Regeneration, conversion, and sanctification are ascribed to the Holy Spirit. He is the divine agent who applies the benefits of redemption, and renders the means of grace effectual to the soul. In regeneration, or in imparting new life to the dead in sin, He exercises creative power; but in sanctification He works in harmony with our own free-will. We are not conscious of force, or violence. We act freely—so freely that the work of sanctification is sometimes spoken of in Scripture as our own. We are commanded to convert ourselves, to be holy, to make to ourselves a new heart, while at the same time we are told that it is God who worketh in us both to will and to do His good pleasure. In the full persuasion that it is God who works in us, and in the full persuasion of our own freedom, we pray with David, 'Create in me a clean heart, O God; and renew a right spirit within me' (Ps. li. 10).

All this is matter of experience. In the work of divine grace accomplished upon the heart of man, there is a divine agency which nothing can supersede. At the same time, the laws of man's intellectual and spiritual being maintain their freedom and integrity. Truths adapted to the understanding are addressed to it; motives fitted to influence the will are applied; and Christ is presented as an object of love to gain the affections. Our whole intellectual and moral nature is influenced in perfect harmony with the laws which govern it. In the work of the Holy Spirit upon the soul, there is nothing at variance with the laws and principles of the human constitution.

We have another analogy in the providence of God, in which we perceive a harmony of the divine and the human agencies, when they meet in and conspire to the same end. God is present in all nature, 'upholding all things by the word of His power.' He has established the laws of nature; and yet, in many instances, human agency is necessary to carry these laws into effect for the accomplishment of special ends. Without the appointments of God, in these instances, human instrumentality could effect nothing; and without human agency, the divine appointments or laws of nature would be equally inefficient. The two co-operate without any interference of the one with the other. Man acts freely in harmony with the fixedness of natural law. We have evidence of this in our actions, and in every voluntary movement of life. In all these we find the power of God uniting with the power of man in its freedom.

We observe the same thing in history, which furnishes us with a commentary upon the providence of God exercised over the world. Take the case of Joseph, who was sold by his brethren and carried as a slave into Egypt. They acted freely; yet Joseph told them afterward, that God sent him into Egypt to save their lives by a great deliverance. Nebuchadnezzar furnishes another example. He accomplished the divine purpose in the punishment of the surrounding nations. He acted freely, while he was merely an instrument in the hand of God. These two instances are not similar to the co-operation of the human and the divine in the case of the sacred writers; for the purpose of God, in each case, was unknown to them, and of course they could not act with reference to it. The sacred penmen knew the divine purpose, and they wrote under the conscious guidance of the Holy Spirit. The cases specified prove, however, the co-operation of the divine and the human agencies under circumstances in which the divine and the human purposes were directly opposed to each other. The human agents were unconsciously controlled by the divine, and yet acted with perfect freedom. They acted in accordance with human motives. If the human and the divine can co-operate, in such cases, without the suspension of man's free agency, why can they not co-operate when they are in accord?

The psychological difficulty, if such it may be called, seems as inexplicable in the co-operation of two human minds, in which one directs the other. The teacher and the pupil work together—the latter working under the direction of the former—in the solution of a question in physics, mathematics, astronomy, or in any other science. The demonstration may, in a certain sense, be called the teacher's; and in another sense it may be called the pupil's; or it may be said to be the work of both. Suppose that, instead of one pupil, fifty were under the instruction of the same teacher, and all employed together in the solution of the same problem. The mind of the teacher would co-operate with all these, acting each in accordance with the laws of his intellectual nature, and displaying each his own individuality in the progress of the solution. The teacher might properly say, I taught them to demonstrate that problem; and the pupils might with equal propriety say, We demonstrated it. Both say the truth. Can any one explain the mode of co-operation, or of assistance, on the part of the teacher's mind with the minds of the pupils? No one will say that the pupils were mere machines. They acted according to the laws of their intellectual nature.

We might mention, moreover, the controlling influence which a superior mind has over others. Every one who approached the first Napoleon, felt, at the first glance, the power of his mighty intellect. His very presence inspired fresh thought in the mind of the dullest. His commands controlled his marshals and generals in battle, while every movement, every thrust of the sword, was an act of their own free-will. Napoleon's will was theirs; and their wills were Napoleon's. At Austerlitz, hundreds of thousands of wills were his, each maintaining its own freedom. It may be said that the army is a mere machine. In a certain sense it is; and, in another sense, it is not; or rather it is a voluntary machine. Every act of every soldier composing it is just as free as if his were the only will in the universe. He can refuse to march, or to shoot, and suffer the consequences of disobedience. The fact that he does march and shoot only proves that his will is controlled by motive. The power of motive, however, is compatible with freedom.

It has been already remarked that we know nothing of the method of the Spirit's operation upon the minds of the sacred writers. We know only its effects; and these effects we learn from the didactic statements of the Bible, and from its actual phenomena. Our ignorance of the mode of inspiration does not disprove the fact, any more than our ignorance of the mode of anything disproves the fact of the existence of that thing. We believe in the existence of the soul and body, though we do not know the mode of their existence. We believe in the divine influence in the work of sanctification, though we know nothing of the manner in which the Holy Spirit operates.

From the Bible we learn that the effect of inspiration was to render the sacred writer who was the subject of it, the infallible organ of the Holy Spirit in communicating truth in relation to all matters which he was inspired to teach. This is clearly taught by the formulas: 'Isaiah said,' 'David said,' and 'the Holy Ghost said,' which mean precisely the same thing, and are interchanged as synonymous in the Holy Scriptures. The nature of the truth communicated makes no difference. It may be a historical fact, a doctrine, or a scientific truth. The effect of inspiration is the same. It renders the sacred writer infallible in regard to each one and all of them. 'The Scripture cannot be broken' (John x. 35), *i.e.* it cannot err. 'All Scripture is given by inspiration of God' (2 Tim. iii. 16).

The sacred writers committed many things to writing, which they knew as matters of history, and as doctrines of religion and morality; but their subjective apprehension of these things made no difference as to the character of the record. It was as fully inspired as any other portion of Scripture. They wrote officially as inspired men commissioned by God to put on record His whole revealed will; and whatever they wrote in that capacity, though it might have been subjectively apprehended by them, had the seal of divine authority and infallibility.

It was not necessary that revelations objectively presented to the minds of the sacred writers should be subjectively apprehended before they could accomplish their object. A man's understanding of a revelation and the revelation itself are very different things; and the objective truth presented to the mind would remain equally true and equally a communication from God, although not apprehended at all by the person to whom it was revealed. It may not have been intended for his information and profit, but for others to whom it may convey truth not understood by the first; just as a messenger may carry a message of which he does not understand the import, and which does not concern himself, from one person to another. The Apostle Peter seems to intimate that this was the case with the prophets: ' Unto whom it was revealed, that not unto themselves, but unto us, they did minister the things which are now reported unto you by them which have preached the gospel unto you with the Holy Ghost sent down from heaven' (1 Pet. i. 12).

It may be a question whether the ancient prophets were entirely ignorant of any of the revelations made to them; but, admitting that they were ignorant of some, such revelations were nevertheless communications from God, intended not for the information and benefit of the prophets, but for the benefit of future times. Their duty was merely to make an infallible record of such revelations, which were to be elucidated by the unfolding of the divine plan.

The infallibility of the sacred writers was not a personal attribute, but a miraculous gift conferred upon them for a special purpose, and available for no other end. It did not preserve them from error in judgment or conduct, in the ordinary affairs of life. Peter erred at Antioch (Gal. ii. 11–14) ; and Paul may have erred in judgment when he complied with the legal ceremonial to conciliate the Jews (Acts xxi. 26). They might, moreover, while inspired, be ignorant of the arts and sciences, and even of theology, in the technical sense of that term. Inspiration does not imply the illumination of their minds with all truth. It does not even imply, as already intimated, that they fully understood what they spoke and wrote (1 Pet. i. 10–12). A distinction must be made between infallibility as the result of omniscience, and infallibility as the result of divine guidance. The neglect of this distinction is the source of many popular objections to the doctrine of inspiration. The sacred writers were ignorant of many things ; but they possessed divine guidance in their official work, and in that work only were they infallible. This work was the communication of what God willed to be communicated in His word. These writers may have differed among themselves in their subjective apprehension of the truth. Isaiah and Jonah, Jeremiah and Nahum, Paul and James, Matthew and John, do not stand upon the same level as to their subjective state. Isaiah had clearer and more comprehensive views of the kingdom of the Messiah than the other prophets ; and Paul's views of the plan of redemption excelled in clearness and compass those of the other apostles. This is perfectly consistent with their plenary inspiration, and the consequent infallibility and perfect agreement of their teaching. Some had greater clearness of intellectual apprehension than others, and were freer from personal and national prejudices; consequently they would possess greater clearness and breadth of views. Had the Holy Spirit inspired Sir Isaac Newton, in the maturity of his intellect, and an unlettered peasant, both would have been infallible in the matters which were the objects of inspiration; but it by no means follows that the peasant would have attained to that comprehensive grasp of those matters to which the great philosopher would have attained. There would be a great difference between an inspired man of large attainments and an inspired child, yet both would be infallible within the limits of their inspiration.

Inspiration being a miraculous gift conferred upon the sacred writers for a special purpose, and available for no other, it follows that the apostles might not always possess infallibility in their preaching, unless their preaching at any time was intended to form a part of divine revelation. The power of working miracles was not a personal attribute. They possessed it occasionally for the confirmation of their divine mission. The infallibility of their preaching may also have been occasional, confined to those occasions when they were speaking under the miraculous influence of the Holy Spirit.

Inspiration extends equally to every part of Scripture. This is what is called plenary inspiration, as opposed to partial, which limits it to parts of the Bible. There are portions of the Holy Scriptures, such as the serpent's falsehood to Eve, and the conversations between Job and his friends, which are not inspired. The sacred penmen have only transmitted to us the record of them, which is an infallible narrative of manners as they occurred, without vouching for their truth or sound morality. But whatever these penmen were commissioned to teach, whether of doctrine or fact, is of inspired authority; and this authority extends to every canonical book, and to every part of it, with such exceptions as those which have been just mentioned, and which every man of common intelligence can eliminate from the sentiments and direct teaching of the writer.

The inspiration of every book of the sacred canon, and of every part of each book, has been admitted as an established truth by both the Jewish and the Christian Churches; the former admitting the inspiration of the Old Testament, and the latter the inspiration of the whole Bible. If any one denies it, he must prove that the Jewish Church was mistaken in receiving into the canon the books that compose the Old Testament; that Christ and His apostles were mistaken in referring to all parts of the Old Testament as the word of God; and that the Christian Church is mistaken in receiving into it the same books and those of the New Testament,—a task which, in view of the overwhelming evidence of their canonicity, would seem to be hopeless.

But admit that some one might succeed in proving any of the books of Scripture to be uncanonical, it would not affect the character and authority of the others, unless the unity and organism of Scripture were thereby destroyed. Inspiration is claimed only for the canonical Scriptures; and until the proof of the uncanonicity of any of them is fairly and clearly made out, we assume, with the Church in all ages, their canonicity, and claim for them inspired authority. They are all alike infallible in what they teach; and inspiration extends to all their contents, whether these contents are moral or religious truths, or historical and scientific facts. In a word, it extends to everything which the sacred writers assert to be true.

The plenary inspiration of the Holy Scriptures is involved in, or follows as a necessary consequence from, the proposition that the sacred writers were the organs of God. If what they assert, God asserts, which is the scriptural idea of inspiration, their assertions must be free from error. Moreover, our Lord expressly says, 'The Scripture cannot be broken' (John x. 35), *i.e.* it cannot err; and both He and His apostles refer to all parts of the Old Testament as the Word of God. They make no distinction as to the authority of the Law, the Prophets, or the Hagiographa. They quote the Pentateuch, the Historical Books, the Psalms, and the Prophets, as all and equally the Word of God. They refer also to all classes of facts recorded in the Old Testament as infallibly true. Not only doctrinal facts, such as those of the creation and probation of man, his apostasy; the covenant with Abraham, the giving of the Law upon Mount Sinai; not only great historical facts, as the deluge, the deliverance of the people out of Egypt, the passage of the Red Sea, and the like; but incidental circumstances or facts of apparently minor importance, as, *e.g.* the temptation of our first parents by Satan in the form of a serpent; the lifting up of the serpent in the wilderness by Moses; the healing of Naaman the Syrian by Elisha, and the mission of that prophet to the widow of Sarepta; David's eating the shew-bread in the house of God; and Jonah's three days' captivity in the whale's belly, are all referred to by our Lord and His apostles with the sublime simplicity and confidence with which they are received by little children.

'It lies in the very idea of the Bible, that God chose some men to write history, some to indite psalms, some to unfold the future, some to teach doctrines. All were equally His organs, and each was infallible in his own sphere. As the principle of vegetable life pervades the whole plant, the root, stem, and flower— as the life of the body belongs as much to the feet as to the head, so the Spirit of God pervades the whole

Scripture, and is not more in one part than in another. Some members of the body are more important than others; and some books of the Bible could be far better spared than others. There may be as great a difference between St. John's Gospel and the Book of Chronicles as between a man's brain and the hair of his head; nevertheless the life of the body is as truly in the hair as in the brain.'[1]

Objections, founded upon the individuality of the sacred writers and upon their personal fallibility and imperfection, have been urged against the plenary inspiration of the Scriptures. Some of these objections have been already anticipated and answered; nevertheless it may not be amiss to state them more fully.

When treating of the individuality of the sacred writers, we intimated that the Scriptures are all of human authorship, and that they are all of divine authorship; that thus they have a double authorship. This was admitted to be a mystery, but not an impossibility, as the illustrative facts then adduced fully show. The admission of this double authorship, of the existence of a human element in Scripture as distinct as though the sacred writers had not been inspired at all, meets and refutes all these objections to plenary inspiration founded upon their individuality, which we see everywhere pervading the sacred volume. We see it embodied in the shape of the expression of their own personal feelings, experience, and beliefs. This is especially observable in the Psalms, which exhibit a vivid picture of the inner life of the spiritual man, and contain a record of the personal experience of their authors. For this reason some of them have been looked upon as mere uninspired expressions of

---

[1] Hodge's *Systematic Theology*, Vol. I. pp. 163, 164. New York: Scribner & Co. 1872.

human feeling. They are certainly expressions of human feeling; but this does not destroy their inspiration, unless it can be shown that these expressions are manifestly immoral. Even the immorality of them would not prove a psalm to be uninspired, in those instances in which the psalmist merely relates his own experience and thoughts, without any claim of the divine approval of them. Asaph describes, in the seventy-third Psalm, his thoughts and feelings when he saw the prosperity of the wicked; but he does not say that these thoughts and feelings were right in the sight of God. No; he confesses the contrary in those humble, penitential words: 'So foolish was I, and ignorant; I was as a beast before Thee' (Ps. lxxiii. 21).

David asserted that, 'The Spirit of the Lord spake by him, and that His word was in his tongue' (2 Sam. xxiii. 2); he belonged to that prophetic order of men upon whom God was pleased to bestow the gift of inspiration; the book which contains his compositions and those of the authors associated with him was recognised and sanctioned by our Lord and the New Testament writers, as belonging equally with the Law and the Prophets to the Old Testament canon; and yet these very same authors give a record of their feelings and experience in words which every penitent and true worshipper can appropriate as expressive of his own. The two things are perfectly consistent, on the principle or doctrine which we have maintained, that inspiration did not interfere with the individuality of the sacred writers. They spoke and wrote like one of ourselves.

We explain in the same way the variety of conception and expression in their statements of the same truth and in their narratives of the same events, which some have regarded as inconsistent with plenary inspiration. The proper statement of the place of the human element is sufficient to account for all these diversities. So also in regard to the inscriptions on the cross, the variations of which are due to the more or the less full statement of the same facts. There is nothing in any of the statements inconsistent with each other, or with the reality of the fact. They are true, viewed as human statements; and what is true in a human writing or statement is also true in one divinely inspired.

The appeal often made by the sacred writers to their own testimony as eye-witnesses, or to their own knowledge as men personally cognisant of the facts or truths which they record, is frequently referred to as decisive evidence against the doctrine of plenary inspiration. But this objection is refuted by the admission of a human authorship, in the way already explained. Moreover, the sacred writers do not disclaim any other source of information. On the contrary, they claim divine guidance.

Different arrangements, which have perplexed harmonists so much, are explained in the same manner.

The fact that the sacred writers exhibited human fallibility by occasional errors of conduct is perfectly consistent with the view of inspiration that we have taken. It has been already intimated that a distinction must be made between their official and their personal character. Officially, they were the recipients of a communication from God, which they were commissioned to convey, without error, to the page of Scripture. This, however, did not involve exemption from error in word or deed in other relations. David and Peter sinned grievously. Indeed Balaam, who is called a prophet, was a wicked man. He had the gift of inspiration, but not the faith which justifies, nor the grace which sanctifies. A failure to observe this distinction has led to many mistakes.

Plenary inspiration is perfectly consistent with the natural deficiencies of the sacred penmen as writers. Some of these were deficient in education, in literary capacity, in intellectual endowment, and in refinement. Those things had nothing to do with inspiration. They belonged to the sacred writers as men; and when they received the divine commission to write, it was not necessary to endow them with the taste and to adorn them with the classic elegance of Sophocles and Plato. Inspiration did not change a single faculty of the mind; neither did it supply information on any subject beyond its sphere. It did not make grammarians, rhetoricians, nor logicians. In these things it left the man as it found him. Had this been kept in mind, the extremes of the Hebraists and the Purists would have been avoided. The Scriptures would not have been represented, on the one hand, as abounding in Hebrew idioms and constructions, and in solecisms; nor, on the other hand, as models of classic excellence, and standards of literary taste.

The exposure of the sacred volume to those causes which affect the integrity of the text has been already considered in the chapter on the 'Integrity of the Holy Scriptures.' It was there shown that the Bible is subject to all those causes that affect the integrity of other books. This is quite consistent with the doctrine of plenary inspiration. Having bestowed upon us the gift of His Holy Word, it has not been the good pleasure of God to preserve it from corruption by a continual miracle. He has given us the light and the atmosphere; but if men exclude the light from their dwellings and poison the atmosphere, He does not miraculously interfere to prevent the pernicious consequences. If we receive a valuable gift, it is our duty to preserve it. Did we depend upon miraculous interpositions to remedy the evil effects of

S

our negligence, all motives to watchfulness and caution would be removed.

Statements in Scripture which do not come from God, and which are not sanctioned by His authority, are consistent with the doctrine of plenary inspiration.

Portions of Scripture have a dramatic character. Persons of different moral character are introduced as speaking and acting. They give utterance to sentiments which accord with their character. The sacred historian gives a record of these; but unless he endorses them, they cannot be used as an argument against his inspiration. No one accuses a historian of holding the sentiments of the characters that he describes; nor does any one accuse Milton of entertaining the sentiments which he makes Satan utter in his *Paradise Lost.* Such sentiments are suitable to the persons in whose mouths they are put, but may be very abhorrent to the historian and poet.

In the matter under consideration, we must inquire whether the opinions expressed are sanctioned by the sacred writer or not, which, as a general rule, can be easily determined by the context; or, as in the case of Job's friends, by a direct expression of disapprobation. In the same way we must determine the character of quotations and actions. We must inquire: Are the quotations adopted by the sacred writer? are the actions approved? A mere record of them, however erroneous and immoral they may be, without adoption and approval of them, is consistent with plenary inspiration.

Many quotations are made by the writers of the New Testament from the Old, which have occasioned difficulty in the minds of many in regard to the subject of plenary inspiration. Some of these quotations are strictly prophetical. In others the language of the Old Testament is incorporated with the body of Christian doctrine. The form in which they are made is not always the same. (1) Some are taken literally from the Septuagint version, where it differs from the Hebrew. (2) Where the Septuagint does not represent the true sense of the Hebrew, the authors of the New Testament abandon it and give their own translation. (3) Some differ from both the original text and the Septuagint version, even where, according to our exegesis, the Hebrew and the Greek translation correspond to each other. (4) When the Septuagint has attached a particular meaning to a passage in the Hebrew, one New Testament writer builds his argument upon the literal sense of the original, while another adopts for his purpose the sense given to it in the Greek version.[1]

In regard to the whole matter of quotations in the New Testament from the Old, we observe (1) that 'It is a point to be determined by the ordinary laws of interpretation in the case of the Bible as much as in the case of any other book, how far and in what way the quotations made by the author are adopted by him as true, and he makes himself responsible for them. If they are adopted by the author as true, and made part of his own statement of fact or opinion, then from whatever source they may come, and how much soever they may differ from the original text from which they are taken, the author, if a merely human author, pledges his own veracity for the truth of the statements they express; if an inspired author, he pledges the veracity of God.'[2]

Were the apostles living now and preaching to English and Germans, they would, for general purposes, quote, as any men of common sense would do, the English and German versions of the Scriptures, with-

[1] Lee on *Inspiration*, Lect. VII. pp. 317–321.
[2] Bannerman on *Inspiration*, p. 532.

out intimating, on every occasion, that in this and in that particular they fail to represent the sense of the orginal. In the same way they quoted the Septuagint, as the version in the language of those to whom they were preaching and writing. But this does not, on the one hand, make the translation infallible; nor, on the other hand, does it furnish an argument against their plenary inspiration. They quoted it as they would have quoted any other book; and the quotations must have been appropriate to their subject, otherwise they would not have made them. The accuracy of the translation was not an object of inspiration, and consequently did not belong to its sphere.

(2) 'The limits within which quotations may differ from the original text from which they are taken, in point of language and form, without being liable to the charge of being untrue or misquotations, must depend upon the purpose for which they are made, and the terms in which they are referred to. There is a wide latitude in this respect allowed in human writings, without the least suspicion of unfaithfulness or even inaccuracy attaching to the author. From the most distant allusion to the language, in which no more than the form of the expression is appropriated, up to the entire transference both of language and meaning from the page of one author to the page of the other, we find quotations employed by human writers, and not justly or reasonably chargeable with misquotation. The object in view, and the manner and terms of quotation, must in all cases determine the limits within which the language and application of the quotation may vary from the original quoted.'[1]

(3) The writers of the New Testament sometimes affix to quotations from the Old Testament ' a meaning unknown to the original author, and not in his

---

[1] Bannerman on *Inspiration*, p. 533

view when he employed the words quoted; and yet a meaning which the words truly and properly bear, and which may be used for the confirmation of facts and doctrines beyond what he could possibly have been acquainted with.'[1]

This mode of quotation could not be justified in the case of uninspired writers, but we would expect it in the case of inspired authors. The subjective apprehension of the truth, we have already stated, was not the same in all. Some had clearer and more comprehensive views than others. It was quite consistent, therefore, with the inspiration of both the Old and the New Testament authors, that the latter, possessing more illumination than the former, should quote as they have done, sometimes giving the exact translation of the Hebrew text; at other times, the words of the Septuagint, in passages in which it differs from the Hebrews; and sometimes confining themselves to neither. The truths of the Old Testament were more fully revealed to them than to its own authors. It was natural, therefore, that they should quote from it in such a way as to convey the ideas of the fuller revelation which they possessed. The Old Testament is inchoate and progressive. It is completed in the New.

A brief statement of the bearing of this theanthropic view of inspiration upon the different theories that have been specified will conclude this chapter.

A distinction, required by the facts of Scripture, has been made between revelation and inspiration. Revelations, which transcend human intelligence, and cannot be attained by human reason, must have been communicated through the medium of human language, or of something equivalent in effect; for the recipients of them were in a passive state. The office of the sacred writer consisted solely in receiving and in

Bannerman on *Inspiration*, p. 533.

recording them as they were given. If they were given in human language, he would use the same words in which they were communicated. If they were made in vision, without the use of words, he would record the vision as he saw it. In the latter case the supposition is that words were not employed. Are, then, the words of the record the words of the Holy Spirit, or the words of the sacred penman? They are certainly not the words of the Holy Spirit, in the sense that He formally dictated them; neither are they the words of the sacred writer, in the sense that he was under no divine guidance. They are the words of both. They are the words of the Holy Spirit; and they are the words of the writer. The human and the divine wrought together in the production of one effect. Both conspired to produce a theanthropic book. This has been already illustrated by an analogy drawn from the constitution of the person of Christ, who is both God and man. He is the God-man, and all His utterances belong to His theanthropic person. The utterances of the Bible are similar. They are the utterances of inspired men, speaking as they were moved by the Holy Ghost. The words are theirs, and the words are the Holy Ghost's; and this is true of the Books of Kings and Chronicles as well as of the prophecies of Isaiah and of the Gospel of John.

This view of inspiration utterly subverts the theory of degrees; for it represents every part of the Bible as equally inspired. As the breath of God animated the whole body of the first man, so the Holy Spirit renders the whole volume of sacred Scripture instinct with divinity.

It is also subversive of the mystical theory; for it represents the sacred writers as possessing complete control over their faculties, to the same degree that they would have possessed had they been writing as ordinary men without inspiration.

It is also directly and irreconcilably opposed to the gracious and the rationalistic theories; for it requires a supernatural element as well as a human in the composition of the Bible. These two elements it unites in the production of one perfect, theanthropic book. This book is the light of the world, the only guide of mankind to eternal blessedness.

To the Divine Author of this wonderful book be ascribed 'blessing, and honour, and glory, and power, for ever and ever. Amen.'

INDEX.

AGOBARD on verbal inspiration, 215.
Alexander, Archibald, D.D., on the canon, 35.
Alexander, J. A., D.D., on the inspiration of the prophets, 221.
Analogies illustrating the twofold agencies in the production of the Scriptures, 258–264.
Apocrypha, 35.
Apocryphal writers, opinion of, on inspiration, 192.
Apollinaris Claudius on inspiration, 199.
Apostles, promise of the Holy Spirit to them—they professed to be the infallible organs of God, 183.
Aristides on inspiration, 197.
Astronomy, 87, 94.
Assumptions, 4.
Athanasius on the canon, 23.
Athenagoras on inspiration, 198, 204.
Augustine on the canon, 24 ; on inspiration, 214.

BANNERMAN, JAMES, D.D., 3, 178, 181, 194, 223–225, 228, 232, 240, 241, 246, 275.
Barnabas on inspiration, 195.
Berosus, chronology of, 65 ; account of creation, 66 ; account of the deluge, 66 ; account of events between the deluge and the time of Abraham, 66.
Bible, has come down to us from remote ages, 1 ; number of books of, 1 ; claims to be a revelation from God, 1 ; professes to give the history of the world so far as connected with the scheme of redemption, 2 ; the miraculous element cannot be eliminated from it, 2 ; historical credibility of, 55 ; scientific accuracy of, 83 ; does not profess to teach science, 83 ; conflict between it and science, 84 ; geology, 92 ; astronomy, 94 ; ethnology, 95 ; Egyptology, 90 ; philology, 98 ; chronology, 98 ; longevity of the patriarchs, 101 ; its doctrines, 107 ; different from all other books, 108 ; its cosmogony, 109 ; its doctrine of God, 111 ; its doctrine of man, 112 ; its morality, 113 ; its precepts, 114 ; its unique character, 116 ; objections to its morality, 122 ; general directions for the treatment of them, 124 ; diversity and unity of, 126 ; books of, written by different authors, 127 ; all the books agree in the same great truths, 128 ; its idea of God constitutes its unity, 128 ; this idea of God consistent with itself throughout both Testaments, 129 ; it represents God's government as moral, 131 ; its teaching respecting the divine government and providence in harmony with its idea and government of God, 130 ; the same teaching in harmony with what it teaches of the nature, condition, and necessities of man, 132 ; it is an organism, 135 ; in some of its features it is a national book, 141 ; at the same time, it is a book for all climes and ages, 141 ; its universality, 142 ; it is adapted to man's moral and mental constitution, 143 ; it is a comforter in the varied experience of life, 146 ; it is adapted to man in his social and domestic relations, 147 ; nature of the knowledge derived from it, and its power, 151 ; its purifying influence upon the individual, 157 ; its purifying influence on society in general, 158 ; its purifying influence on the State, 159 ; its exceptional position in the world, 162 ; its testimony to its own inspiration, 173 ; it contains two elements, human and divine, 252.
Bleek, *Introduction to the Old Testament*, 24.
Butler, Bishop, 6, 11.

CAIUS on inspiration, 202.

T

INDEX OF SUBJECTS, ETC.

Canaan, conquest of, 74.
Canon, discussion of, distinct from, and preliminary to, that of inspiration, 15 ; Romanists and Protestants in relation to it, 15 ; books received as canonical, 15 ; canon of the New Testament, 16-26 ; this collection considered by the Church as a harmonious and complete whole, 17 ; historical division of, 18 ; ante-Nicene catalogues of, 19 ; the Peshito, 19 ; Origen's catalogue of, 20 ; Eusebius' catalogue of, 21 ; Council of Nice in relation to the canon, 22 ; catalogues of the fourth century, 23 ; catalogue of the Council of Laodicea, 24 ; catalogue of the Council of Carthage, 26 ; recapitulation of testimonies, 26 ; canon of the Old Testament, 26-35.
Captivity, 79.
Carthage, Council of, on the canon, 26.
Chalmers, Thomas, D.D., adaptability of Christianity to all men, 143.
Chedor-laomer, expedition of, 68.
Chrysostom on inspiration, 213.
Coleridge, S. T., on inspiration, 231-233.
Cyril on the canon, 23.
Cyprian on inspiration, 206.

Daniel, Book of, 79.
Davidson, Dr., *Biblical Criticism*, 41.
Discrepancies, origin of, 41 ; design of, 54.
Dionysius the Less on the canon, 24.

Egyptology, 90.
Epiphanius on the canon, 24, 213.
Ethnology, 95.
Eupolemus, testimony to the Mosaic authorship of the Pentateuch, 60.
Eusebius of Cæsarea on inspiration, 213.
Exodus, 69.
Ezra, formation of the canon of the Old Testament attributed to him, 28.

Faith the true rest of the mind, 144.

Gaussen, S. R. L., on the canon, 17-19, 24, 26 ; on inspiration, 217, 254.
Genesis, Book of, 63.
Geology, 88.
Great synagogue, its relation to the Old Testament canon, 28.

Gregory the Great on inspiration, 214.
Gregory the theologian on the canon, 23.

Hagenbach on inspiration, 216.
Haley, J. W., A.M., *Discrepancies of the Bible*, 42-44, 47, 48, 52-54.
Hecatæus of Abdera, testimony to the Mosaic authorship of the Pentateuch, 60.
Hegesippus on inspiration, 199.
Henderson, Dr., on inspiration, 222.
Heppe on inspiration, 216.
Hetherington's *Apologetics*, 194, 223.
Hippolytus of Portus on inspiration, 203.
Historian, criteria of the credibility of a, 55.
Historical criticism, canons of, 56.
History, testimony of, to the beneficial effects of the Bible, 159.
Hodge, Charles, D.D., on the canon, 15 ; on inspiration, 186, 226, 227, 229, 231, 233.
Horace, 8.

Ignatius, 18, 196.
Inspiration, importance of the doctrine to the Christian system, 15 ; importance to the Church of maintaining the infallible authority of the Scriptures, 13 ; relation of, to biblical interpretation, 13 ; proofs of—(*a*) doctrines and precepts of the Bible, 107 ; (*b*) diversity and unity of the Bible, 126 ; (*c*) organic character of the Bible, 135 ; (*d*) universality of the Bible, 141 ; (*e*) beneficial effects of the Bible, 148 ; (*f*) prophecy, 165 ; (*g*) testimony of the Scriptures, 173 ; definitions of, 189 ; opinions and theories of—(*a*) opinions of the apocryphal writers, 192 ; (*b*) Josephus, 192 ; (*c*) Philo Judæus, 193 ; (*d*) the Jews, 194 ; (*e*) subapostolic Fathers—Barnabas, Clement, Polycarp, Ignatius, Papias, and Hermas, 195 ; (*f*) the apologists — Justin Martyr, Tatian, Athenagoras, and Theophilus, 197 ; (*g*) Fathers of the Church of Asia Minor—Hegesippus, Melito, Claudius Apollinaris, and Irenæus, 199 ; (*h*) Fathers of the Roman Church—Caius, Novatian, and Hippolytus, 202 ; (*i*) Fathers of the North African Church—Tertullian and Cyprian, 205 ; (*j*) Fathers of Alexandria—Clemens Alexandrinus and Origen, 207 ; (*k*) Eusebius, Chrysostom, Jerome, Epiphanius,

INDEX OF SUBJECTS, ETC. 283

Theodore of Mopsuestia, Augustine, and Gregory the Great, 213; (*l*) Schoolmen, 215; (*m*) Reformers, 215; (*n*) theory of verbal inspiration, 216; (*o*) mystical theory, 220; (*p*) theory of degrees, 221; (*q*) latitudinarian and rationalistic theories, 226; (*r*) theory of Schleiermacher, 227; (*s*) Coleridge's theory, 231; (*t*) theory of gracious inspiration, 232; (*u*) dynamical theory, 234; (*v*) theory of the Roman Catholic Church, 235; distinguished from revelation, 237; nature and extent of, 252; did not destroy the conscious self-control of the sacred writers, 256; the Bible contains two elements,—divine and human,—so combined as to produce one individual result, 257; the union of these two elements inexplicable, 257; they have an analogue in the person of Christ, 258; the Bible is theanthropic, 258; inspiration is limited to the nature of the object to be accomplished, 266; it is a miraculous gift, 267; it extends equally to every part of Scripture, 267; objections to it considered, 270; bearing of the theanthropic view of inspiration upon the different theories of it, 277.
Irenæus, 200.

Jerome, 24, 213.
Jews return to Palestine, 80.
Joshua, Book of, 27.
Josephus, 169, 192.
Justin Martyr, 197.
Juvenal, testimony to the Mosaic authorship of the Pentateuch, 60.

Laodicea, Council of, 24.
Lee, Archdeacon, 176, 238, 275.
Longinus, testimony to the Mosaic authorship of the Pentateuch, 60.
Lysimachus, testimony to the Mosaic authorship of the Pentateuch, 60.
Luther on inspiration, 215.

Manetho, 65.
Melancthon, 216.
Melito, Bishop of Sardis, 199.
M'Clintock and Strong, *Bib. Theology and Eccles. Encyclop.*, 215.
Milton, 158.
Miracles, no presumption against, 5; capable of proof, 8.
Morell, 228.
Moses, autograph of, 27.

Neander, 228.
Nebuchadnezzar, 79.
New Testament, historical credibility of, 82; organism of, 139.
Nitzsch, 228.
Noah, descendants of, 67.
Novatian, 202.

Old Testament, organism of, 138; organic connection with the New Testament, 139; quotations from, in the New Testament, 178; divisions of, 181.
Organism, definition of, 136.
Origen, 20, 21, 210, 213.

Patton, F. L., D.D., 243-245.
Peshito version, 19.
Papias, 196.
Phœnicia, connection with Judea, 75.
Philo Judæus, 193.
Prophets, 176.

Quadratus, 197.

Rawlinson, George, M.A., *Historical Evidences*, 9, 56.
Reformers, 215.
Rogers, Henry, *Superhuman Origin of the Bible*, 116.
Rufinus, 24.

Schaff, P., D.D., 258.
Scrivener, 52.
Scriptures. *See* Bible.
Schleiermacher, 227.
Septuagint, 34, 194.
Smith, John Pye, D.D., 223.
Sun, miracle of, standing still, 74.
Solomon, relations with Egypt, 76.
Spring, Gardiner, D.D., 161.

Tacitus, testimony to the Mosaic authorship of the Pentateuch, 60.
Tatian, 198.
Tertullian, 205.
Theodore of Mopsuestia, 214.
Theophilus of Antioch, 198.
Tholuck, 228.

Westcott, *Introduction to Study of the Gospels*, 196, 199, 202, 204, 207, 213.
Williams, Rev. John, 161.

www.ingramcontent.com/pod-product-compliance
Lightning Source LLC
Chambersburg PA
CBHW050339230426
43663CB00010B/1913